*The psychology of
character development*

JOHN WILEY & SONS, INC., New York · London

The psychology of
character development

by

ROBERT F. PECK
The University of Texas

with

ROBERT J. HAVIGHURST
The University of Chicago

and

RUTH COOPER, *The University of Missouri*

JESSE LILIENTHAL, *Hillsborough, California*

DOUGLAS MORE, *Nicholson, Kohn and Associates,*
St. Louis, Missouri

Preface

There is perhaps no study of human behavior more fraught with risk of subjective bias and culture-bound prejudice than is the study of moral character. Yet in no aspect of life is objective knowledge and understanding more essential to human happiness, perhaps even to racial survival. Although much wise thought has been accorded the subject through several millennia, relatively little scientific research has yet been done, particularly on the inner forces that shape and determine character.

A generation ago, the Character Education Inquiry, under the direction of Hartshorne, May, and Shuttleworth, devised some ingenious ways of testing children's honesty and other aspects of their moral behavior. When they described their findings, they were careful to point out that their tests tapped only a small segment of school behavior. They felt that the important features of character in the child's total life behavior remained to be investigated. In *Studies on the Nature of Character*, Volume III of their publication, they described the ways in which they attempted to probe these broader characteristics and more general moral problems. However, they concluded that moral behavior was highly specific to each situation. It was, as they defined and tested it.

Their studies removed the ground from under some widely held beliefs to the effect that moral behavior was "all of a piece," with good behavior in one area of behavior assuring the presence of good behavior in other areas. Character, they found, was much more specifically related to particular situations than had been supposed. The Character Education Inquiry also showed that the supposed "character-building" agencies, such as church, schools, and Scouts, were not nearly so effective as many had supposed.

One unintended result of the Character Education Inquiry was that it apparently discouraged the proponents of experimentation and objective study in the field of character education. Most educators and psychologists reacted to the Inquiry by turning away from this complex area of human behavior. Thus it was a decade before people began to theorize and experiment again, with the conviction that they could accomplish something useful in this field.

In the 1940's, we undertook a new study. If behavior were viewed from a different angle from the one Character Inquiry adopted, that of persistent attitudes and ways of relating to people, it seemed to us likely that "popular opinion" about the generality of moral character, which Hartshorne and his colleagues felt was discredited by their studies, might turn out to be not so far wrong after all. We were prepared to find any and all discrepancies in moral behavior that the children might exhibit; but we also believed it possible to discover certain stable general tendencies—character structure, in other words. As the results of this study suggest, it seems an accurate description of the facts to say that some individuals have a predictably unstable pattern of moral behavior, whereas others show a consistent pattern of morality in the broad sense of respecting and considering other's needs and rights. In fact, the intercorrelations of honesty, loyalty, etc., which we found, were quite large and were significantly different from the low correlations the Character Education Inquiry reported, probably because their measurements were more particularistic and situationally restricted than the ones we used.

The chief difference is probably one of emphasis. The Character Education Inquiry stressed the variations that individuals show in their overt moral behavior on certain specific tests. It cannot be gainsaid that this is a matter of observable fact. We have gone more in the other direction, not to ignore variations in a person's behavior, but to look for some consistent, underlying orientation the individual may display which makes him "all of a piece," even if it be in the very inconsistency of his obvious, overt behavior. As will be seen, we recognized and tried to show fully the discrepancies which almost always exist within any one person's behavior pattern, but not to the extent of throwing out such persistent, predictable trends as may also characterize his behavior. This emphasis runs the opposite risk of overgeneralizing. We have tried to strike a balance between depicting consistencies and pointing to inconsistencies; between recognizing general character structure, if it exists, and recognizing that a person seldom behaves in exactly one way in all situations—particularly if these situations are highly specific tests, within a narrow range of "in-school" behavior.

This line of inquiry has had increasing attention in the years since the Character Education Inquiry. Vernon Jones's comprehensive review of the research studies on character up to 1953 (Jones, 1954) points out the complexity of the intrapersonal forces that produce conduct, the complexity of the nature-and-nurture forces that produce character, and the central role of motivation in determining moral conduct. This view of character, though more implicit than explicit in his writing, seems to have been Ligon's throughout his years of study of character education. (Ligon, 1956.) Thus, the ideas which shaped our research have a long history. (Roback, 1952, 1955.) If it is new in any respect, it is, perhaps, in its attempt to comprehend all these aspects of character and character development in a single study. To apply all the varied appraisal techniques and statistical techniques in such a way that an integrated final pattern could be discerned, also required certain innovations. In method as well as in subject matter, therefore, this has been an exploratory research rather than a definitive one.

Its findings must also be regarded as provisional because it was necessary to limit the study to a relatively small number of cases. We believed, however, that at this stage in our knowledge of character it was more important to achieve a thorough understanding of each individual in a relatively small cross-sectional sample than to take more superficial measurements on a very large population.

As Gordon Allport has said, in his introduction to *An Experiment in the Prevention of Delinquency* (Powers and Witmer, 1951), "The basic principles involved in building character are not known. . . . To discover the how and why [of character development and change] a deeper study of cause and effect would be needed. And this study would have to focus on single cases because only in single cases can the factors producing the change be identified."

The course of this research has been typical of a new venture: a launching-out with only hazy, general direction; a gathering of facts which presumably might be useful; the slow emergence of more specific hypotheses; and only after a long while, the finding of certain vantage points from which to survey and map the area traversed.

GENESIS OF THE MORAL-CHARACTER STUDY

The present study was the second of two investigations of moral character in adolescence. In 1940 a committee of the Committee on Human Development was formed to plan for a research program. The committee met several times and finally proposed that a longitudinal study be made of child development in a Midwestern community. This study would be started with a group of children at birth and carried through to adulthood. It would have biological, psychological, and social-anthropological aspects. In particular it would employ the new social-anthropological methods of studying a modern community, which had not hitherto been used in any longitudinal study of child development. The decision was made early in 1941 to choose a community and get started on the program. W. Lloyd Warner took responsibility for collecting data on Midwestern communities between 5,000 and 25,000 in population. Eventually, by using a number of criteria of "typicality," some twenty communities between 5,000 and 15,000 were selected. In the spring of 1941 a committee consisting of W. Lloyd Warner, Ralph W. Tyler, Mandel Sherman, and Robert J. Havighurst visited "Prairie City" and talked with the superintendent of schools, the president of the school board, and the ministerial association. "Prairie City" seemed to be satisfactory, and the people who were interviewed all expressed interest in and approval of a study.

Late in 1941, three subcommittees were formed dealing with the biological, psychological, and social-anthropological aspects of the study respectively. At this point the United States declared war and it became evident that the time was not auspicious for the beginning of the longitudinal study. Even if money could be obtained, it would probably be difficult to obtain the technical personnel for the study. Accordingly, the longitudinal-study idea was modified into a series of more or less related investigations of various aspects of child development.

One area of major interest was the social structure of Prairie City. The work since 1942 is reported in three publications: *Democracy in*

Jonesville by Warner and associates, *Elmtown's Youth* by A. B. Hollingshead, and *Social Class in America* by Warner, Meeker, and Ellis. These studies were made in an effort to describe the web of life in Prairie City and the way it affects the behaviors, beliefs, and feelings of the growing child.

As a number of small studies were planned and executed, it began to be apparent that it would be extremely useful to concentrate on a specific group of children and follow their development in detail. Consequently, two groups of children were chosen for intensive investigation. One consisted of all those presently living in Prairie City who had been born in the year 1926. The other group was composed of all the children who were born in 1933.

It was at this time, in 1942, that the committee decided to undertake a study of the nature and development of moral character. Accordingly, instruments were designed and administered to the 1926 group, and a series of conferences was held which eventuated by 1945 in a report on the correlates of moral reputation. This work has been published in *Adolescent Character and Personality* by Havighurst and Taba.

Meanwhile, information had been gathered on the 1933 group for various purposes. In 1945 it was proposed that a full-scale study of the psychological and social development of these children be undertaken. Thirty-six children were chosen for intensive study and a large number and variety of instruments were used with them. This resulted in a "clinical conference" in 1946 and 1947 under the direction of Dr. Carolyn Tryon and Dr. William E. Henry. The population for that study was the same one that was used in the present research, though with the main focus of attention on psychosocial development and the forces affecting it. Three of the present authors, Havighurst, Peck, and More, participated in that project. During the course of it, methods for intensive case studies were developed which proved invaluable when the time came to design the present research.

During that study new methods of psychological inquiry, such as projective instruments, sociometric tests, and the like, proved so fruitful that in December of 1948 a new research on moral character was proposed. It was decided to use the 1933 group of children since there was such a wealth of information on them.

CHRONOLOGY OF THE MORAL-CHARACTER STUDY

The study of moral character had always been one of the central purposes of the whole Prairie City research program under Havighurst's continuously active direction. By December, 1948, it seemed time once more to undertake a specific study of this problem. After Havighurst called an initial meeting to survey the whole Prairie City program, a series of meetings was held to plan a new investigation into moral character. The earlier project, reported by Havighurst and Taba, had confined itself to a study of factors related to moral reputation. Reputation was used in the belief that it gave a reasonable approximation to the actual moral behavior of the children. However, in the years since 1945, several of the staff had had experience in personnel assessment, both in the Tryon-Henry project and in other studies, which convinced us that we could now penetrate much more deeply into the motivations, as well as the surface appearance, of child behavior as it pertained to moral issues. Therefore, a trial theory of the motivation patterns in moral behavior was presented for discussion by Robert Peck.

This theory about the psychodynamics of character grew out of some ten years' study of Jung, Freud, Horney, Sullivan, and the "neoanalytic" school. The specific stimulus was Fromm's *Man for Himself*. Inspired by this, a theory of five character types, psychogenetically arranged, was evolved. At the same time, very much in the spirit of Henry Murray, an effect was made to specify and measure a rather large set of attitudinal and personality variables which it seemed reasonable to suppose were related to character and moral behavior. There was still no synthesis of these variables with the character types into any organized, comprehensive theory. They were ideas inductively derived from previous experience and reading. Their power to explain and order data was as yet untried.

This theory appeared to make sense, nonetheless, and to involve areas of feeling and action which were accessible by the instruments already developed and used. A research team was then formed, under Peck's chairmanship, to carry out a new study.

The next step was the draft of an outline for the analysis of each individual case. The earlier project had made clear the necessity for an organized framework for case analysis. In the early days of that conference, when the group simply sat down and decided it was going to "study a child," it found itself with case reports which were extremely difficult to compare with one another, and which often did not cover the same points from case to case. Therefore, slowly and rather painfully, a case outline was evolved, appropriate to the purpose of that study of psychosocial development.

This experience gave us a long head start in preparing for the present study. Having decided upon the necessity for a specific conceptual framework and having decided upon the facets of individual personality which seemed to be relevant to moral functioning, we were able quite quickly to agree on a workable outline.

Weekly meetings were held, to improve the case outline and the theoretical framework. At this time it was decided to take an additional step beyond the qualitative case studies which had been done in the previous projects. It was agreed that rating scales should be constructed so that, when all the cases had been studied, detailed, quantitative comparisons could be made within and between cases. Without the ratings, it would not have been possible to achieve nearly the degree of clarity and specificity in the results which ultimately proved possible.

The chief reason for citing this chronology in so much detail is to show the slow, gradual emergence of concepts and procedures. The study did not begin with a full-fledged, satisfactory research design and methodology; rather it was evolved, often with hours of seemingly redundant discussion, until it appeared that a reasonably clear, sensible plan of operation was in hand. The six months spent in this kind of preparation were importantly responsible for whatever effectiveness the subsequent study may display.

On the twenty-fifth of June, 1949, the staff included Clara Berghoefer, Ruth Cooper, Gerald Handel, Walter Hartmann, Robert Havighurst, Douglas More, Robert Peck, Jeremy Sarchet, Robert Schmidt, and Stuart Wright. Semiweekly case conferences continued, together with the inevitable discussion and redefinition of variables, through the end of August, 1949. The month of September, which was a vacation period, brought a few changes in staff. When work resumed in late September, the staff consisted of James Abegglen, Clara Berghoefer, Harold Finley, Gerald Handel, Robert Havighurst, Philip Katch, Wilma Lux, Douglas More, Robert Peck, and Stuart Wright. The only change in staff after this point was when Philip Katch left and was replaced by Jesse Lilienthal. From this point on, a regular schedule of case analyses was maintained, in two two-hour conferences per week.

At every meeting lengthy discussions took place, concerning trait definitions and points of theory as well as interpretations of the particular case at issue. On October 25, for instance, the question of the rationale for the rating system was reopened. During December, 1949, and January, 1950, a systematic revision of the trait list and a set of operational definitions for all the traits were worked out. Thus, it was actually not until the first of February, 1950, that the theoretical framework and the trait definitions were on paper, in full. Some kind of definition existed in black and white, of course, from the previous June; but although there was quite good agreement on the interpretation of the traits, their meanings had not all been spelled out explicitly. At this time, therefore, that task was completed.

During the fall and winter months the case studies had been progressing, and by the fifteenth of April the last of the thirty-four cases had been presented. At this point Mr. Handel and Miss Lux left the staff and eight people remained. A schedule of three conferences per week was set up, to go over the twenty-four cases which had been originally presented and rated prior to February 1, 1950. (That was the point at which the final trait definitions were completed.) From April 17 to June 10, the staff of eight rerated one case per day, three times a week. All the quantitative analyses which are reported in the rest of this study are based on the case ratings made after February 1, 1950.

By late 1950 the authors prepared several working papers, looking toward a report on the study. Havighurst described the social structure of Prairie City and its relationship to character. His writing constitutes a good half of Chapters II, VI, and VII of this book. Cooper began her obverse-factor analysis, with the eventual results described in the Appendix. More prepared papers on the reliability of the conference ratings (see Appendix) and also on the social reputations of the adolescents in the study. It was the ideas and leads in the latter paper which were later followed in locating and analyzing the data for Chapter VI. Lilienthal prepared a description of the families in the study, and also wrote disguised versions of five case studies. Chapter III contains substantial portions of those case studies, and some of the description of families in Chapter V is derived from his work.

In keeping with his responsibilities as formulator of the theory underlying the study, Peck was responsible for constructing a coherent, overall view of the data, and for seeing to the appropriate statistical analysis. He therefore undertook the following steps.

First, a correlational analysis was made of all the ratings on all the cases. This was largely an inductive step, since no comprehensive pattern of character-personality relationships had yet been foreseen and formulated. At first, the result seemed to be chaos. Simple intercorrelations of variables showed a tendency for most of the personality variables to be negatively related to the Amoral-character-type scale. At the other extreme of morality, many personality variables appeared to be positively related to the ratings of the subjects on the Rational-Altruistic scale. No meaningful pattern could be discerned, however, for the intermediate character types—which is to say, the intermediate degrees of morality. At this point, inductive exploration seemed to have become relatively fruitless.

Two further steps suggested themselves, however. First, the correlation matrix of the personality variables looked very much as though factor analysis would produce just a few distinct personality dimensions, out of the thirty-odd variables. With the aid of William Stephenson, such an analysis was applied. It "boiled down" the personality measures to six well-defined "vectors," whose meaning seemed to have definite implications for moral behavior, if some way could be found to relate them to the measures of character. (Peck, 1951.)

The second step involved a change of view on the character-type measures. Up to this point, the ratings of the thirty-four subjects on any one of the five character-type scales had been treated as a separate measure, with little useful result. Now it was decided to take into account the total character profile of each individual on all five types together. In the end, it was decided to classify each subject by his *dominant* character type—or type combination. This had the effect of giving a single overall score for "maturity of character" to each subject. When this kind of scale was constructed, and it was compared with the six personality vectors, at last it became possible to see a distinctive personality pattern for each of the character types. It could be shown, too, that character was closely related to personality throughout its entire range, from amorality to the most mature form of ethical behavior.

Meanwhile, as much by good fortune as by planning, certain ratings on the subject's families had been made by a research group in 1946–1947, and stored untouched. These independent family ratings were exhumed, factored, and compared with the character and personality measures, with the results reported in Chapter V of the present book. A somewhat similar procedure was applied to peer sociometric data which had been available, but not analyzed, during the conference phase of the character study. These results are given in Chapter VI.

The achievement of a coherent view of the total problem, the inclusion of appropriate new data and their appropriate analysis, the discovery and description of a "simple structure" in the total body of data—this required several years and the writing of several successive drafts of the manuscript, before this book achieved its present form. Havighurst gave editorial advice on the manuscript throughout this process.

In summary, this book represents the end product of years of exploratory study, largely inductive, by a good many people. If it now appears to present a simple theory, in reasonably clear terms, with some provisional evidence to support it, this is a consummation for which we are profoundly grateful. To the degree this clarity is approached, success might be said to have crowned the sixteen years of exploring, in largely uncharted country, by a goodly company of inquiring minds.

One final word about authorship responsibility in this study: the factual data were provided by the work of many people; the undersigned, however, should be held solely responsible for all interpretations or speculations that appear anywhere in this book.

Throughout the years of this study we have been indebted to two organizations for their indispensable financial support. The Lilly Endowment, Inc., provided funds during the 1940's, when the field work was in progress. Thereafter, the actual analysis of the data by the Clinical Conference group, and the preparation of the first manuscript, were made possible by support from the Grant Foundation. Their support came at a crucial time and is therefore doubly appreciated.

ROBERT F. PECK

Austin, Texas
September, 1960

A note on reading this book

The most complete picture of the character study is to be gained by reading the chapters in sequence, with reference to the Appendix for the more detailed definitions and procedures. Some specialists might even prefer to read the Appendix first, for method, then read the main body of the book.

An effort has been made to make the main chapters as comfortably clear as possible for the non-technical reader. There are, however, a number of terms which require careful definition, some of them new to many readers. These are defined in the text the first time they are used, or at the most appropriate place. If any question arises, reference to that term in the index will show the page on which the term is defined.

Those interested in some special aspect of character development can read the appropriate chapter or chapters. The titles are intended to be self-explanatory, and each chapter can be read as a separate unit, with some side references to definitions that occur earlier in the book.

The non-technical reader who wishes, can gain a reasonably adequate picture of the theory and findings of the study by reading Chapters I, III, IX, and X. In fact, Chapter IX is a rather complete summary of the findings, though not of the research design or the procedures.

Contents

xvii

List of tables

I

A motivational theory of character

At the outset of this inquiry, "character" presented a series of unanswered questions: What is moral character? Is it all of a piece or are people too unpredictable and inconsistent to be said to have definable, stable character? What personality elements make up character, or are importantly related to it? What is the relative influence on character development of home, school, church, age mates, and other formative agents? What kinds of experiences produce poor, average, and good character? When is character formed, and at what age is its formation largely completed?

William James, William McDougal, and Sigmund Freud, among many others, used the term to represent a pattern of acts, rather consistent through time, which may be said to "characterize" and define the human individual. In both its general sense and its specifically moral aspects, they emphasized the inward elements of motivation and intent as the major determinants of character. Paraphrasing Freud, Fenichel observed, "Character [is] the habitual mode of bringing into

1

harmony the tasks presented by internal demands and by the external world. . . . [It] is necessarily a function of the constant, organized, and integrating part of the personality which is the ego. . . . The latest complication in the structure of the ego, the erection of the superego, is also decisive in forming the habitual patterns of character. What an individual considers good or bad is characteristic for him; likewise whether or not he takes the commands of his conscience seriously, and whether he obeys his conscience or tries to rebel against it" (Fenichel, 1945, p. 467).

The concept is not new that character is to be defined by the intent as much as by the deed: "As [a man] thinketh in his heart, so is he." Insofar as concerns *moral* character, the intent that counts is the intent to do good or ill to other people. This, too, is at the heart of the definitions of ethical character that have come down to us from many sources: Christ, the Biblical prophets, Buddha, Confucius, Lao-Tze, Mahavira, Zoroaster, and Mohammed. Whether to explain present character, or to trace it to its original sources, it appears essential to investigate the individual's feelings and attitudes toward the other people in his life.

To bring all the strands together into a unified theory of character, however, was and remains a formidable challenge. First to achieve it in part, if chiefly for the "shadow side" of man's nature, was Freud. As Fromm notes, "Freud developed not only the first but also the most consistent and penetrating theory of character as a system of strivings which underlie, but are not identical with, [overt] behavior" (Fromm, 1947, p. 54).

Freud described personality, *and character,* developing through the "pregenital" stages of orality, anality, and phallic striving. An adult who showed the attitudes characteristic of a very young child could, figuratively speaking, be said to show "oral character"—i.e., marked, uncritical self-centeredness, insatiable demands for personal attention and indulgence, a low tolerance for any kind of frustration, quick changeability of mood and interest, and other, dynamically allied re-actions. An "anal character"—one more object oriented, whether thing collector or thing user—would be more self-disciplining than the "oral character," though not necessarily with any great spirit of affection or concern for other people. Thus Freud, who was primarily concerned with unraveling the causes of disordered behavior, devoted most of his attention to those kinds of character which represent stalled or very imperfect development. He only briefly, though pithily, summed up the nature of the matured, "genital" character as possessed of the ability to love and the ability to work.

Fromm, in adapting Freud's developmental stages to a character typology more specifically ethical in nature, vividly portrayed the "non-productive" orientations: receptive, exploitative, hoarding, and marketing. His "productive" orientation, a notable elaboration of Freud's "genital" character, is spelled out at considerable length, with emphasis on two themes: *loving* and *reasoning*, as the hallmarks of the ethically mature person. If there is any limitation in Fromm's characterology, it seems to consist only of the completeness with which he made his types descriptive of different motive systems, and did not explicitly relate them to one another. If the organic, developmental continuity of Freud's stage-concept could be preserved, while focusing attention on the ethical aspects of human behavior, as Fromm has done, a maximally useful picture of character might be constructed. This is what has been attempted in this study, with a certain added emphasis on the individual's *reasons* for acting morally, or not, in terms of the inner or outer authority to which he consigns directing power in his life.

This last aspect led to a character typology which at points resembles the typology that Reisman independently advanced at about the same time, in *The Lonely Crowd*. (Adherents of the *Zeitgeist* theory of cultural history may find this coincidence of interest, although it can probably be traced to the common interest of the two writers in neo-Freudian theory.)

DEVELOPMENTAL LEVELS OF CHARACTER: A THEORY

In an attempt to answer the first question, "What is character?", a set of five character types was defined, each conceived as the representative of a successive stage in the psychosocial development of the individual:

Character Type	Developmental Period
Amoral	Infancy
Expedient	Early Childhood
Conforming Irrational-Conscientious	Later Childhood
Rational-Altruistic	Adolescence and Adulthood

This set of character types was intended to: (1) be defined and labeled in terms of the control system the individual uses to adapt his search for satisfaction to the requirements of the social world; (2) include all the possible modes of adaptation; (3) be defined in terms of motivation (so long as it achieves behavioral expression); (4) represent both operational patterns of behavior, and the stage in psychosocial development to which each pattern presumably is most appropriate.

Since few people are so completely all of a piece that they have only one kind of motivation at all times, it is more accurate to think of the five motivation patterns, or "character types," as *components* of character. Indeed, that is the way they were treated throughout most of the research. However, for purposes of exposition, it is convenient to define them in terms of five pure "ideal types." This serves an additional purpose in thinking about the motivation patterns as an ascending developmental sequence, from childlike reasons to mature reasons for behaving morally. Consequently, while these five "main motives" are henceforth treated as *components* of moral character, the term "character type" is used in defining and discussing them.

The first "pure" character type represents the absence of any self-imposed control, or any concern for adaptation to the moral requirements of social living. The last four represent the four kinds of reasons why a person may behave according to the moral standards of his society. (At least, it seemed that these four modes of adaptation to society covered the gamut; this may or may not hold true when other people have had an opportunity to reflect on the problem.) Names were selected for the types which would, as far as possible, indicate the chief dynamics operating in each. This becomes a little unwieldy at points, but it may have the virtue of conveying the central concept in quick, brief fashion.

The definition of each type was phrased in terms of a hypothetical individual whose character structure would be a "pure" example of the type. Actually, one would expect to find only rarely a person who operated so exclusively in one way as to constitute a pure type. In practice, what was assessed was the relative proportion of each person's dynamic structure which belonged in each of the five type categories. It was found that one component often tended to predominate and make the person a reasonably clear-cut example of one particular character type. In every case, however, there always were some times when the person acted according to other type patterns.

Amoral

This type corresponds to what is often called clinically the "psychopathic personality." Such a person follows his whims and impulses, without regard for how this affects other people. He considers himself the center of the universe, and sees other people or objects as means to direct self-gratification. If his basic emotional attitudes are mainly hostile, he is apt to be found committing delinquent or criminal acts. If he has a positive, pleasant view of others, he is more apt to be known as "charming but irresponsible." He may form temporary alliances with people, but will abandon them the minute he sees a richer source of gratification.

He has no internalized moral principles, no conscience or superego. He feels no need to control his personal impulses, and exhibits no control. His impulses may or may not be actively *immoral*, antisocial, or destructive in intent; but in any case he disregards the moral connotations and consequences of his behavior.

In a real way, this is a picture of an infant, in its first year. Adults who show such a pattern are spoken of clinically as fixated at an infantile level. To the best of our knowledge, they act so because they have never learned to accept prohibitions or sanctions from others. The percentage of near-complete psychopaths in our society is probably small. More often, a tendency of this sort may be present to some degree, partially repressed or suppressed, within a person who is otherwise responsive to social demands.

Expedient

A person of this type is primarily self-centered, and considers other people's welfare and reactions only in order to gain his personal ends. He tends to get what he wants with a minimum of giving in return. He behaves in ways his society defines as moral, only so long as it suits his purpose. For instance, he may act in "honest" ways to keep an advantageous reputation. If he can gain more by being dishonest, particularly if he can avoid detection and censure, he does so. He is not particularly concerned about other people's welfare, except as he may observe it in order to obtain their approval. Like the amoralist, he regards himself as the only person who is really important; but he is more aware of the advantage of conforming to social requirements in the short run, in order to achieve long-run advantages. Hence, his outward behavior may often be honest or responsible, in the main, as far as others can see. The key to his low-level morality is his "me-first" attitude in a critical situation, where an unmoral act may bring advantages that outweigh any disapproval.

A clue to his basic motivation, despite any outward conformity to social patterns, is that in the long run he may be inconsistent in living up to moral principles. He may or may not have a well-organized, rational system of personal values, firm self-control, and realistic perception of how to get what he wants; but he has no internalized moral principles, no conscience or superego.

Such a motivation-behavior pattern is characteristic of many very young children, who have learned to respect the reward-punishment power of adults, and to behave correctly whenever an adult is around. External sanctions are always necessary, however, to guide and control their behavior, and keep it moral. In the absence of such controls, they immediately relapse into doing what they please, even if this involves shoving other children around, taking what they want, or otherwise gratifying their self-centered desires.

Conforming

This kind of person has one general, internalized principle: to do what others do, and what they say one "should" do. He wants to and does conform to all the rules of his group. He wants to do what others do, and his only anxiety is for possible disapproval.

The conformist is seen most often, perhaps, in stable folk societies. He learns, more by habit than by awareness of moral cause and effect, to behave in each specific situation in a certain prescribed way. He is kind and loyal to his family and tribe, because he is rewarded for acting in such a way on this occasion, punished for transgressing the rule on that occasion. He may learn that he should be polite and considerate of male relatives on his mother's side, but is freely permitted to insult and take advantage of men from his father's family. He has no generalized principles about being "honest" toward everyone. He follows a system of literal rules, specific for each occasion, with no necessary overall consistency as to the degree of morality in different situations.

A convenient way to distinguish this type may be to ask whether the person feels bad when he breaks a rule, out of *shame* or *guilt*. We define shame as fear of disapproval by others. Thus, a person who acts morally because he would be ashamed if others found him violating the moral rules is controlling himself according to external sanctions:

a violation is not wrong in itself, nor because of its effects, but because other people say it is wrong and their approval is at stake. This is a childlike attitude, uppermost in Piaget's heteronomous period, no doubt (Piaget, 1948). It differs from the Expedient approach in that social conformity is accepted as good for its own sake. A Conformist may frequently ignore chances for personal advantage, if they require departure from the prescribed rules of conduct.

In a sense, such a person might be said to have a crude conscience, since he may feel very uncomfortable about departing from the rules. However, he does not follow them for a moral purpose, that is, because he is concerned about the effect of his behavior on other people. He defines "right" as acting by the rules. If this sometimes hurts others, he feels no moral responsibility, no guilt. Further, he has no abstract principles of honesty, responsibility, loyalty, etc. The rules he lives by may call for kindness to some people, cruelty to others. This does not concern him.

This kind of pattern is visible in middle and late childhood. It may be an alternative solution to the problem of living in society, parallel with the Irrational-Conscientious kind of orientation. Both types ultimately spring from and depend on external rules and sanctions to make their behavior consonant with a code of morality.

Irrational-Conscientious

This is the person who judges a given act according to his own internal standard of right and wrong. In the adolescent or adult of this type, conformity to the group code is not the issue. Rather, it is conformity to a code he has internalized and believes in. If he approves of an act he sees as honest, he carries it out whether or not the people around him approve. He appeals to an abstract principle of honesty, applying it as he interprets it to any situation where it seems relevant. If he fails to live up to his own idea of what is moral, we call his anxiety "guilt." It is a feeling of having violated one's own integrity.

The irrational component is visible in the individual's customary rigidity in applying a preconceived principle, somewhat in the manner of the Conformist. An act is "good" or "bad" to him because he defines it as such, not necessarily because it has positive or negative effects on others. This is the "blind," rigid superego at work. It is characteristic of children who have accepted and internalized the parental rules, but who have not attained awareness that the rules are man-made and intended to serve a human, functional purpose. Consequently, they may be so rigidly "moral" that they sometimes act to the detriment of others. This would seem to be an alternative form of childlike morality, occurring at the same developmental level as the Conforming type, and thus parallel with it as far as concerns any measure of the maturity of character development.

On the positive side, this may be reasonably effective in insuring outwardly moral behavior at all times. We assume this strong, blind conscience to be "the heir of the parental superegos." If the parents' code fits in well with a moral code which has been produced in the society by long, empirical testing of what is good for people, then it probably contains few seriously destructive elements. This would not be true, of course, of the Irrational-Conscientious child of a criminal subgroup in a society, if such a combination could exist.

Rational-Altruistic

The Rational-Altruistic type describes the highest level of moral maturity. Such a person not only has a stable set of moral principles by which he judges and directs his own action; he objectively assesses the results of an act in a given situation, and approves it on the grounds of whether or not it serves others as well as himself. (He may do this either consciously or unconsciously; the issue is not the consciousness, but the *quality* of the judgment.) In the ideal case he is dependably honest, responsible, loyal, etc., because he sees such behavior is for everyone's well-being. He is "rational" because he assesses each new action and its effects realistically, in the light of internalized moral principles derived from social experience; and he is "altruistic," because he is ultimately interested in the welfare of others, as well as himself. He is not interested in pursuing a principle for its own sake, without regard to its human effects. He has a strong, firm conscience or superego, but he tests, modifies, and applies its directives in order to achieve the ultimate purpose of the rules it contains.

He observes situations accurately, sees implications beyond the immediate, and can experiment mentally to decide on the most moral course of action. He recognizes objectively what other people want and how they feel. He is able to feel as they do, or know how he would feel in their position, without losing perspective by completely identifying with them.

He is as much concerned with assuring the well-being of others as with assuring his own. He is capable of self-sacrifice, but only if it genuinely helps others, not for neurotic self-satisfaction. He enjoys seeing others live a full life, and his efforts to aid them are based on what they need and want. His motives are not primarily to win personal gratification, using others as a means to this end.

He wants to work constructively in some area and produce results useful to everyone. He sees his relations with others as a pleasant, cooperative effort toward mutual goals, whether vocational, social, or recreational. As an adult, he assumes an appropriate share of responsibility in his role as member of a family, community, nation, and the human race. His moral horizon embraces all mankind, as his behavior demonstrates. He is honest with all, kind to all, and respects the integrity of every human being.

He is actively *for* his principles, neither a passive conformist nor an intolerant "reformer." He does not interfere with others' constructive activity; but he uses voice and action to prevent anyone from acting destructively.

He reacts with emotion appropriate to the occasion. This does not mean he is unemotional, for he is enthusiastic about promoting what is good, and aroused to prevent what is bad. He knows himself, and faces his own reactions honestly. He does what is morally right because he wants to, not because it is "the thing to do."

His behavior is both spontaneous and rationally oriented. He accepts responsibility for his own acts, and blame if it is deserved. He judges other people's discrete actions without making a blanket approval or condemnation of the person as a whole. He knows what is good for himself and others, and acts accordingly. He is consistent in principle, but not rigidly ritualistic. He assesses each situation in its own terms, but follows his principles in deciding what to do. He has no logic-tight compartments in his thinking.

His public and private values are just about identical. He sees himself as he is, works for deeper perception and understanding, and respects his own capacities as he does other men's. He feels no irrational anxiety or guilt. If he errs, he feels guilty; but his response is to take steps to rectify the error. If he succeeds, he no longer feels guilty. He justifies his actions by their moral effect, not by rationalization or defensive misperception. Such a person, it was proposed in this study, is moral to the highest degree. He is also mature, emotionally "well-adjusted," and using his constructive capacities to the fullest.

This picture of the Rational-Altruistic person represents an ideal goal, of course, to be sought, perhaps to be approached by adulthood, but probably never to be perfectly achieved and unfalteringly maintained by the best of mortals. None of the adolescents in the study were expected to reach this ideal. They were appraised for the proportion of their character that resembled this pattern, in ways one could reasonably expect of boys and girls their age.

Comparing these types with Freud's stages, the Amoral type represents a character structure which has never developed beyond the "oral" stage in its basic attitudes and style of behavior. The Expedient pattern retains some of the primary narcissism of the oral stage, but displays a more discriminating perception of external reality—an achievement that might be said to represent partial advance into the "anal" stage. There is no resolution of primitive internalizations into an organized conscience, however; not an effectively guiding one, at any rate. In Freud's terms, this represents a failure to resolve the Oedipal problem (which can be seen as an authority struggle, a la Adler, quite as well as a rivalry for affection). For the most part, though, the crucial selfishness of the Expedient type would seem to resemble most closely the later stages of the oral period.

Both the Conforming and Irrational-Conscientious types might be said to represent fixation at the later pregenital stages, extending through the latency period. In either case, there is developed a firm, unquestioned set of rules which repeats the prescriptions laid down by the parents and other adult authorities. Theoretically, the Conforming phase could be conceived as coming first, followed by an internalization that leads the Irrational-Conscientious person to be free from the dictates of specific people around him. In effect, however, the irrational conscience precludes ego-directed autonomy just as completely and as blindly as does the drive to conform to those around one. Neither seems any more or less mature, or rational, than the other. In neither is Piaget's heteronomous stage outgrown.

The Rational-Altruistic type corresponds to Freud's "genital" character and to Fromm's "productive orientation." Its full emergence and synthesis probably is possible only as adolescence brings the establishment of an examined, differentiated identity (cf. Erikson, 1950). Its perfection being unlikely this side of the Styx, the development of such a character is a life-long process. Indeed, it is in the nature of this character pattern to continue to grow, to experiment, to incorporate new facts, and to develop new depths of understanding as long as life permits.

Piaget's formulations significantly affected the development of this typology. It embodies the movement he described (Piaget, 1948) from adult constraint, through the "moral realism" of uncritical conformity to external rules, to an autonomous morality based upon co-operation among individuals who separately examine and rationally validate their own moral decisions.

There are well-known dangers in any attempt to "type" people, no matter what the system. This character typology was mainly designed as a rough, provisional way of classifying the adolescents for research purposes, in an effort to find out if there were any significant, correlated differences in two other sets of factors: their personality characteristics and the interactional dynamics of their families. Only if the subjects classed together according to character type proved to be similar in the other factors, would there be any evidence that this character typology might have some validity as a way of describing people's character.

The character type assessments were treated in a number of ways when the research data were analyzed. The ultimate procedures were to arrange the subjects into "character type *groups*," for certain analyses, using as the criterion the dominant type in the individual's character profile; by assigning scores increasing from "predominantly Amoral" through the types to "predominantly Rational," a score was given to each individual on overall "Maturity of Character." Details of these procedures will appear in Chapter IV.

PRESUMED PERSONALITY CORRELATES OF MORAL CHARACTER

In a very real sense, assessing moral character is simply one way of assessing an individual's personality. However, there were certain personality characteristics that seemed especially relevant to moral functioning. It was decided to study the subjects from a number of angles, none completely independent or separate from the others, in order to attain as full and well-rounded a picture as possible of the reasons for each person's moral behavior, and, more generally, to determine the place of personality in moral character.

Several aspects of personality were selected for study: the perceptual and cognitive system; the personality structure; attitudes toward other people; and the self-concept system, including the person's own rationale for his behavior. These areas were subdivided into more than thirty characteristics, and rating scales were developed for use in the case analyses. (See Appendix for complete definitions.)

Perceptual system

It was postulated, first, that effective morality must require at least enough intelligence to perceive the nature of a social situation, and relate it to some moral rules, however crude they may be. Mere level of test "IQ" is probably less significant than the subject's ability to see relationships among various elements in a real-life situation, to generalize and apply a principle in terms appropriate to the situation, and to foresee the results of any action he takes. His *potential intellectual capacities* are of interest in these respects, since they indicate the highest level he is capable of achieving, under ideal conditions. At the same time, it seems well to assess the level at which he is actually functioning, which may be well below capacity for any one of several reasons, including lack of motivation, lack of training, or disturbing emotional difficulties that divert or distort attention.

Good intentions are notoriously a poor substitute for accurate perception and appropriate action. Thus, to be very highly moral, one must probably have the ability to perceive fairly complex situations realistically, to relate abstract ideas above the level of observation of immediate details, and to include a number and variety of factors in forming a general, integrated picture. Further, one must be able to envision and mentally test various solutions to a problem involving moral issues. In its highest form, this permits new insights and syntheses, such as the first man must have had who voiced the principle of the golden rule, in an age when barbaric competition was presumably the norm.

At its most crucial point, this involves one's perception of other people: its degree of accuracy and its depth of understanding. It appeared useful to distinguish three modes of perception: observation, insight, and empathy. *Observation* consists of watching people, seeing how they behave, and recognizing how they structure their social relations. *Insight,* here, means insight into other people. This involves objective, intellectual understanding of others' wishes, needs, and motives. It seems important for anything beyond literal, rule-determined morality. For instance, to give only candy to a child who is hungry for affection may betoken a well-meaning donor, but it shows little effective concern for the child's real needs. It is "kind," but not the most effective sort of kindness, because it lacks insight.

Third, is a capacity called *Empathy*. This is the ability to feel with another person, to experience the same emotions, for a short time at least, and to appreciate another's attitude from his point of view. If this existed alone, and to excess, it might lead to quite irrational, ill-considered action which was not to the other's benefit in the long run. However, some degree of it seems necessary if morality is to be other than a cold, mechanical application of rules.

As a way of summarizing the degree to which the individual's perceptual and adaptive behavior is in accord with the realities of the social and moral situations he faces, it was decided to make an overall rating on the typical *rationality* of his behavior. This was conceived as a measure of the extent to which his actions are adapted to the facts of each situation, and the extent to which his behavior is effective in achieving the moral objectives he has in mind.

It might be noted that when this characteristic was defined, it was thought that some individuals might be highly rational in seeking selfish ends, so that rationality might not necessarily imply good moral behavior. It was thought, on the other hand, that the most effectively moral behavior would probably require highly rational perception and choice of action. A significant distinction should perhaps be drawn here: this measure was not intended to assess merely the capacity to consciously *think* logically, but the demonstrated tendency to *behave* logically. Thus it was defined for rating purposes as *Rationality of Behavior.*

Personality structure

In order to study and understand human beings, it is necessary to understand what is going on "inside" the person. Two different people who behave in an apparently identical way may have different motives for this piece of action. One could predict behavior most accurately, it seemed likely, by knowing the private, personal world of the individual: the different things he wants or hopes to do in life, the intensity and nature of his emotional reactions, and the ways he has of handling and expressing his deepest desires.

One important measure of the way a person views the world might be termed the *maturity of his emotional reactions.* For example, when children respond to events with strong feeling, they do so without tempering their response to any of the subtle differences between situations. When they are happy, they are exuberant, uncritical, and have a hard time not to jump and run all over the place. When they are angry, they are angry "all over"; and they respond just as strongly to minor frustrations as to big ones. As they grow and mature, healthy children more and more respond to events with feelings that are appropriate to the particular situation. They display differences in the intensity of their emotional reactions according to the relative importance of events. They learn to accept inevitable frustrations without flying into a rage. By adulthood, ideally, everyone will have learned to make these discriminations.

However, appearances can be deceptive. A child may learn that it is considered socially undesirable to express intense, primitive feelings openly, and learn to "cover up" his reactions in public. Outwardly, he may act quite "grown-up," but inside, as those who know him well may realize, he may still have the same strong, blind emotional reactions of an infant. Therefore, one must look beneath the surface, and see the person's spontaneous reactions. Later, of course, it is desirable to know how he handles them; but at this point the question is how discriminating he is in responding emotionally. The more mature he is in this respect, the more perceptively he can react to people. His motivation to act should be appropriate to the unique features in each new situation. This quality was measured as *Emotional Maturity*.

Closely allied to the above, is the nature of a person's most pressing drives and impulses. There is a great difference between a girl who has strong affectional tendencies which lead her to view others in a warm, favorable light, and another girl who feels rejected, bitter, and whose strongest private desire is to strike back and hurt people. Such negative impulses may never be expressed openly, but by their very nature, the best morality such a girl can show is one of *not* actively hurting people. She has no motivation to act in a truly warm, positive way.

Some of the main kinds of impulse to be considered in each case are those of relating to other people in terms of affectional responses, aggressive or hostile action, and sexual responses. It is not that these cover all areas of human behavior that makes them crucial. It is rather the fact that in our culture it seems to be these kinds of impulses, more than any other, which are the focus of difficulty. The latter two are entirely taboo in many ways, and the problem of handling and channeling them usually occupies a good portion of an American's energy. This is often outside the consciousness of the individual concerned, but that makes it no less a problem, personally and socially. In any case, it seemed worthwhile to identify the nature and direction of these vital drives. The generalized social attitude of each subject was measured by two variables: *Absence of Overt Hostility* and *Absence of Covert Hostility*.

It is axiomatic in modern dynamic psychology that a person can effectively and thoroughly control only those impulses or wishes of which he is aware. A desire that is "denied" is no less real, simply because the person cannot admit to himself that he feels it. Such impulses often appear in disguised forms, so that other people feel their effect, even though the person himself is unaware of the meaning his behavior conveys. On the other hand, the more impulses one recognizes in himself, the better one can test how realistic and reasonable they are, and, if desirable, learn to modify them.

It is the fact that consciousness of one's major impulses often has an important influence on the degree to which they can be modified or re-educated that made this seem relevant to moral behavior, especially to moral education.

A person's impulses to act are only half the story, of course, in accounting for his behavior. The other half concerns the nature, the stability, and the internal congruity of the system he has evolved for expressing or controlling his various impulses. Urges can be expressed directly; but much or most of the time they require repression, suppression, or redirection, in order for the individual to fit in acceptably with his society.

In moral terms, the ideal would no doubt be a person who always actively wants to do only what is morally right. Humanly speaking, however, almost everyone has moments when his desires are less than perfectly moral. Most people contain such desires, or modify their expression. The adaptive personality mechanisms by which such modification is achieved are what is meant by "control system."

For example, in describing a person who acts "loyal," it should be helpful to know whether he *feels* loyal, or is outwardly conforming to a socially approved code while inwardly he would like to behave quite differently. At one time or another, such a discrepancy between inner impulses and outer behavior seems almost inevitable. In any case, the way they are reconciled must be considered. The "ideally moral" person would have no problem of control. The rest of us must choose one of several ways of curbing spontaneous reactions, at such times as they are not in accord with the moral code.

One method is repression. In this, the individual denies to himself and the world that he has anything other than acceptable impulses. As long as he can command his behavior, no non-acceptable impulse will be expressed. But the notorious difficulty with repression is that impulses often "leak out" in ways which are disguised. The individual is not conscious, for example, that his "slip of the tongue" conveys a hostile intent. Others, however, may have little difficulty recognizing that, for all his professions of amity, on this particular occasion he would "really" like to hurt someone. It is clear not only that his outward morality has a flaw in its appearance, but that this unconscious expression if the repressed impulse, perceived as it is by others, has an adverse effect on them. To the degree that this is true, his operational morality is less adequate than he realizes.

There is another way of conforming to the socially defined code in the face of contrary impulses. This is to recognize whatever feelings one has, but consciously select which ones are to be expressed. Such a method is commonly termed "suppression." In practice, hostile or otherwise non-constructive impulses which are this close to the surface may be quite apparent. The person is able to conform to the moral rules overtly, and perhaps quite reliably. However, if he does it "unwillingly" in a sense, the same qualification holds as for the repressively controlled person. He will not go out of his way to show active concern for others in an area where his real desires are counter to the code he observes officially.

Perhaps the most "mature" type of impulse control is that where the impulse is positively toned toward others to begin with. It may be necessary to defer personal gratification, in order to observe others' best interests; but there is no essential conflict between what one wants to do, and what would be "good" in its effect on others. One might call this a "conscious-adaptive" system, although such a label does not convey the essential identity of the impulse with "that which is morally good."

Whatever control system typifies a given individual, it is important to know how consistent it is, and how flexible. In a given person, for instance, his sexual impulses may be firmly controlled, so that potential sex partners are not exploited for selfish gratification. At the same time, his aggressiveness may be checked when dealing with people of equal or superior status, but freely released toward people of subordinate status. Thus there can be consistency or inconsistency among his expressions of different kinds of feeling in different social situations. Presumably the greatest degree of morality involves consistency of both kinds.

In more specific terms, it was decided to look at the ways in which individuals reconcile their personal desires with their wish to adhere to a moral pattern of action. Some people defer personal gratifications until others' interests are no longer affected adversely. Others release feelings such as aggression through substitute outlets with no moral connotation. The farmer who is annoyed at his wife but takes his hostility out by splitting a pile of cordwood is a case in point, especially if he returns to the house in a more amiable frame of mind when he has finished.

A less productive and less moral approach is that of "projecting" onto other people one's own negative feelings. This amounts to distorted perception, and also to denial of responsibility for one's own immoral impulses. If this process is carried far enough, it may lead to projection of blame for actual behavior. To call it "paranoid" or "psychoticlike" is not to remove moral responsibility from the individual. This is recognized in our society by legal provision for institutionalizing such people, either as psychotic or as socially dangerous "psychopathic personalities."

Most of us indulge in rationalization to some degree to justify our actions. In the moral sphere, this is an attempt to avoid guilt or blame by calling an immoral act something else that we can "justify" on other grounds. It is nonetheless a misrepresentation of moral responsibility. Rationalizing is not a realistic way of facing and accepting moral responsibility. Nor is rigid, literal insistence on formal rules the most perceptive, realistic way to insure the highest moral ends in dealing with other people. These are only some of the ways in which people can be defensive rather than honest, put blame somewhere else, rather than put the responsibility where it rightly belongs.

In positive terms, the development of reasoned self-control, in order to insure other people's well-being, is one of the hallmarks of the ethical person: an essential ingredient for social living. An important aspect of such self-control is the presence and influence of some set of moral rules or principles, usually referred to as the conscience or superego.

In order to measure some of the salient features of the individual's control system, ratings were made on the following things:

Identity of overt behavior with inner impulse.

Autonomy (ego-directed behavior, free from arbitrary outer pressures or from irrational inner pressures).

Accuracy in assigning responsibility.

Emotional stability (overtly demonstrated control).

Superego strength (*effectiveness* of the subject's conscience in guiding his behavior).

A subject for summary study was the value system actually at work in an individual's behavior. It included study of both motivation— what he wants to do, and actual behavior—what he does. The latter was conceived to be the resultant of two forces: personal motives, and the pressures enforcing the socially defined moral code. It was asked, in summary, what the subject's operational values are, and how consistent they are. Are they a set of generalized principles, stably followed, or are they particular to certain people or situations? Is he honest about money transactions, but not honest in card games if he can avoid detection? To put it another way, are the moral principles on which the subject acts integrated into a coherent, consistent system, or are they compartmentalized? Is he honest, loyal, responsible, etc., to about the same degree; or is he thoroughly honest, but not very reliable in carrying out responsibilities? Such questions helped sketch a subject's moral character as he is seen in action.

There were two kinds of consistency observed. The first is internal, the degree of consonance or contradiction among a person's aims and values. In a real sense, it is a measure of personality integration. The other factor is the consistency with which he conforms to the moral code in his outward behavior. The latter is a sort of summary evaluation of his moral character in its social aspects. The internal measure focuses attention on the effect on the individual himself; what it "costs" him in terms of emotional energy, to reconcile his private impulses with social directives. One might expect that the most vigorous, actively moral person is one whose energy is not bound up in an internal war between acceptable and unacceptable impulses. This would imply, perhaps, that neurotic features of personality functioning have an adverse effect on moral character; that mental health is important to good character. The hypothesis seemed worth investigating.

The two kinds of consistency were rated as: *Inner Consistency* (personality integration) and *Overt Conformity* to the (conference-defined) moral code.

Self concept

We believed it would help us understand a person's behavior if we knew how he sees it, and how he explains and justifies it. Here, we were concerned with the subject's concept of himself as a moral person. He may not be doing at all what he thinks he is doing. Bill K., for example, may feel he is really dishonest, remembering a childhood episode of petty stealing. Yet his every action may be that of an unusually honest youth, as all who know him can testify. On examination, we find that he feels he *should* be honest; and that his suspicion that "really" he is not reinforces his determination to overcome his "sinful nature." This is a clear case where the self concept is a motivating force, and therefore relevant to our understanding of Bill's moral behavior.

While one's self concept may or may not coincide with one's behavioral self, there is a practical utility in studying it. We wanted to know whether a person feels he is "good" or "bad" in general. Specifically, how does he rate himself on honesty, kindness, and each of the other traits? Is he calm or anxious, self-satisfied or guilty, when he evaluates his behavior morally? Perhaps most important, how accurately does he recognize identities and discrepancies between his inner impulses and his outward behavior?

One of the major difficulties that hamper re-education or therapy with certain "maladjusted" people is their defensive refusal to examine objectively the ways in which everyone else sees them acting. Particularly if they tend to project blame, and refuse to acknowledge that they may be responsible for things that go wrong, they are apt to continue inflexibly, robbing themselves as well as others of certain satisfactions they would like to have. Since all interpersonal behavior can be viewed from a moral aspect, it is important to know the individual's own rationale. Especially if education toward a higher level of morality is to be undertaken, we must know whether the person is open to reorientation; whether he is able to modify his self concept in the light of new conditions or goals.

The aspects of this area which were rated were: *Guilt about Outward Behavior, Guilt about Inner Impulses, Accuracy of Self-Perception.*

Attitudes in major relationships

As an aid to understanding why a person acts as he does in moral respects, it seemed useful to find out how he feels about the significant people in his life. It is known from other researches, for instance, that one tends to carry over his attitudes toward parents in reacting to other people in positions of authority, even much later in life. This appears true in work situations, and in reacting to governmental authority. Similarly, attitudes developed early in life toward brothers and sisters are often carried over in reacting to age mates in later years.

Feelings of good will or of antagonism to such people have an obvious and direct bearing on how much consideration and unselfish concern one is likely to show in dealing with them, or in dealing with other people who summon up the same strong, often unconscious feelings. It therefore appeared likely that one could find in these deep emotional reactions much of the explanation for a person's moral behavior.

Consequently, it was decided to investigate the subjects' attitudes, both openly displayed and covert, toward father, mother, siblings, and other significant family members or their substitutes. In addition, since the world of age mates becomes increasingly important as a learning and testing ground for values, particularly in adolescence, the feelings and attitudes toward peers of both sexes were studied. Such attitudes were measured by ratings on the following variables: *Out-*

ward Acceptance of the Father's Code of Behavior, Positive Feeling toward Father (intensity), *Negative Feeling toward Father* (intensity), *Outward Acceptance of the Mother's Code of Behavior, Positive Feeling toward Mother* (intensity), *Negative Feeling toward Mother* (intensity), *Feeling Tone of Outward Relations with Same-Sex Peers, Inner Feeling toward Same-Sex Peers, Feeling Tone of Outward Relations with Opposite-Sex Peers, Inner Feeling toward Opposite-Sex Peers* (hostility-to-friendliness scales).

It might be stated at this point that sexual behavior, as such, was not defined as moral or immoral for the purposes of this study. The question would be, in sexual just as in other areas of behavior, what are the motives involved and what are the effects on the people concerned? It is clear that sexual behavior involves moral issues, but it was hoped to locate the general, definitive factors which give sexual interaction a moral aspect, like any other interpersonal relationship. Undoubtedly, because of the intensity of human feeling and the potential social and physical consequences involved, this is an area where morality is particularly significant.

A generalized attitude was summed up in a variable called *Locus of Concern.* This is a continuum from completely egocentric self-interest, where other people are viewed only as a means to a personal end, to sociocentric concern, where the person is as much interested in the well-being and happiness of others as in his own welfare. At this high end of the continuum one might find a person who will sacrifice his own interests in order to benefit others, when the necessity arises. Since this is a measure of inner motives, an overt act of apparent "martyrdom" does not inevitably imply a highly socialized locus of concern. Everyone is familiar with cases in which neurotic, long-suffering "martyrdom" has been used to tyrannize the unwilling beneficiaries of such "self-sacrifice." However, sincerely unselfish behavior, which results in good for other people, would clearly place a person high on this scale.

An allied concept, which was tested for its possible usefulness, is the *Range of Moral Horizon.* Some people feel duty bound to act morally toward their family and immediate friends, yet consider rivals or strangers "fair game" for exploitation. Others include in the circle of people toward whom they feel they should be moral all others who are "like them" in manners, in social affiliations, or in religion. They may still feel that people in other groups are somehow less deserving of thoroughly moral treatment. There may be some, too, who include all citizens of their own nation, but exclude "foreigners." Some few, such as Albert Schweitzer perhaps, hold every man as brother, no matter what his race or nation, and act by that belief. In short, it seems insufficient to say that a person is moral in his behavior. It further appears necessary to ask, "moral toward whom?"

After the subjects had all been studied and rated, the many positive correlations among these personality variables suggested the advisability of a factor analysis. When this was performed, it turned out that not thirty, but six significantly separate dimensions of personality had been measured. (See Appendix, pp. 243–249.) The six dimensions were identified as follows: Moral Stability, Ego Strength, Superego Strength, Spontaneity, Friendliness, and a Hostility-Guilt Complex. The relationships of these dimensions to character are discussed in Chapter IV.

THE SOURCES OF CHARACTER

During the course of the individual case studies, estimates were made of the relative influence of various people and institutions on the value system of each adolescent subject. The results of this appraisal are presented in Chapter VII.

Independent appraisals had been made some years earlier of the children's families. These measures of the families' emotional dynamics and interaction patterns made it possible to look for general relationships between family experiences and character formation. The results, for each level of moral effectiveness, are presented in Chapter V.

The relationship of individual character to peer acceptance and peer reputation was studied both in the case studies, and by detailed analysis of certain sociometric measures. A comparison of family dynamics and peer reputation was also made. The findings from these analyses will be found in Chapter VI.

THE TIME SCALE OF CHARACTER FORMATION

While only retrospective evidence was available for the years before age ten, in the case of these subjects, it was possible to study directly the consistency and pliability of their characters from age ten to age seventeen. The results are discussed in Chapter VIII, together with related information from other sources.

II

The setting,
the research population,
and the research procedure

The community called Prairie City was selected because it is small enough to be studied intensively, and at the same time it is typical in size and complexity of the many small cities of the Middle West.

According to the U.S. census there are about 250 small cities with population between five and ten thousand located in the twelve North Central states, from Ohio to Missouri and from North Dakota to Kansas. One hundred and eight of these cities are the largest centers in counties which are agricultural-industrial. This type of county has between 25 and 50 per cent of its gainfully employed males in agriculture, and the remainder in industry, business, and other occupations.

Prairie City, the county seat of Prairie County, is one of these 108 cities. There are communities of twenty to thirty thousand population in the adjacent counties, and there is a metropolitan area within a hundred miles. The total population of this community is about ten thousand, of whom six thousand live within the city limits and four thousand in the surrounding rural territory.

Prairie City was chosen for study after a survey had been made of the census data on all the small cities of this type within two hundred miles of Chicago and after Prairie City and other cities had been visited. These preliminary studies showed Prairie City to be typical of small Midwestern cities according to a number of significant census criteria.

The town is about a hundred years old. Its population grew rapidly until 1900, and since then it has remained relatively stable; it has not changed as much as 10 per cent in any decade since 1900.

The city has shared in the development of the Middle West from a simple agricultural society to a complex industrial-agricultural society. The community is now economically dependent equally upon agriculture, manufacturing, and retail sales. It has a favorable location on railway and waterway lines and serves as an important shipping point for the surrounding region. Census data show that the proportion of people paying an income tax is about the same as in other small cities.

A community like Prairie City tends to be relatively complete and "self-sufficient." Lying outside a metropolitan area, it has an independent social life; there is no college, university, or state institution in the community, nor is it a health or summer resort. Its local autonomy and coherence are therefore undisturbed.

Approximately 90 per cent of its inhabitants are native born; there are two distinguishable ethnic groups—a substantial group of Norwegians and a small Polish group. There is one Negro family and one Chinese. Thus Prairie City has the usual American diversity, though it is not as highly diversified as most of the large cities.

Although the community is simple and unified enough so that the scientist can describe its social structure after a relatively short period of study, at the same time it offers "everything" in American life— factories, a complete school system, library, movies and other commercial recreation, banks, hospitals, and specialized medical service. Although it is small enough so that a boy or girl can grow up and be acquainted with "almost everybody in town," it gives a youth enough experience with modern industry and society to enable him to step into a more complex metropolitan world and act with decisiveness.

Like the other communities of its type, Prairie City is a vital source of new life for the metropolitan areas of this country. The great cities, which fall considerably short of reproducing their populations, continue to draw from smaller communities. Thus the welfare of the great cities, as well as small, depends to a considerable extent on the quality of the children who are reared in Prairie City and its kindred communities.

The families of Prairie City fall into five major groups or "social classes." A social class is a group of people who think of themselves as belonging to the same social level and who generally are willing to associate intimately with one another, to have their families intermarry, and so on (Warner, 1949*b*).

It is worthwhile to study the social structure of Prairie City and to locate the families of the subjects on the social scale because various social classes have different ideas of what is right and wrong, interesting and boring, important and unimportant. Therefore there may be differences among the social classes in moral character.

The five social classes of Prairie City have been described by Warner (Warner, 1949*a*), and their general social characteristics may be studied in his book. In their general moral reputations the boys and girls of the several social classes differ, as has been shown in the earlier study of Prairie City by Havighurst and Taba. Those of higher social status tend, on the average, to have better moral reputations.

THE VALUES OF PRAIRIE CITY

In the things it values Prairie City is faithfully representative of the American Midwest. The community values the general moral virtues of honesty, responsibility, loyalty, and kindliness. It expects industry and thrift, except for some of its lower-lower status families. Boys and girls are expected to get part-time jobs while they are in high school and to learn that the individual should always be responsible for his own economic security.

Though not a wealthy community, Prairie City has been comfortable since the prosperity period of World War II. It tends to forget the grim days of the Depression thirties, when farmers sold their product below the cost of producing it and could not make payments on their mortgages, local industries closed down or employed workers for less than a full work week, and the town was economically stagnant. The community is more interested in economic security than in economic progress. Population growth is not desired. People like the town because it is quiet.

Like other Midwestern communities, Prairie City shrugs its shoulders at a degree of mild political corruption which allows illegal gambling, and in general maintains a cynical attitude about the relations between politics and certain kinds of "shady" business. Boys and girls grow up hearing their elders speak with respect, indifference, or condemnation of one or another public official, and they come to think of civic virtue as something which must be worked for and cannot be expected unless the citizens are alert all the time.

Growing up in Prairie City is an integrated process for most boys and girls. With a few exceptions, they find the values of community, church, school, and family to be in substantial agreement. There is no break in the moral experience of children as they move from one age to another, or from one part of the community to another. They are not forced to shift quickly from one value system to another as were so many German children in Nazi Germany, when they had to combine the values they learned at home and in the church with those they learned under Hitler Youth Leaders and from the Nazi textbooks. Prairie City has such social and political homogeneity that few children are exposed to the moral conflicts of active race prejudice, of labor strife, or of rapid social change.

The exceptional cases who find a degree of moral conflict tend to come from lower class families whose value systems clash with the dominant middle class value system of school, church, and community. For a small minority of boys and girls, mostly from deviant families, their association in school and the community institutions brings them into contact with strange moral expectations, and they must eventually come into conflict with the schools and the community agencies or they must break away from the values of their homes.

Children in Prairie City are subjected to the same government, newspapers, schools (with some exceptions), public library, movies, radio and television programs, and recreation places. Children see the most common American movies, they hear the most popular radio programs, and they have access to the most widely read books. There is no book store in Prairie City, and very few people purchase books by mail.

Insofar as it is a valid statement about American society that it tends to have a mass-production moral code and outlook on life, influenced by the radio, movies, and newspapers and periodicals of the greatest mass circulation, Prairie City shares fully in this situation. Certainly this tends to produce a kind of all-American ethnocentrism that might be called moral smugness. Children tend to grow up with a moral horizon limited to the American whose standardized features they have learned from the mass media of communication. They do not get a chance to look at life from the point of view of the non-American, or even from the point of view of the non-middle class American.

DIFFERENTIATING FACTORS IN THE COMMUNITY

In spite of the powerful difference-destroying factors in the experience of Prairie City children, they are exposed to some differentiating moral forces.

Social classes are a differentiating factor. The various social classes of Prairie City have somewhat different sets of values. The differences in moral values among them are probably greater in practice than in words. People all up and down the social scale in Prairie City tend to agree verbally with an official moral ideology, from which their actual moral behavior departs in various ways. For example, upper class parents undoubtedly tell their children that gambling is wrong, although adults in this class do gamble. Parents of the lower-lower class tell their children that stealing is wrong but do not punish it consistently and may themselves set an example of stealing.

The official value system and moral ideology of Prairie City is that of the middle class. This was found to be true when boys and girls were given the Moral Ideology Test, in which they were asked to name examples of good behavior and bad behavior. There were few differences between children of the different social classes.

In the particular group studied in this research, there was much less social class differentiation than is usually found. There was not a single upper class child in the group, and only three upper-middle class children. A comparison of the social class distribution of this group of children with that of the entire population of Prairie City is given in Table 1. The children born in 1933 are much more homogeneous, socially, than the community as a whole. Four-fifths of them belong to lower-middle or upper-lower class families, which are already the least differentiated pair of classes in terms of values.*

Lower class life in Prairie City differs in one important way from lower class life in a metropolis. The great city presents the disturbing

---

* This fact makes the picture of social-class differentiation among adolescents somewhat different from the research group that was reported by Hollingshead in *Elmtown's Youth*. Although the general trend of Hollingshead's findings for the group of adolescents he studied is valid for our research group, we do not find as sharp differences between social classes as he found. With practically no upper or upper-middle class youth in our group, the positions of leadership and honor had to go to boys and girls lower in the social scale. Thus our lower-middle and upper-lower class youth have had a somewhat different experience than those described by Hollingshead. However, our lower-lower class youth are quite similar to Hollingshead's Class V in their moral experience.

TABLE 1. SOCIAL CLASS AND SEX DISTRIBUTION OF POPULATION

Social Class	Research Group				1933 Group, Prairie City				% in Prairie City, All Ages	% in U.S.A.
	Boys	Girls	Total	%	Boys	Girls	Total	%		
Upper	0	0	0	0	0	0	0	0	3	2
Upper-Middle	1	0	1	3	1	2	3	2	11	8
Lower-Middle	4	5	9	26	11	13	24	20	31	30
Upper-Lower	9	10	19	56	47	26	73	61	41	40
Lower-Lower	3	2	5	15	8	12	20	17	14	20
Total	17	17	34	100	67	53	120	100	100	100

phenomenon of "disorganized areas" in which, from the middle class viewpoint, social values have gone awry. In these areas, there usually is a minority subculture in which it is normal for a child to steal, to lie to the authorities, and to be sexually delinquent. In a subgroup of this kind, delinquency is normal, and only those children who deviate from that norm have a chance of adopting middle class values. This phenomenon of a "delinquency subculture" is possible because of the geographical fragmentation of the city, which forces thousands of lower class people to live together, with their own schools and places of recreation, and which effectively prevents their children from having contact with children from other social classes. Even in such circumstances, of course, non-delinquent youth outnumber the delinquents four or five to one.

In Prairie City there is very little segregation by social class, and there is no "disorganized area." The people of the lower-lower class live in a fringe around the town, as well as in the poorer parts of the business district. Their children are found in all the elementary schools. Thus they are exposed in the school and on the playground to middle class influences among their own age group. There are no delinquent groups in Prairie City, though of course some groups of young people have lower reputations than others.

THE RESEARCH POPULATION

The "universe" of subjects from which our research sample was drawn consisted of all the children born in 1933 and living in Prairie City in 1943. They numbered 120. Beginning in 1943, when the children were ten years old, all of them were tested and rated in a variety of ways. Intelligence tests, achievement tests, attitude questionnaires, the Moral Ideology Test, the Emotional Response Test, and social-personal sociometric measures were obtained on all 120 children from year to year. Character ratings by teachers and by children themselves were also obtained at ages ten, fourteen, and seventeen. Thus, the entire 1933 population was measured on their moral behavior, and on many aspects of ability and social reputation.

However, in order to obtain information about motives, attitudes, and other inner personality characteristics, more intensive study was required, using much more searching and more time-consuming techniques. Therefore, in 1946 a cross-sectional sample was selected, consisting of seventeen boys and seventeen girls who ranged evenly from the top to the bottom of the 1933 group in measures of character. Their social class distribution can be seen in Table 1 and their character reputation ratings by teachers and peers in Table 2.

This research is based on case studies of these thirty-four children, comprising about one-third of the total 1933 group. They were studied from their tenth to their seventeenth year (1943–1950). Earlier data were used in assessing character only insofar as they helped explain the existing pattern of behavior at age sixteen. For the developmental phase of the study, of course, all data were used. This permitted the gathering and analysis of a great deal of information about each subject; not only his behavior, but his motives and personality structure. A study of several hundred would undoubtedly have given us a better cross section, a better statistical sample of the American population; but we hoped, by this more intensive method, to find the *meaning* of the behavior we were studying.

The choice of this adolescent population was made in order to permit close inquiry into the development as well as the nature of moral character. We had at least some information about the earliest years of these children, and had first-hand data on them from the time when they were ten until they had almost reached maturity, at the age of seventeen.

TABLE 2.   1949 REPUTATION D SCORES
(AVERAGE OF RATINGS ON FIVE MORAL TRAITS) *

Case	Peer Ratings	Adult Ratings
T-3	24.4	24.4
T-4	15.3	21.0
T-6	22.6	22.9
T-8	16.7	16.9
T-11	12.0	14.5
T-16	20.2	20.4
T-17	21.8	17.9
T-22	21.3	16.4
T-25	17.4	15.7
T-28	22.5	25.3
T-34	21.4	22.3
T-37	20.6	19.4
T-39	19.2	22.1
T-40	22.8	18.9
T-42	15.3	17.0
T-47	20.8	21.7
T-49	24.1	24.0
T-50	26.7	24.4
T-51	22.6	20.1
T-52	23.3	20.3
T-53	25.0	24.1
T-55	12.5	16.3
T-57	17.0	22.9
T-60	21.6	20.4
T-64	12.3	no data
T-76	22.8	17.8
T-78	19.6	16.4
T-79	23.9	23.8
T-83	22.9	25.2
T-86	21.0	17.3
T-88	15.2	17.6
T-89	16.2	16.9
T-95	16.0	14.6
T-99	17.4	19.8

* These are standardized scores (mean at 20; sigma, 4) derived from the distribution of scores of all 120 children in the 1933 group. These research cases cover the entire range of the total group on moral reputation.

THE COLLECTION OF THE DATA

There were two principal groups of agents in the collection of the data: full-time field workers who lived in the community, and the teachers in the Prairie City public schools. Each year, a different woman field worker was employed to interview the thirty-four children, their parents, and other people in the community. She also was trained to administer the TAT and Sentence Completion techniques. (The Rorschach was administered by experts who visited Prairie City for that purpose in 1946, 1948, and 1949.) An important feature of the field worker's role was her ability to establish friendly, informal relationships with the children in the study and with the people in Prairie City. She worked closely with the teachers, also, and administered many tests and measures to the entire 1933 group each year. Consequently, the field workers were chosen for their personal qualities as well as for technical ability.

The cooperating teachers greatly aided the work of the study by giving behavior ratings and character ratings for their pupils, and by administering some of the tests.

The individual intelligence tests were administered by university specialists who, like the Rorschach testers, briefly visited Prairie City for that purpose.

The data-gathering stage of the study lasted from 1943 through 1950. A list and description of all the instruments used will be found in the Appendix.

THE WORK OF THE CLINICAL CONFERENCE

A research team of ten people spent January to June of the first year organizing the conceptual framework for the study, preparing a case outline based on that framework, and defining the personality and character variables on which the subjects were to be assessed. (See Appendix, pp. 220–236.)

From July through the following June the conference made a case study of each of the thirty-four children, including an investigation of the developmental background. Each staff member performed three roles. The first was that of a specialist in the "blind" analysis of one or more instruments. When all such analyses had been completed, each staff member was, secondly, assigned to collate all information and instrument interpretations which bore on a given section of the case outline. The complete case document was then presented in conference, and discussed until consensus was reached on the picture of the child's behavior, personality structure, and formative experiences. This procedure was patterned after Murray's diagnostic council (Murray, 1938).

The third function of each staff member was that of a judge of behavior and motivation, expressing his judgment in the form of ratings. It was decided during the planning stage of the research to use a system of ratings in order to permit more precise comparison of one case with another, and to permit a systematic, quantitative analysis of the entire body of data after the individual case studies were completed. Therefore, following the conference on a case, the staff members separately rated the case on all the variables selected for study. (The reliability of the average of the eight judges' ratings, at this point, was .96.) In a second conference these ratings were discussed, wherever sizable interjudge discrepancies existed, until agreement was reached on the most representative rating to assign the subject on the trait in question. There were particular reasons for using this system, rather than one of totally independent, blind ratings prior to any conference on the cases. The rationale, method, and validity of the ratings are discussed in the Appendix.

Three different, complementary kinds of data were used in building up the picture of each individual. One consisted of scores on standardized measures such as IQ tests, interest inventories, and personality questionnaires. A second kind of data consisted of scores derived from measures on the entire age group of 120 children. Sociometric scores on character and personality traits are an example. Finally, there were the idiosyncratic data, different for each person, such as the interview protocols, projective techniques, essays, and the like. These were qualitatively analyzed, to describe the life pattern unique to the individual. They were also analyzed for evidence that would bear on the variables which were to be rated. The final case document was a synthesis of the information and appraisals from all three sources.

Case studies
of three character types

A few excerpts have been selected from the hundred and fifty or so pages of data and analyses in each of three case files. These are arranged chronologically for each of three children, representing three character types. In the first case, "Arthur" (a pseudonym), the data are given at some length, in order to sample most of the major kinds of data. In the other two cases, some highlights are more briefly indicated. All data have been heavily disguised.

There are three reasons for presenting these data. In the first place, they illustrate the kinds of behavior on which the character study ratings were based, and which they represent. Secondly, the reader can make comparisons and contrasts among children at the various levels of the character type scale, by inspecting the comparable test responses and interview data. In the case of interpretive excerpts, all instrument analyses were done independently of one another, except for the 1948 Sentence Completion and the 1949–50 TAT's, which one person analyzed. Consequently, repetitive interpretations represent agreement between independent assessments made by analysts who did not know what other analysts would report from other kinds of data. Lastly, fragmentary though they are, the excerpts from each case illustrate some of the chief changes and consistencies in the child's character, from age ten through age seventeen.

ARTHUR ADAMS: AN AMORAL BOY

1943

Moral Ideology Test Responses

Good Things to Do: 1. go to the store for old people; 2. don't yell around old people; 3. do good work at school; 4. don't fool with the telephone; 5. carry coal for your parents; 6. don't talk in school; 7. don't swear at people; 8. go to sleep on Christmas night; 9. don't hit children.

Bad Things to Do: 1. fool with the telephone; 2. knock snow forts over; 3. brake the fire alarm; 4. talk at school; 5. swear at people; 6. stay up and see Santa Claus; 7. hit children with sticks; 8. make funny pictures of the teacher; 9. spill garbage on the sidewalk.

1944

Emotional Response Test Responses

I Was Angry When: 1. A girl called me a sissy because I ran away from a big boy; 2. My sister got a dollar from my uncle and I didn't; 3. I had to entertain some kids I don't like.

I Was Ashamed of Doing: 1. Took a nickel away from my sister; 2. I called my big sister a snot; 3. Called my aunt and uncle a big fat baboon.

The Best Thing That Could Happen: Become a rich boy with diamonds, rubies, emeralds and other jewels.

Worst Thing: Kill my best dog and best cat.

1945

Essay

THE PERSON I WOULD LIKE TO BE WHEN I GROW UP

The person I would like to be probably is not real. He is real rich, and he lives in a big castle, estate, mansion or palace. He has

kennels full of the most beautiful dogs in the world. (mostly collies)
He should have a treasure house with a lot of diamonds, rubies, opals,
sapphires, emeralds and other precious stones. Also he should have
a wardrobe of the finest clothes money can buy.

I want him to be so rich and powerful that his name is in every
paper. He should be medium tall and have blue eyes. He should
be a little stuck-up.

His dogs won every prize including the sweepstakes for dogs.
That's the kind of person I would want to be when I grow up.

The End

Interview Excerpt

Mother: . . . For instance, this matter of appreciating things—a
couple of years ago, his aunt brought him a green wash suit. It
put her out some. It was more that she could really afford, but
she liked it so well and she just wanted to get it for him. He took
one look at it and he said, "That thing! Why I wouldn't even wear
it. It's awful. I wouldn't be seen in a thing like that." She felt
pretty bad about it, and she went into the other room and cried.
Then a few minutes later he went down to see his friend (he used
to play with a couple of boys who lived here in the building) and
said, "Gee, you oughta see the swell suit my aunt got me." He
wore it after that more than any other suit of his, but he'd never
give her the satisfaction of knowing that he liked it. You can't
tell what he means by what he says at all, and nothing ever pleases
him.

1946

Interview Excerpt

Interviewer: How does he get along with his sister?
Mother: Just the same way. He'll fight with her and if he can, boss
her around. They don't get along at all. . . .

He's so changeable. There'll be some days that he'll come in and
he'll be just as nice as he can and we'll talk and we have a fine
time; and then other times you can't do a thing with him. . . .
Now once Addie told me he was over to her apartment and he
waited purposely until he knew it was late enough for his uncle
to be in bed, then he called him up. When his uncle got out of bed
and came to the phone, Arthur said that all he wanted to do was

to say, "Hello," and then he hung up again.   I guess he thought that was funny.   Addie said that if she had been his uncle she'd 'a been furious. . . .

Interviewer: . . .   Just as we were talking about this, Arthur came into the room.   He made a number of derogatory remarks and I asked him if he was feeling rather cross that day.   He said yes, because it was a rainy day.

Rorschach Interpretation Excerpt

His inner disturbance, anxiety, oppositional tendencies, withdrawal from and unconnectedness to reality would tend to make him an isolate, or even a scapegoat.   His relationship to the group is apt to have an avalanche effect, i.e., he has a low, if not negative, social stimulus value in terms of his inner maladjustment, which in turn affects his intrapersonal organization negatively, which probably continues to reinforce the negative opinion and reaction of the group. In terms of his own conception of himself in relation to the group, he reacts oversensitively, withdrawing like a "burnt child."   In view of the above, he should be below the norm on his reputation scores throughout—and especially judged as one who is apt to do mean, sneaky things.   Ratings should be low from both peers and adults, peers being possibly somewhat lower than adults.

In this case it seems somewhat difficult to talk about a "basic emotional attitude"—it seems like a contradiction of terms to say that his "basic" attitude is characterized by instability and rambling; by a childlike, succorance-craving passivity at one time; by an abortive attempt to reach out for interpersonal contact and affection, which quickly is replaced by rebellion and hostility, which in turn gives way to self-attack, anxiety, and insecurity of depression; while at times there might be some earnest self-scrutiny in a vague, short-lived attempt to tackle emotional problems and inner conflicts.   Chiefly his emotional attitude is marked by confusion, anxious withdrawal, occasional outbursts of temper, and depression.

There are no indications of positive identifications in the entire record.   Inferentially, I am inclined to state that probable sources for his anxiety pattern would include:

1. His own fantasies, and feelings of hostility
2. Experienced rebuff from interpersonal relationships both in and outside the family
3. Although there is evidence of existing sex anxiety (see sequence

analysis), the data do not allow a "determining cause" hypothesis in that area.

Emotional-social growth is at present at a prepubescent level of development with deep cravings for succorance (oral satisfactions).

Ego defenses consist chiefly in complete withdrawal, which contains an element of rebellion and "I don't care" attitude. This may be accompanied by occasional temper outbursts of authority defiance and self-assertion (e.g. "I want to have my own way.") Positive ways of self-comfort should consist in sensuous fantasy escape and pleading for affection from sympathetic adults.

TAT Interpretation Excerpt

Arthur's relationships with peers are probably extremely poor— poor in the sense that he has few positive ties to them and in general is received negatively by them. This is an instance where the social stereotype will probably operate strongly against him to give him a reputation of rejection. Actually he has very little hostility against his peers, but his feelings of self-martyrdom, his strong introspection, and his rather sensuous and full inner vitality will be received with suspicion by the group. I should expect that his sociometric scores would be heavily on the rejection side. While he is a good object for scapegoating, I doubt if he receives much of that kind of attack at present.

Basic emotional attitude is essentially passive though it is accompanied by occasional wild, aggressive flares. These aggressive moments are not directed outward. That is to say, he attacks the images of his frustrations in fantasy rather than any specific individuals in his environment.

His ties to other people are only present as they relate to his succorance needs. In general, in his stories, older women are seen as rejecting and restraining; men are seen as impersonal but good and desirable; peers are non-existent.

Sexual adjustment: Pregenital, undifferentiated sexuality of oral character. Has latent many of the features of passive male homosexual. Anxiety over masturbation and castration fear.

1947 Conference Summary Excerpt

All the evidence (except his answers on the California Personality Test) indicates that T-39 is an isolate in the peer group, at least during the years of 1945–1946. "His classmates respond to him negatively, apparently not for what he does or says, but because of some 'queerness' which they find distasteful" (sociometric data).

The two projective tests agree that "his relationships with his peers are extremely poor—poor in the sense that he has few positive ties to them, in general is received negatively by them." (TAT) The question is raised whether he is the object of scapegoating. There seems to be no evidence that this is true in any of the data. On the 1946 Guess Who, for example, he is not mentioned as grouchy, not nice to people, or on similarly negative items.

1948

Sentence Completion Test Responses

2. Sometimes I feel like—I would like to save all the money in the world.
3. With other people I—No idea.
7. Boys—more mindful of sex than girls.
8. When I'm alone—I sometimes get sex minded.
9. Secretly I—wish I could see what goes on in the world at night.
11. A person's life—is their own personal problem.
13. I would do anything if—I got enough money.
22. There are times when I—am so mad I could yell at anybody.
27. I am usually—very selfish.
28. It is more important to—have friends than to be alone in the world.
39. My only trouble is—I am sex minded.
43. If I am left behind—I am mad.
44. As I child—I was mean.
47. I am very—selfish.
49. I cannot understand what makes me—so sex minded.

Sentence Completion Interpretation Excerpt

He is impulsive, and is having a hard time to keep even a sufficient minimum of these impulses in hand and to get along with society as a whole. He will often break into attacking, non-social, situationally inappropriate kinds of behavior. He is acutely aware of this pressure from his inner life, in both the major areas of hostility and sex, and it makes him very uncomfortable when interacting with people. His awareness, unfortunately for him, does not seem to prevent such impulses from breaking out, and their strength is such that they probably burst through his controls quite often.

He is a highly constricted person whose controls are such that impulses break through into spontaneous behavior a large part of the time. He is anxious and uncomfortable about this, feels guilty, basically bad in his inner being and in his resultant behavior. For a boy with as strong intellectual interests as he has, it may seem somewhat surprising that we must call him very non-rational in his approach to the world. His judgments are personal, idiosyncratic to an extreme. He lays the blame for things either too heavily on himself, or too thoroughly on others, as the spirit arises. Projection onto others is itself a spotty character feature. Mother particularly is selected for blame.

What moral principles are manifest are those of a very punitive set of rules about sex introjected into something that we might call a superego. He has become obsessed with questions of sex, and it is in this area that he is experiencing the greatest difficulty in adjusting his behavior to the rules as he perceives them. There is little stable in the whole personality picture—let alone the moral area, particularly.

While he thinks of himself at a conscious level, in the main, as a fine fellow, and thinks that the world is wrong not to recognize his worth, he also sees himself as somewhat of a selfish stinker and doesn't really wonder so much that others avoid him, and don't want to have much to do with him. This latter feature is what nearly everybody sees, what they don't like in him and in truth that is probably what he acts like in the public eye. There is thus a large discrepancy between his self-evaluation as a wonder boy, and what others would accord him.

1949

Interview Excerpt

Arthur: I think I differ greatly from what people think I am. For example, a person who doesn't know me as a personal friend thinks I am stingy and selfish when I won't give them anything of mine, but a real friend would only have to ask and I'll give it to them. Some people think I am stuck-up because I won't speak to some one I dislike. I think I am as friendly as the next person. Others think I am not so good-looking. I think that while I am not as handsome as some, I *am* good-looking.

Some think I am shy and bashful in front of strangers while I am really cool and calm in front of strangers. Some people think I am showing off when I sing, but I think I can sing very well. I can sing just like opera—like a girl. I can also sing like a boy.

(You don't like to go in a large group?) No, just a few; I'm snobbish you know and I don't like to have anything to do with some of the other kids. I go with one person for awhile, one fellow or so and then I get tired and I go with someone else. I don't go with the boys in school very much; I prefer to be by myself.

(Are there any girls you can think of that you admire?) I can't think of any qualities I admire in girls, but I don't hate them. Now, M., I know her pretty well. . . . But I can't think of any qualities that I think are particularly good in any of the girls.

(What qualities do you admire in boys?) Oh there is one boy at school that I think is swell, he is so snobbish and I would like to be like him. He's very selfish, and well he's just snobbish. I always wanted to be rich and not speak to him or anybody. . . . I would like to be rich and not speak to him or anybody. . . .

. . . I just have a knack for saying mean things. I can get even my best friends, I can get'em, you know when they know I'm doing it on purpose, I can get them mad, even. I can just provoke people. And I can tell things out that I just guess at and get the truth; they get so mad! (What do you consider an insult?) . . . Depends on how mad I was, I mean, what I was going to insult them. If you say something about their family, talk about the mother or father or something, that usually gets them mad. You could laugh at them, tell them to their face how you made a fool of them or something. Or just call them names. Hell, you know, not to say it out loud but be kind of subtle about it. It gets them so mad, I can see that. . . . I'm not insulted at all, I don't think. If they did I wouldn't feel hurt, I'd feel mad and insult them back. I guess they don't want to insult me because I wouldn't feel hurt about it, I'd just feel mad and insult them back. Insults wouldn't affect me any.

Like my little cousin, he'll squeal and cry. He's spoiled. I won't give him any thing, mostly because I'm selfish but if I don't feel good, if I'm mad, I like to hear him cry and I laugh. It's terrible but I do. He's so spoiled and you know he is really cute. . . . And everyone thinks he's nice. He'll do anything he's so spoiled. So I just out of meanness let him know he can't have everything. . . . I slap him hard as I can and as often as I can. I like to hear him cry anyway. . . .

I get them something I like (for Christmas) so if they don't like it they can give it to me easily enough. . . . I'm a terrible snoop.

I follow them around and look at price tags and then I—I know last year, mother was so mad at me, everyone was mad at me, after Christmas, after I got my presents, the next day I went down and found out what everyone paid for my presents. I went around asking how much things cost and then I told them. Oh, everyone was so mad. . . . I wanted to embarrass them, I wanted to embarrass them. So I went down and found out how much things cost and told them how cheap they were, and how much they paid for it and everything. You know, I wanted to say it right off, I'd say, "Gee, you're kind of cheap" and they'd ask why, and I'd say, "Gee, you only paid so much for this and that and it'd get them so mad and I thought that was terrible after I was done. . . . I like to do that for meanness.

They're not giving it to me out of the kindness of their heart, they're giving it to me because it was Christmas anyway, so why should I thank them, and besides I gave them something so—I don't see why I should thank them so I don't. They think I do but I don't.

Rorschach Administrator's Comment

In both his reactions to the Rorschach test and his free verbalizations, he showed much introspection as well as an attitude of making fun of himself. This poking fun at himself is not done in an easy, carefree manner, but rather with a cynical undertone.

Sample TAT Story

Picture No. 2

Well these people come from a great civilization, they were Western pioneers and settled and got along fine. They built a school and a church and everything went along fine. Then the crops suddenly went back on them and things got harder. The woman against the tree is standing there thinking and the father is plowing the ground but he's old and can't do it very well anymore. The girl is on her way to school, a little country school. The girl looks up and sees the sky and there is a big cloud there and she is afraid it is a tornado and she calls but no one hears her and then she runs and falls and breaks her neck. Her parents run to her when they see her lying there but they don't know that she is dead. Then they see the tornado and it comes and sweeps the mother and father and both are blown away and killed. The horse is gone and the buildings are gone and the fields are blown different ways and everything is desolation. Another family moves in and the same thing happens that a tornado comes along. That always follows. No one wants to farm the land. Everybody is superstitious, and no one will live there because it's always bad luck.

TAT Interpretation Excerpt

Observations are weak, so self-oriented as to lose meaning much of the time. Insight is seldom good, if that, and he sees only himself in everyone and everything. Empathy with the deserted child is the forte of his emotional repertoire. On that he can let go, and does in several places. He knows what the lost child feels like, and when faced with one of them would be likely to respond with impulsive help and warmth. Otherwise he understands and feels with no one else.

Locus of concern: The simplest statement here, unelaborated, may be the most true one possible. This boy is so narcissistic that he is unable to concern himself over the welfare of anyone else. He has no goals in common with any consciously seen group, nor is there an indication that he wants such.

The motives of the community are something he not only does not see clearly, but he also denies the validity of the application of those he does see to himself. It is rare to see such a primitive person . . . one who does not bother to project rules onto others, who does not rationalize his own behavior—he just says, "I want" and then, wanting, tries often to take. Still, fearing people, running from them constantly, living in his own inner fantasy world of power and romance, guilty about his hostility at an unconscious level, he is actually a constricted personality . . . but the constriction is the result of outer fear more often than not . . . impulses are not integrated under any consistent control plan.

1950

Essay

THE PERSON I WOULD LIKE TO BE LIKE

The person I would like to be like when I grow up is imaginary. He is very rich, and owns an estate in the country and a house in town. The country estate has many prize collies and horses on it and is famous for them. This person is quite tall, black hair and deep grey eyes. He has slim waist and hips and broad shoulders. He is not married and can come and go when he pleased. This person is well known in the community but isn't liked too well because he is quite stubborn and selfish. He refuses to let anyone pay him after something is due, but rather makes them pay on time. His collies and horses are famous and he takes great pride in them. He is between the ages of 21 and 25. He likes to swim and bowl and to write. In fact, a novel of his has already been published. This man is attracted to a girl, he knows well, but isn't quite sure that he is in love with her. He likes the way he lives, and is happy.

Interview Excerpt

Arthur: Well, there were a few kids over there who wanted to be friends with me and I don't know . . . maybe this is conceited but I thought they were kind of poor and I didn't know whether I'd like them or not. And I just haven't been friendly with them. The first of the year I thought I would but now I don't. I don't even speak to them.

Interviewer: How does what other people think of you differ from what you think of yourself?

Arthur: I don't think of myself as greedy or selfish or conceited while almost everyone else I know does. My friends tell me I am a snob.

Interviewer: Do you know why they think so?

Arthur: Well, because I am, I guess. The things I do—at the time I don't think of them as selfish but when I stop to think about them I see that they are and they probably look that way to other people. I don't feel like I'm being selfish or conceited when I do something but later on I can see that I am really. Some people—I meet when I do something I meet 'em on the street and I just don't speak to them, and I can see how they might feel about it, but I don't know, I just don't do it. I always think I won't be that way but I am. Then it seems like practically every week I am mad at some of my friends—get in a fight with 'em or insult 'em or something— say something that makes them mad. I try too hard to stop it but I just can't seem to.

TAT Interpretation Excerpt

We have in this record what may be the first glimmering of growth of attention to the values of the community. This is at such a primitive level as almost to beggar consideration, and we can give it little weight on the problem of rating consistency of values with those of the community in any constructive sense. His inner needs remain the pressures of importance to him, and it is through these that he sees the world. His own inner life is disorganized, has a strong tendency to be self-defeating to an extreme, has few if any goals that can be said to lead to positive action in guiding his behavior over any length of time. The superego is in such an amorphous state as to make it impossible to say that his inner system is consistently generalized. This is not to say that parts of the superego are not present and violently punitive; but even at this late date they contain highly inconsistent elements.

ARTHUR'S CHARACTER AND GROWTH

Arthur is a boy full of primitive, contradictory needs, which are easily excited and directly discharged in behavior. His "locus of concern" is almost entirely within himself. His goals, as he states them at seventeen, are to have a lot of money and the rich material comforts it can buy. Even in fantasy, he cannot make up his mind whether he should be selfish or generous with his money. The money seems to represent omnipotent, self-sufficient power, through having inexhaustible supplies (inferentially, of love and emotional support). None of this has anything to do with what he can realistically expect. It is an obsession with him, but not one toward which he is likely to take any actual steps.

His ability to perceive social reality is highly "spotty." His intellectual potential is estimated at an IQ level of 130, but emotional disturbances interfere and reduce his usual functioning to about the 115 level in quality. He shows flashes of excellent ability to observe how people behave, and how the world works. He is keenly sensitive and empathic, but only for very short periods; and as often as not, he has used this sensitivity to locate people's tender spots, and then jab them hard where it hurts most. As his remark about hitting on unpleasant truths about his friends illustrates, he can make sharp, intuitive insights into how others feel and how they will react. However, his attention span is very short (corroborated by an exceptionally low Memory score on the Primary Mental Abilities test, where he was well above average on other factors). He no sooner identifies a real fact about people, than his own reactions surge up and blind him to what is going on around him.

Arthur has had a very difficult time keeping himself in hand. In his thirteenth to sixteenth years in particular, he was regarded with some distaste by his classmates, for he was "queer" and uncomfortably unpredictable. This was a good deal more than the "storm and stress" of adolescence. He lived as much or more in a world of vivid, strange fantasies, than in the real world. He managed to keep the distinction fairly clear, but there were times when he came close to schizophrenic dissociation from the world around him.

There was nothing "flattened" about his emotionality. Rather, he behaved strangely under the press of intense feelings. These feelings were seldom appropriate in nature and intensity to the immediate situation in which he was engaged.

His emotional immaturity and lability, his erratic powers of perception, and his difficulty in controlling himself might be summed up by the phrase "weak ego structure." That this has recently changed in the direction of somewhat more stable, controlled behavior instead of progressing to a complete personality disintegration, can only be credited to some remarkable stamina which Arthur possesses. Nothing and no one in particular has helped him of late years, but he seems to have learned to find a little more satisfaction by becoming more passively conforming to the social and moral code, instead of continuing to rebel fruitlessly.

Through the years, while he was fighting for some kind of attention, part of his behavior was dictated by certain very primitive moral rules which he had apparently internalized. In telling the interviewers about slapping his cousin and hurting his friends' feelings, he was almost deliberately inviting censure. Throughout his life he has shown a painful awareness of the badness of his behavior. And often, he seemed to do destructive, hostile things in such a way as to insure punishment.

Clearly, Arthur is not a complete psychopath, lacking in any socialized principles or sense of morality. Indeed, he is qualitatively different in this respect from the utterly amoral person who has no emotional concern at all about moral issues. Arthur felt extreme guilt about his insistent sexual urges during adolescence and knew it. Such guilt only later became attached to his hostility, and only to a small degree.

The difficulty is that Arthur's conscience consists almost literally of "parental voices" which he carries within him, but which have not become enough a part of him to exercise effective control over his behavior. They tell him he is horrid, *after* he has done something contrary to their dictates; but he has been engaged in fighting them at the same time that he has felt the guilt they arouse. At best, they are undigested, unintegrated parts of a superego, too confused and confusing to provide any consistent guidance, even if he were completely willing to follow them—which he is not.

Until he was sixteen, Arthur more often than not behaved just as his primitive, irrational impulses dictated. He managed to avoid serious trouble with his community, since much of the time he withdrew from any form of activity and discharged his intense urges toward securing love, power, and the destruction of his enemies, in vivid daydreams. He learned, too, to express his hostility in verbal attacks which often passed for wit, rather than in frontal, physical attacks. Thus, his chief mode of control was a crude expediency, suppressing impulse, or releasing it in hidden or solitary ways. He used withdrawal from social interaction to prevent destructive outbursts; and fantasy, to relieve the resultant tension. He never gave up the hope of receiving love and attention, and got enough occasional notice of a positive kind, to keep him going somehow.

In addition, his "superego parts" provided powerful repression of some impulses. He never has really realized the depth of his longing, nor the intensity of his hostility. He has always rationalized himself as being not really as bad as he paints himself to other people.

As a result, his behavior has been highly unstable; unpredictable from moment to moment; yet usually within the outside limits of what his peers and his community would accept. It has been an anxious, unhappy life for him, for all his bravado and cynicism. He has wanted and sought warm, protecting older men and women, only to flee when he got too close; or only to bite the hand that fed him.

He has looked all too "independent" on the surface, but he has been far from truly autonomous. Pushed around by primitive emotions from within, and stimulated unwillingly by the people and events around him, he has directed his own life with only partial success and at the cost of continual struggle.

The behavior that emerges from this has not been notable for its rationality or consistency. He has struck out blindly more often than he has behaved in a way appropriate to the circumstances. His judgment has been subjective to an extreme degree. He lays the blame for moral infractions either too heavily on himself or too completely on others, as his mood of the moment determines.

At times, he is acutely and accurately aware of what he is doing, and how it relates to the moral code of the community; but he does not know why. Since sixteen, he has learned to adopt and live within a more socialized facade. It gets him in less trouble, and it has even brought a few mild rewards. This increasingly passive adaptation is no great change for him, since it is still aimed at getting gratification for his unchanged infantile needs; but it does give him a better chance of receiving some kind of approval.

It is a significant change, socially, for he has become much less actively destructive. He has begun to appreciate, just a little, the virtues of honesty and kindness, as he receives a little of them. What is more, his actively destructive behavior has importantly declined. As a moral being, he contributes almost nothing constructive to the well-being and happiness of those around him. He seems no more loyal, responsible, or honest than he ever was; and that puts him at the bottom of his age group. Still, he now is more actively kind, perhaps, to younger children, with whom he identifies and feels safe. He is more self-controlled, in that he no longer flies into a raging physical or verbal attack so frequently.

However, in his last year in high school he was still regarded as a deserving scapegoat for criticism and ridicule; and as one who too often disrupted activities in and out of the classroom by inappropriate, disturbing behavior. He now gives a surface impression of a masculine lad, but inwardly has not resolved the intense conflict between his frightening homoerotic responsiveness to men and his primitive desire to have a passive but motherly woman as an object for the impersonal release of his sexual urges.

What few active moral principles he has come to recognize and appreciate he applies only to the few people he knows well who treat him decently. His "range of moral horizon," despite his intellectual capacity for seeing beyond his community, is actually limited to a very few persons, and is not dependable even for them.

His picture of himself is as contradictory as everything else about him. At times, he condemns himself wholesale, almost wallowing in self-recrimination. But increasingly he seems to view himself as a decent enough person, justified in his lack of consideration for other people by their lack of good will toward him. He prides himself on his aloof loneliness, even while he finds the isolation cold comfort. His anxiety about getting something from the world, and escaping its threatened punishments, still appears far more fundamental a motive for what conformity he does render, than the sporadic, ineffective feelings of guilt he experiences.

In everyday behavior, Arthur seems likely to maintain a very marginal place in his community, working "off and on" through the years at jobs which are far below his abilities. If he marries, which is questionable, he is not apt to stick at it or be a dependable husband.

If he stays in Prairie City he is not likely to become criminal. He will probably "scrape by," but never be counted on to do much good to anyone else.

ARTHUR'S FAMILY HISTORY

Arthur's parents were married in 1924. Until they separated in 1943, when Arthur was ten, they had lived with Mr. Adams' parents, in a makeshift apartment in the once-stately homestead. Arthur's father had always been close to his mother. Indeed, for several years before 1943 he reportedly lived downstairs with her most of the time, while his wife and children lived upstairs by themselves. Never a steady worker, he became even more erratic in his comings and goings after his mother died in 1942. It was shortly after this that he completely separated himself from his wife and children.

Mr. Adams attended elementary school in Prairie City until the seventh grade, when he dropped out of school. He has had an occasional odd job, but there is no record of his ever having a permanent job until World War II, when he worked at the mill for a few years. Apparently, his chief financial support all along has come from his parents.

Mr. Adams has no record of either church membership or attendance. He has belonged to no organizations in the community. His community reputation in general is summed up in three brief statements by three different informants.

Male informant No. 1 (UL): "I can't say much for him. What I should say is I can't say anything for him at all. He's sure not much."

Male informant No. 2 (LM): "He's just floated around. He's never done anything as far as I know, except run away from his wife and kids and follow the ponies. He's got one of his race track cronies living over at the house with him right now. His folks were nice people, too."

Male informant No. 3 (UL): "He has always been no good at all. He couldn't keep a job if he wanted to, and I don't think he ever wanted to. I don't know what he does and I'm glad I don't."

As far as it is possible to tell, Mr. Adams at no time subsequent to his marriage took any constructive interest in establishing a family characterized by any stability. His interests are primarily self-centered.

Apparently, since Mr. Adams cut himself off from the family he has made no effort to see either his wife or children. However, he does nothing to keep Arthur from seeing him. Actually, in his own narcissistic way, he seems to be somewhat fond of his son; but he never thinks of himself as being in a position to meet any of Arthur's needs. So for Arthur he is there as a passive, rather neutral person, providing occasional relief from a more distasteful environment with his mother.

Mr. Adams' relationship with Arthur, incomplete as it is, is better than the relationship between Mr. Adams and Mrs. Adams ever was. The entire period at the grandmother's house was characterized by extreme disharmony, in which Mr. Adams sought frequent refuge with his mother. In describing Mr. Adams to interviewers, Mrs. Adams used the word *ninny* repeatedly. In general she is bitter and derogatory.

The father's relationship with Arthur's sister, Edith, was similarly bad. Arthur reports, "My sister never sees my father. She says she won't have anything to do with him. Gosh, I guess I'm the only one in the family who does."

Mrs. Adams is about two inches taller than Mr. Adams. She is quite stout. Around the apartment she customarily wears a house-robe with a Navaho motif, and her hair is generally in pin curls. Outside the apartment she uses generous quantities of make-up.

Mrs. Adams attended elementary school through the fifth grade. At that time she stopped school and started to "help people in their houses." When she was fifteen years old she met a twenty-year-old boy from Prairie City who was visiting a relative in her home town. Shortly after this meeting she went to visit the boy in Prairie City, and never returned home again. She succeeded in supporting herself, living in a small room in a private house, by doing domestic chores. She met Mr. Adams over two years before they were married, when she was twenty-three. From the time of the marriage until 1940 Mrs. Adams did no steady outside work; she did some occasional "helping out" for local housewives. From the time Mr. Adams left she has had fairly steady work. During the war she was employed as a packer at a nearby war plant. Since the war she has been working part-time as a waitress; she has had three different jobs as a waitress since 1945. In 1950 she says, "I get awful tired of this working. I get headaches all the time. I can't work steady like I used to. My oldest brother, Otto, helps us out now more than when I first went to work."

Like her husband, Mrs. Adams is not a church-goer, nor does she belong to any community organizations. Nevertheless, she is not an invisible person in the community. Arthur himself succinctly summarizes what many community informants have reported to the staff of this study in more words: "She likes men who have the same habits she has—go in a car and stay away all night—drink—smoke—and play cards." A slightly different angle is provided by a teacher: "His mother's no one to help him if he has any real problems. She's an argumentative, bossy person and doesn't understand him at all. She just doesn't seem to care."

Mrs. Adams has never bothered much about the maintenance of her home or about providing comforts for the family members. Although she can cook well, since 1943 Arthur has been doing a large part of his eating outside the home. Mrs. Adams told an interviewer, "It's so much trouble to cook. And really it's as cheap to eat out." A community informant (female, LM) says, on the subject of Mrs. Adams' housekeeping, "She's the laziest person I've ever seen when it comes to taking an interest in her own things."

Mrs. Adams has given Arthur very little attention, affection, or response. She probably never wanted him in the first place. She is not interested in him and she does not like him. She is openly derogatory of him. (In several interviews she discussed his obesity and lassitude while he was listening.) She knows that she does not understand him and she sometimes indicates, not in the least subtly, that she wishes she could get rid of him. (For example, "I'd give anything if I could afford to send Arthur to a military academy.") She talks loosely and glibly about his problems and always with reference to herself. Her general rejection of Arthur is apparent throughout the interviews.

She frequently compares Arthur with her estranged and strongly disliked husband, as, "He and Arthur are a lot alike. He was always sarcastic himself and never appreciated a thing that anybody ever did for him."

At another point she says, "You just have to clamp down on Arthur hard. He's so mean. You can't trust a things he says. He lies about everything."

Similarly, "He's a smart aleck. I tell him all the time he's a nasty little boy, but it doesn't do any good. He keeps on with the same tricks."

Arthur is equally outspoken and negative about his mother. Again, brief examples have been selected.

"She's a crosspatch. She always wants me to take care of little Johnny (Otto's child). They dump him here on me all the time. She tells me I should love him 'cause he's my cousin and Uncle Otto is so good to us. She's always giving him cookies, and when I sock that kid I never hear the end of it. He's a brat and somebody's got to keep him in line. But will she play with him? No, that's me. It's always Johnny this and Johnny that. She thinks he's so cute. Well, he is cute with those blue eyes and that blond hair. I really like him. But what a brat!"

And, "You can't do anything to please her. She always finds something wrong. And boy, can she scream around. But not when Uncle Otto's there. Then she's like apple dumpling, with him anyway."

Mrs. Adams' lack of interest, understanding, concern, or affection for Arthur, and her own narcissism, are everywhere evident in the interviews. Comments one interviewer, "She ignored Arthur's presence completely. So far as she was concerned there was no one there but herself and me. She showed no sign of concern about the real purpose of my visit, telling her about Arthur's test scores. When I mentioned that his score on the computation area was low, she said, "I never liked anything about arithmetic," etc., etc., talking about herself. The interviewer concludes, "Before I got downstairs I could hear a woman's voice nagging away—Mrs. Adams scolding Arthur about something."

For Arthur, home has been a battleground, a place of various crises. While his father was still in the home there was marked discord between the parents, to say nothing of the discord created by the grandmother. After the father left, there was discord between the mother and sister, between the mother and Arthur, between Arthur and his sister, between Arthur and his uncle. All along, the home life has been characterized by confusion, accentuated by the geographic break-up of the family. There has never been even a semblance of routine. Even when the father was in the picture his erratic work life did not necessitate any regularity. The mother never cared about establishing a regular routine in the home. She says: "I hate to be tied down."

In conjunction with the pronounced irregularity of the home routine, Arthur was never delegated any responsibilities in the home. The mother says, "I can't even get Arthur to help with the dishes. All he will do is cook. Some cooking he does too! Nothing but pies and cakes and creamed vegetables. You can't expect me to put up with that, can you? And do you think he'd fix up that couch for himself to sleep on? He just takes a blanket and throws it over himself at night. Sometimes he doesn't even take off his clothes, sleeps right in what he's had on all day."

Neither Arthur's mother nor father has any clear-cut moral standards. Arthur's notion of principles of right and wrong is similarly confused. He has never known what to expect. Mrs. Adams tells us about her own disciplinary practices:

"I guess you might say I've given up about Arthur. A person who tries to watch a kid all the time would go nuts, especially Arthur. I got to a point a long time ago, when I'd see him doing things, I just wouldn't bother. Sometimes, especially when I was tired or something like that, I'd let him have one. But it never helped much with Arthur."

In short, control has been sometimes harsh, sometimes absent, never consistent. The lack of consistent control has set the stage for conflict and confusion. The lack of affection has left him with a hunger for kindness and attention; but because he does not know how to accept them, and is also very hostile, he is left with a deep inner loneliness. Arthur himself sums up the area of emotional deprivation in one of his statements in the interviews:

"I don't think I was spoiled. I was mostly let to cry it out. I didn't get as much attention as Johnny does. He just cries till he gets it. If I cried like that I'd get a spanking. I know I'd cry after I got spanked, to get my own way. First I'd try crying, and if that wouldn't do it, then I'd just cry and I wouldn't speak to anyone for a while. And then I'd just forget all about it. Now I don't cry. I just don't speak to anyone. I get mad."

While never satisfying his needs in a motherly fashion, Mrs. Adams has aggravated Arthur's inability to relate positively to any male by appearing as a seductive figure to him. Thus, at the same time that she rejects him, she goads him into jealousy of the men she favors. Arthur is in the position of never having had a male sufficiently interested in him, to enable him to adopt a stable male pattern. Combined with his mother's way of actually encouraging certain feminine interests of his, this has resulted in Arthur's development into an almost feminine kind of person.

It is difficult to make any statements of a positive nature about the supportiveness of his family. About all that can be said is that the home has been a source of some physical support; but even this is not too reliable (e.g., eating out). It is not surprising that Arthur does not see even the physical side of his home in a positive way. "I always criticize the stuff we have around the house. I always say to my mother, 'Why don't we have better stuff? If we had money we'd have better stuff than this.'"

This disorganized, loveless home, with its self-centered, irresponsible parents, has had a predictably unfortunate effect on Arthur's character, just as it has made him a relatively unhappy boy for most of his life.

His sister Edith shows a more stable character. It is worth noting that her first ten years were spent in an Adams family where both parents were living together, apparently in a more friendly relationship than existed eight years later when Arthur was born. Whatever its disadvantages, living in the home of Mr. Adams' parents may also have had some stabilizing effect during Edith's childhood. In any case, Edith was eighteen when the divorce took place, after several years of increasingly bitter discord; whereas Arthur was only ten, and had known little but discord since infancy. In short, although the members of the family were officially the same, the "Adams family" of 1933–1943, in which Arthur grew up, was a good deal different kind of world for a young child than the "Adams family" of 1925–1935, in which Edith spent her first ten years.

The shaping of Arthur must have been accomplished, at least in broad outline, in his first ten years; for from the age of ten on, when our first-hand observations began, he has shown certain persistent attitudes toward people and toward himself, and certain characteristic ways of behaving which have not altered fundamentally. There have been some changes as he has grown up, of course; but his character and personality have remained at about the same relatively low level of adequacy through the years, when compared with the other children of his age. The consistencies, and also the changes, can be seen by tracing his development from 1943 through 1950.

It seems particularly noteworthy that Arthur's behavior and peer reputation, which were superficially average or "normal" in 1943, became distinctly worse after that year, and stayed poor from then on. That was the year in which his parents finally broke apart completely and were divorced. The parallel appears too striking to be mere coincidence.

CATHERINE CRANEK: A CONFORMING GIRL

1943

Moral Ideology Test Responses

Good Things: 1. Mind your teacher, 2. Mind your mother, 3. Mind your Father, 4. Pick up the papers for the janitor, 5. Don't talk out loud in school, 6. Help the teacher, 7. Help your mother, 8. Help your father, 9. Help your sister.

Bad Things: 1. Don't use good language, 2. Be mean to your sister or brother, 3. Talk out loud in school, 4. Don't do anything teacher asks you to do, 5. Don't do anything that your mother asks you to do, 6. Don't do anything your father asks you to do, 7. Don't pick up the papers for janitor, 8. Step on the American flag, 9. Don't be good to your classmates.

Interpretive Excerpt

It is almost startling to note the clarity with which she depicts the dominant theme of her morality: do what grown-ups—and everybody else—tell you to do. Indeed, her "good things" are almost devoid of specificity, except for two extremely innocuous, not to say superficial, acts. In her "bad things," except for "be mean to your brother and sister," and the faint, very much displaced symbolic rebellion of "step on the American flag," she similarly displays a very mild, emotionally passive desire to "be good" in a vague but completely generalized way, following whatever rules adults lay down.

That she quite happily accepted this wholesale adaptation to the moral stereotype—with definite emphasis on *morality* as an essential attribute—can be seen in the essay she wrote when she was eleven.

1944

THE PERSON I WOULD LIKE TO BE LIKE

If I was a grownup person now I would be seventeen years old. My character would be kind, friendly, happy all the time, and honest. I would wear nice clothes and be clean in my appearance. I would be a secretary and a student in High School.

By contrast with what the other children wrote (see the other case studies), there is a striking lack of self-initiated *action* in this picture. She literally does not show herself *doing* anything specific. Instead, she presents a static portrait, in abstract descriptive generalizations: "kind," "friendly," "clean." At the same time, however passive a creature of her environment she showed herself to be, Catherine's values were firmly entrenched and very much as her parents and teachers wanted. She was, indeed, a good girl. (She is *still* this good little girl, in her inmost emotions and wishes, by the time she reaches the threshold of official "adulthood," seven years later.)

At this time, Catherine was rated very high on all moral traits by both teachers and age mates. Moreover, she was highly popular with everyone. Mrs. Tryon, analyzing the 1944 sociometrics, said:

"Catherine was outstanding in participation (one of the three extremes) for always doing things with others, working hard for club or team, liking parties, play, always cheerful, smiling, sticks by her friends and keeps secrets.

"She was considered *about the most outstanding person* for being kind, helpful, careful of others' feelings, nice to everybody. Almost always calm and controlled in temper.

"She was rated very responsible about finishing tasks, getting things done before she played, seeing what needed to be done and going ahead with it, doing her share, etc.

"She was also rated as extremely honest; and not a person who let her friends persuade her to do things that are wrong. However, there was some question about her willingness to stand up to teachers and leaders for what she believes is right.

"She was admired very much for her sweet, friendly, rather gay participation which seemed to be marked by an almost complete lack of assertiveness, and by cooperativeness and agreeableness. This is the 'little lady' pattern found so status-laden in the University of California study at the seventh-grade level. Boys are still disregarded or actively ignored. It is a pattern usually very much approved and rewarded by teachers."

Catherine maintained her high status unchanged until she was thirteen, although, as was pointed out by many test analysts,

"In spite of the fact that Catherine has had the same 'friends' and has belonged to the same high-status clique (the Secret Six), she has shown little evidence of warmth, close personal ties, or spontaneous affection. Her belongingness seems to have resided in an awareness of, and conformity to, group expectations and codes; absence or withholding of hostility or aggressiveness; and a sort of generalized docility."

Nevertheless, she was very active in her peer world, in overt ways. She played games and early took part in sports ("played house," "played jacks," "rode horseback," and rode a bicycle). She went to school games, and even had dates, later.

1947

However, a rather dramatic change occurred in her fourteenth year. It was described by Mrs. Tryon as follows:

"Catherine's status in the peer group has changed more sharply between seventh and eighth grade levels than probably any other case we have studied. From a position of almost the highest prominence and prestige at the late childhood level, she dropped to a position close to invisibility at early pubescence according to the Sociometric Data. However, she did maintain ties in a clique group. In an interview (Nov. '47) she says she liked junior high school better, explaining that "they don't hold back as much for the dumb kids there.'"

What happened? The evidence suggests that it was not Catherine who changed, but the peer code. In fact, it was her inability to change, to match the increasing maturity of her adolescent age mates, which left her behind. Her "little lady" characteristics, which made her so popular at ten, by fourteen caused marked loss in her prominence, although she was still considered highly moral. By 1947, it was said of her:

"Catherine is not a prominent person in the total eighth grade group, but she apparently has a secure position in the most prominent clique. In general her picture is one of a rather passive, possibly dependent kind of person, quite 'feminine,' rather cheerful and happy. There are no evidences of assertiveness. Instead, she is considered rather quiet and demure, although gay-spirited with her feminine group."

1948

At sixteen, she wrote about "A Good Person to Have in Our Community":

"This person must be able to get along with all types of people in all types of conditions. A community is a place where all life is centered."

Interpretive Excerpt

If we are able to assume she carried these sorts of ideals out in her own behavior, it is probable that she is well liked and has many friends. She must be, by her own definition, accepting and uncritical of everyone. This does not mean that she condones amoral behavior, nor that she behaves amorally or immorally herself. Presumably, however, we should be able to use her as a yardstick of what her peer group is like—an assessment of the morality of Catherine becomes very nearly an assessment of the general morality of her age mates, at least the group with whom she interacts regularly.

That same year, she gave these responses to the Sentence Completion Test:

2. Sometimes I feel like—working.
3. With other people I—have fun.
7. Boys—lots of fun.
8. When I'm alone—I listen to the radio.
9. Secretly I—write in my diary.
11. A person's life—is his own.
13. I would do anything if—I could write.
22. There are times when I—feel glad.
27. I am usually—am having fun.
28. It is more important to—be liked than disliked.
39. My only trouble is—that I'm too slow.
43. If I'm left behind—I find something else to do.
44. As a child I—played.
47. I am very—slow.
49. I cannot understand what makes me—do the things I do.

On the surface, these are quite normal, happy responses, and on the surface, that is just what she is. However, the analyst of this test had these additional remarks to make, based on all her responses:

"While she will give the appearance of spontaneity to a casual observer, this is hardly true of her inner emotional life. The record is shot through with social anxiety, but not with neurotic anxiety. The feeling was, during analysis of this record, that she is not very high on rationality of judgment nor on accuracy of perceptions, that she

does indulge herself in projective mechanisms, is defensive to an un-
necessary degree. She seldom blames herself for things that happen
to her, does blame parents, sibs, and the world. Peers seldom come
in for censure, nor is she sure enough of herself to incriminate teachers or other adults."

1949

In 1949, her *own* responses to the sociometric test were analyzed:

"This record is distinguished by the tremendous number of names
entered to some items, together with frequent phrases indicating she
would name even more people if she could, e.g.:

". . . boys and girls who always seem to have a good time . . . 'I
am mentioning only a few' (She names ten.)

". . . ones who always know how to start things . . . 'A few are
mentioned' (She names eight.)

". . . ones who would seldom let a friend persuade them to do something wrong . . . 'The ones mentioned before plus:' (She names four
more and then adds 'Others too numerous to mention.')

". . . boys and girls you run around with . . . (She names 16, of
whom five are boys.)

". . . Who are the ones everyone seems to like to be with because
everyone has a lot of fun when they are around? 'All the kids mentioned before' (To arrive at this number, sum all her nominations:
this comes to 38. Several of the names appear more than once, however. It should be noted, further, that up to this point, item 17, she
has not entered a single name to a negative item.)

"To only one of the approximately twenty negative items does she
enter any names: 'ones you sort of stay away from.' Here she names
two rather aggressively outgoing girls. To all other negative items
she either makes one of the responses quoted above or she simply
draws a line through the answer space."

1950

The next year, in telling an interviewer about her social life, she said:

"We're just all together, we don't form any couples or anything.
(About how many are in your gang?) About ten or twelve. Oh, I
can't even name them all. Norma goes with Dick sometimes. But
we don't get along too well, I don't know, sometimes she's friendly

and sometimes she isn't. She's sort of odd sometimes and doesn't fit in. Sometimes she's OK. She's changeable but I guess I don't have any room to talk, I am too."

(What kind of fellow would you pick out?) "Oh, a lot of fun, not too crabby or choosy about what you do, they can always find something to do. Willing to teach you things, that's what I need."

Lest it be thought that Catherine has been an inhumanly proper girl, here is an item she mentioned to an interviewer when she was seventeen:

"Well, I don't have such an awful temper but when I do get mad I get awful mad. I don't just get mad about any little thing. It takes quite a bit to make me mad. When I do I usually throw things. I broke a vase once, or a teapot I guess it was. My mother was disgusted with me. I don't throw things at people. I just throw them on the floor. It's a good thing I don't throw them at people."

(I asked her what kind of things made her angry.) She said, "Oh, when people keep nagging at me to do something, and they ask you to do something and you don't get it done and they keep nagging at you. I get mad."

In fact, between her sixteenth and seventeenth years, Catherine showed signs of some restlessness and partial rebellion against her "nice little girl" hyperconformity. Her very feelings showed increasing spirit, although she still did not act on them much more openly. To illustrate this change which occurred—still within the same basic character pattern—here are some pairs of TAT stories to the same pictures. The first story was given in 1949; the second, in 1950.

Picture No. 2 (1949)

"Oh, gads. (17 second interval) Oh, I know I just thought of something. This girl has been going to school and came back to the place where her parents live and worked on the farm. This background is what she's thinking of, is that her grandfather works in the field and her grandmother is standing by a tree. That's about all. (What made her come back?) She was probably away at school and never thought much of what her parents went through, and she's just come back to see what it was like. (Then she's visiting her grandfather's place?) Yes. (Does she like it?) There's not much expression on her face, she's just taking it all in, there's not much to say about it."

(1950)

"I remember the trouble I had with this one the last time. (Long pause—about three minutes.) Well, this girl over here has gone away to a school in some big city just to further her study. I guess she went to college a couple of years and she doesn't know whether or not to go back on the farm where she was born with her parents, or to continue her schooling some more and get a job in the city some place, so she goes back to her place in the country, and she looks over the field and land and the way her father and mother have worked to build up the place, and thinks that since they have worked so hard to get what they have got—that she thinks she ought to go back to school and finish her course and go on with what she had set out to do."

Picture No. 1 (1949)

"Oh, gads. (5 seconds) This is something. (12 seconds) Looks like this boy was outside playing baseball or something he wanted to do and his mother called and told him to come in and practice his violin lesson. He's just sitting there looking at it as though he doesn't want to practice, and yet he wants to be outside with the rest of the kids. Mm—that's about all, except it doesn't look as if he was playing the violin very much."

(1950)

"Oh, dear! Well, it looks as if the little boy has been told to practice his violin lesson and he doesn't want to. He doesn't seem to be interested in it. He just seems to be sitting there thinking about it, probably thinking of going outside and playing with the rest of the kids— baseball or something. Probably end up practicing; mothers usually make you do that."

Her 1950 story to Picture No. 1 indicates what other evidence also says, that despite her more lively struggle to find herself and be more the captain of her own soul, "mothers usually make you do (what they think you should)."

Her career through adolescence has been summed up:

"Catherine's interaction with girls is one of long and successful associations. She has been a member of a high status girls' clique throughout most of the eight year period, and has had a close mutual friend for the whole period. She has been active in nearly every club or organization that was open to girls, both in and out of school. Almost the only one she seems to have missed is the Girl Scouts. Often a chairman or committee member for special group projects like parties and dances, she held few elected offices that carried any continuing responsibility. It has somehow been sensed that her motivations were in being with and acting like a group, and not in the group's goals themselves.

"In interacting with the opposite sex she lagged a bit behind the norm for the girls' group. It was almost as though they had to establish that pattern of behavior, and provide her with a model of some sort to follow, before she could begin dating. Since then she has had two steady boy friends, seeking those who could teach her things, and would take the responsibility for determining what they and she did. She is rated higher by the Conference on surface adjustment than on inner feeling toward boys. This is similar to her relations with girls, also. That is, while the strength of her positive feelings toward people is only average, her outer behavior gives the impression of much greater emotional interest in them."

CATHERINE'S CHARACTER STRUCTURE

By eighteen, Catherine dreams of college, and an "artistic" career, but has no real expectation of fulfilling these aspirations. Indeed, she seems quite happily settled, on the whole, in a life in Prairie City, with fairly early marriage a strong likelihood. Now, as ever, she has an excellent moral reputation; except, that is, on "moral courage." She never, at any age, was considered more than average in that quality.

"I really don't know what people think of me. It's not something you go around asking people. We mostly do the same things. I do what everybody else does, so I guess they probably think the same thing of me."

This was Catherine's reply to an interview question in 1950; and a more succinct description of her conforming character would be hard to imagine. She wants the approval and friendly recognition of those around her. The best way to insure this, in her view, is to be just the sort of person they like. This means doing the same things, the same way.

Her pleasant daydreams are simply more vivid variations on this basic theme. Though she is now a telephone operator and will in all likelihood marry and settle down in Prairie City, she has not given up her dreams of being a gay, glamorous actress. Though she has switched the background for her visions from the movies to T.V., even here she has followed the crowd.

Fame and fortune seem to represent to her a delightful fairyland where she would be important in her own right; and where she would have the security of being admired and "loved" (as she understands it) by millions of people.

Catherine is not lost in her cloud-land. She keeps it as a refuge for fleeting moments of escape, and will probably always dream her dreams of "what might have been." However, she feels too much the importance of getting on well with the people in her immediate life, to be impractical or detached from the everyday world.

In some ways, she will probably always be a little childlike in her desire to have everything "nice," as well as in her reluctance to get involved in the strong currents of emotion that flow in a mature human relationship. She prefers to keep the "light touch"; to be pleasant and friendly; and live by the rules of the local "Emily Post."

That she has stronger impulses, and sits on them sternly, is evident in her 1950 TAT story to Picture No. 4 (the young couple, with a "sexy" girl in the background):

"That's interesting. (Long pause) Gee! (Another pause) I must be blind. (Another pause) Can't think of anything. Can't even get a good location for it, let alone a plot. Oh, dear; oh, dear. (Short pause) Oh, I just thought of something. This man is an escaped convict, morbid mind I have. He broke out of prison and came to his girl friend's house, and he wanted to hide, and he thought he was safe, but he just heard a knock on the door and he's frightened, and the girl tries to comfort him. Be calm and quiet; it might not be the police. But he thinks it is. She goes to the door, then (pause) quick! quick! It's the police and—as the police is coming in the front door the criminal is sneaking out the back, but since they have the place surrounded, they get him and send him back to prison, and he finished out his term."

As usual, a great deal is condensed in here, including her fixed insistence on living by the rules. Not even personal affection can stave off the just penalty for wrongdoing. (Though of course Catherine, as the heroine, didn't "really" send her boy friend back to jail to finish his term. As the story teller, she simply saw to it that the law triumphed —and triumphed over those same dangerous, "criminal" impulses which she unwittingly introduced into her tale; attributing them to the male, of course.) It scarcely needs comment that she was completely "blind" to the "other woman" in the background of the picture. (The correspondence to the emotions and behavior pattern of the feminine "soap opera" fan is striking. See Warner and Henry, *The Radio Daytime Serial.*)

Actually, her unconscious anxiety about letting out "bad" impulses is not warranted. She has more hostility toward her mother than she is aware of, or expresses; but it is not of unusual intensity at all, and no more than many people would openly express. She occasionally hates her little brother, humanly enough; quite genuinely liking him at other times. She is more strongly attracted to her father than she could comfortably recognize; but no more than would be quite healthy and normal in many families.

The important thing is that she would feel ashamed of *any* feeling that was more than mild. As far as she is concerned, the safe and proper way to behave is to treat everyone well and neither love nor hate anyone with any depth of feeling. In this, she is playing it safe; and her self-concern becomes apparent. It would be most untrue to say that she does not consider others' wishes and feelings; but, to some degree, she does it in order to strike a bargain. She is nice to them so that they will be nice to her. This sounds quite reasonable, of course, and very like anyone's reason for acting in a well-socialized manner.

However, this is not the same as being concerned for others' feelings because she likes them for themselves and wants them to be happy in their own way, whatever it may be. Catherine does not feel sure enough of herself to stand on her own. She would be extremely upset if she felt disapproved or unliked.

She operates, that is to say, more by careful, sensitive observation than by insightful understanding of other peoples' desires. She does show some ability to share others' feelings, having almost as much empathy as the average adolescent. But her rapport is fleeting and rather shallow. She usually cannot let herself feel deeply enough to match the depth of others' feeling.

Her control is still highly heteronomous—Piaget's morality by constraint. (In her case, some constraint by inner, but extra-ego forces, as well as by external, social pressures.) While she adapts "flexibly" on the surface, her actual controls are themselves quite rigid. She cannot act on impulse, or certainly not while she is aware of it. Her pattern is one of initial caution and hesitancy, then growing directness of action. But this seldom gets to the point of true spontaneity. At the first sign of difficulty with the outer world, she retreats to passive, safe, innocuous conformity, and restricts her activity to familiar, well-enclosed areas of group participation.

Her major technique is to "lose" herself in a group, to guide her behavior by its sanctions, and to conform to its pattern in active, positive ways as well as guarding against any untoward impulsiveness. Her deceptive gaiety and "spontaneity" have a faintly hectic tone. That is, she does not understand that emotional participation is a central purpose of adolescent group action. She knows all the words, but she "doesn't know the music." Social action, per se, is her idea of being "in." (Note her reply to the sociometric question, Who is not dependable?: "Lose friends this way.")

By defining herself as a "happy, thoughtful, kind and sociable" girl, and doing her best to act this way, she succeeds very well in appearing to be a normal, typical, well-adjusted girl. In her own way, she genuinely wants to be nice to people, and thoroughly moral. By spending her energies in sociable activity, doing the right things with the right people, etc., she does succeed to quite a degree. It is not that her inner impulses are "bad," antisocial, or completely egocentric, that prevents her from finding really deep satisfaction, and giving it to others. It is rather the fact that her rather childlike level of perception and socialization never makes her behavior quite as meaningful to herself or others, as it would be if produced by mature motives and mature perceptiveness.

When impulse slips out, and her behavior is not in accord with her official code, she tends to excuse herself, to rationalize, and in general to avoid seeing herself as she really is, if this means taking any view less than wholly favorable. She is not insincerely sweet, or "goody-goody," but she is an incurable optimist about her own motives.

As a summary assessment, we might say that Catherine's morality of duty and obedience makes her a thoroughly acceptable member of society. It is true that those close to her may slowly and dimly come to feel that they are living more with an institution than with a woman. She makes herself too much a stereotype to give warmly and deeply to others. But she will doubtless always be likable and dependable in carrying out the duties which society expects of a wife and mother. If there is not much more to her contribution than the outward observances, she will be cheerful and good-natured in offering what she does know how to give.

CATHERINE'S FAMILY HISTORY

Catherine's father was born in Yugoslavia and came to this country as a small boy, with his parents. He has worked at the largest lumber yard in town since 1927. The yard foreman recently reported, "I'm the only one who's been here longer than him. I don't think he's missed five days of work in the last ten years. When he started to build his house, the boss give him the materials practically for nothin'. The boss said to me, 'Hell, if you can't give a guy like that a break, life isn't worth livin'.' But you know, it's the damndest thing about that guy. He always does the same thing with the paper from his lunch sandwiches—folds them up in neat little squares and puts them back in his lunch box. What the hell do you think he does with them papers?"

Mrs. Cranek says of her husband, "He's just a plain working man." His participation in the community is in accord with this statement. He attends church fairly regularly, although he does not belong to any church organizations. He belongs to one of the high school parents' organizations and attends meetings without taking an active role in them. He used to belong to a men's fishing and hunting club, but he dropped out when he started to build a new house for his family.

In the home the father's role is essentially that of provider, and he has provided all along for his family in a stable, steady, unspectacular fashion. An upper-middle informant says, "You might say he's one of our stalwarts around here. Never any trouble from him. I wish I had him working for me." As far as the upbringing of the children is concerned, the father is definitely secondary in importance to the mother. Mrs. Cranek says, "He leaves most things up to me. He just tells the children, 'Do like mother says.'" At another time when the mother was asked by an interviewer whether the father had done most of the disciplining and spanking of the children, she replied, "No, I'm more home with the children always." However, Mr. Cranek is apparently not always passive in his support of the mother. Thus he says, "I don't go for the rowdy business you see nowadays. But we've never had any real trouble from our children." And Mrs. Cranek added, "He won't allow it."

Mrs. Cranek has been aptly described by a lower-middle class informant as a "benevolent despot." In this home, it is the mother who does most of the controlling, and indeed she is a forceful disciplinarian. The mother of one of Catherine's friends partially sums up the effect of the mother's severity: "Catherine is a sweet child. Friendly in a way. But you always have to push her into a group to get her started. Of course, not but that Mrs. Cranek is a good mother. She is; but I told her, 'Cora, don't you think you're a little too severe on Catherine sometimes?' She demands so much. She's sort of domineering."

In the process of supervising, Mrs. Cranek, of course, knows a good deal about Catherine's activities and has considerable interest in the girl's doings and achievements. She says, "A mother has to keep right up with her children if she's going to teach them behavior and manners. That's the main thing for a mother to do. I always blame a lot of the trouble children get into on their mothers. If they don't know what their children are doing, how can you expect them to behave themselves? I've had my worries with mine, but never anything serious. They know they just can't get away with certain things. If you make that clear to a child from the beginning, you don't have to watch them so close as they get older. It makes you feel good when you go over to school, like I did the other day, and the teacher tells you your child is so well behaved and never causes any trouble. I had that always with Catherine. I never had to be ashamed of the way she behaved in school. She always did her work the way she was supposed to."

Mrs. Cranek portrays her distrust of autonomy for her children in a briefer statement she made in regard to Catherine's forthcoming post–high school work: "I kinda believe she'll really make something of herself—and yet you just can't be sure."

Mr. and Mrs. Cranek attend together the meetings of the school parent organization to which they belong, but Mrs. Cranek is a bit more active in the organization than her husband. Thus, she has several times volunteered to be a chaperone at school dances. Once, she telephoned several of the mothers before the meeting to inform them of a report by Catherine to the effect that there was considerable necking occurring on the school bus to out-of-town games. During the meeting she was one of the mothers who offered to go along on the bus to see that necking was stopped.

Although she does attend church fairly regularly with her husband, Mrs. Cranek is somewhat apologetic about not taking an active role in church organizations. She says in addition, "Maybe Catherine should take more interest in church activities. But I suppose as long as she's so active in school activities it's all right. You know she belongs to [the mother here recited the names of eight organizations in which Catherine has participated]."

Mrs. Cranek sees herself as an efficient person, and she has the reputation of being efficient. An upper-lower–class acquaintance says, "She can do more with little than anybody I've ever seen. She don't have to apologize for her home, or for her kids. She's a hard worker. You know, she worked at the hospital all that time till Catherine was born. And there's no reason for her to work now, but she still takes in laundry all the time. She's a very ambitious person." Mrs. Cranek's efficiency, which she values so much, seems to be achieved at some sacrifice of deeper emotional ties. There is no indication of any real personal closeness between her and her husband or between her and any of the children. She is definitely interested in the family, but essentially from the point of view of getting things done and getting them done well. She says, "I never was one for hemming and hawing away about nothing. Catherine knows if she has any troubles she can bring them to me and I'll be glad to advise her. But talking's never an excuse for not doing what has to be done."

In general, the Cranek home is a rather impersonal, restricting place that fosters dependency while giving positive approval for good behavior. Parental authority permeates the air of the home. The father supports and confirms the mother's edicts and both parents have very consistently demanded obedience. What is expected of Catherine has been made clear to her from the beginning. The mother of one of Catherine's friends has commented on the effects on Catherine of her life at home: "I think she wouldn't be quite so diffident if she had a little more freedom at home." The "at home" could be left off this statement without violating the evidence. Mrs. Cranek has consistently and closely controlled Catherine's outside contacts as well.

This is a rather authoritarian home, very regular in its routine. The main approval Catherine receives from her parents is in return for close conformity to their demands and expectations. Attempts at self-expression are not encouraged or rewarded very much. Catherine's character structure appears to be a natural product of this rearing, and in most respects she is just what her mother has wanted.

RALPH REED: A RATIONAL-ALTRUISTIC BOY

1943

Moral Ideology Test Responses

Good Things: 1. To help people, 2. Obey patrol rules, 3. Wash before meals, 4. Mow lawns, 5. Do not fight when you are mad, 6. Don't break windows, 7. Put out the flag, 8. Don't trip people, 9. Don't make noise when people are sick.

Bad Things: 1. Break windows, 2. Hurt your brother or sister, 3. Fight on the playground, 4. Gobble up your food, 5. Talk back to your parents, 6. Don't mind the teachers, 7. Kick things around, 8. Swear at people, 9. Acting smart.

Like almost all the children, Ralph's chief moral "problem" at this age was learning to control his aggressive impulses. Instead of revealing violent, infantile hostile impulses, however, most of Ralph's aggressive responses showed a built-in control which tended to suspend attack or displace it into relatively harmless outlets.

He was certainly "all boy" at this age, but compared to the other ten-year-olds, he showed more complex and more specifically differentiated thinking in his responses. Not literal-minded, they were yet concrete, likely illustrations of everyday moral issues, mixed with abstract but decidedly lifelike ideas, such as "acting smart." (In the original "blind" analysis, the quality of his responses was correctly interpreted as reflecting intelligence in the superior range.)

The same picture of active, outgoing boyishness was evident in his Emotional Response Test, when he was eleven. At the same time, he revealed more concern and sympathy for other people (and pets) than most of the children, by the simple act of mentioning as important, things that happened to those others, instead of events which affected only himself.

In his eleventh year Ralph was rated very high by his age mates on all the moral traits (average D score for all traits, 24.3, with a high of 26.5 on loyalty). Teachers also rated him high, except, curiously, for a below-average score on honesty. There is no available evidence to explain this, and two years later they rated him very high on honesty, as well as on all the other traits. One can only speculate that one or two of his teachers in 1944 may have taken affront at his frank independence and rated him down on honesty as an expression of their distrust of such determined self-direction in a schoolboy. Certainly, there was never any evidence of dishonesty in his behavior.

1944

Sociometric Interpretation Excerpt

Ralph had extreme scores for being a leader in work and play, enthusiastic, enjoying things he does, able to sit still or move about quietly (in adult-controlled situations), and for being "someone you would choose for your best friend." He was also rated high on being willing to take chances, and on being well-groomed. On the sociogram of the total T group, he was chosen by eleven classmates as one they would like for their best friend. These were all boys, except for one prominent girl.

1946

Sociometric Interpretation Excerpt

When he was thirteen, Ralph's social position and reputation was almost exactly the same as in 1944: among the best-liked and most influential in the group. Now, three girls named him as a "best friend" choice; girls who were themselves highly popular. (In 1947, his sociometric status was still as high as ever, as was his moral reputation with both peers and teachers.) Ralph was not "standing still." On the contrary, his continuing high status was evidence that he was growing up steadily, keeping pace with the changing, maturing code of values of his age group.

That Ralph was a boy with normal self-indulgent tendencies is apparent in an essay he wrote in 1946, at thirteen:

"If I were sixteen I would get in my convertible, five passenger coupe. I would go to a dance and get introduced to a girl and make a date for the next Saturday night. I would stop in on Bill Miller and we would go for a ride all afternoon and then we would pick up his girlfriend and I would go pick up the girl that I had dated. Then we would go take in a show. After the show we would go get something to eat. If it was a nice day we could go for a ride after we ate, or else if we wanted to, we could go skating."

Certainly, this seems a rather aimless fantasy, and it is. It is necessary to know from other sources about Ralph's hard work and ambitious purpose, to realize that this is a wishful daydream he had when he "let down" temporarily and thought of what he would like to do. Nonetheless, he automatically assumed that anything worth doing would involve other people—by *his* active choice.

Interview (with father)

He said that Ralph enjoys taking tests very much and has been interested in them and talks about them at home. He also commented that unlike most boys, Ralph was very fond of school and seems to enjoy everything that goes on at school.

I told him that Ralph seemed to be among the children who got along especially well in this group. Mr. Reed smiled and said, "Well, we think a lot of Ralph." I said I thought that he had reason to be proud of the boy and he talked a little more about him. "Yes, Ralph can do just about anything. He likes school and he likes to tinker around with machines. I think he first started learning when he was about five years old and has been at it ever since. It just seems to fascinate him. He's a great help to me."

1947

Interview Excerpt

While another interviewer was talking with the mother of another boy on the football team, the mother said:

"Of course Ralph is the thinker of the game. He really figures the way for all the good plays of Earl's and Jack Flaherty's. (You don't say. I always thought of Earl and Jack as the stars of the team.) Well, Earl says that he couldn't get along if Ralph didn't do some of the planning. He thinks Ralph's awfully good." (Earl was her son.)

Interview (with mother)

"Ralph likes to be with a crowd—and there is no holding him down when there's company around. He likes to tease and act foolish. They get quite a kick out of him. (He's pretty much of a family boy, Ralph?) Yes, he likes to be with us—at home or going out to games and shows. We all like a good show. (He isn't going out with girls very much?) No. He isn't interested yet (not implying disinterest, but rather preoccupation with rural life and basketball). He doesn't run around a lot with boys, spending money. There's one advantage to living out here. It keeps them in more to read and get to bed early."

1948

Sentence Completion Test Responses

1. The future is—a husband and farmer.
2. Sometimes I feel like—shooting myself.
3. With other people I—enjoy.
7. Boys are—better than girls.

8. When I'm alone—I don't get scared like some people.
9. Secretly I—like to drive.
11. A person's life is—worth having.
13. I would do anything if—I could be like Henry Kaiser.
14. She—is my girlfriend.
15. My mind—is made up to be a farmer.
21. I can't—vote yet.
22. There are times when I—am sleepy.
27. I—would like to be a boxer.
28. It is more important to—work and earn a living.
39. My only trouble is—girls.
42. He—is my buddy.
43. If I'm left behind—I try to catch up.
44. As a child I—was small.
46. Most girls—are O.K.
47. I am very—young.
49. I cannot understand what makes me—look at girls.

Sentence Completion Interpretation Excerpt

There is a well-differentiated responsiveness in Ralph's case, without much involvement at the emotional level. He avoids the direct emotional response and keeps close check on what he wants to do in terms of the current situation. He is aware of his impulses, and both positive and negative ones are channeled into appropriate expressions, by and large. He uses rather often the technique of displacing his hostile feelings onto some inconsequential object as in "Nothing annoys me more than—flys and mosquitoes." It may be that there is more than the usual amount of suppression going on in this boy's life. He is one of these cases, of which we have several, who will appear to be rather spontaneous in outer dealings, but who in inner life is thoroughly a controlled person. Still, it is impossible to say that he is affectively constricted. Actions are deferred, some responses may be repressed by the superego, but this is less the case than that other rational mechanisms are in force as a stable, adaptive, and consistent system.

1949

Sociometric Interpretation Excerpt

Ralph had top or near-top ratings on the moral traits in everyone's eyes, except for a few months when his peers temporarily rated him no better than average in self-control. He continued to be a sought-after leader, rather than a bossy or aggressive one.

Interview Excerpts

Ralph: I'd as soon have sports with teamwork myself. I don't know, of course, maybe you can do better sometimes by yourself than with teams when some guy just doesn't seem to care—that'll ruin a team.

There's some who just don't care for a team—there's always a certain group of boys who are just together all the time and there's some who just go off by themselves all the time. Won't come around, just don't care, won't go out for sports, just don't do anything. Most of them don't even come to watch. Just sort of cut off from the rest of them. (What makes them do this?) I don't know. (Any idea?)—Long pause—I don't know what it could be.

(About how would you rate yourself with the group?) Well, about in the upper half (this slowly and hesitatingly) quite a ways up. This year I didn't try to get on any honor roll. I remember though in the eighth grade I was afraid I was going to be an honor student. Earl Eddy and I found out that we could work just a little bit more and be honor students but then we found out we would have to give a speech if we were, so we dropped everything, and instead of picking up our work we slowed up enough so that we got into high school but would not have to be honor students, and then we managed it too.

But I got the Legion award (for outstanding character). I didn't know I would get it. I didn't work for it, I didn't even think about it, I don't know how it's awarded. I didn't even know until they handed out the medals at graduation. (So it was a big thrill?) It was the biggest thing in all my school life.

By late 1949, Ralph was definitely moving into sustained heterosexual activity, though with his eyes wide open, in a rather emotionally detached way, as this interview quotation testifies:

(Are you going to the dance tonight?) Yes. (At this dance the girls invited the boys.) I'm going to do some square dancing. (Do you mind telling me with whom you are going?) With Jean Muirson, she's a junior. (You have been doing some dating lately?) Yes, quite a bit, since I can have the car anytime I want it. (That helps.) Yes, but you don't always need a car; it's nice to have though. Some girls won't go with a fellow unless he has a car, but I don't like that kind. I don't go with girls if they only want the car, or if I think that is why they are going with me.

1950

Interview Interpretation Excerpt

Ralph likes people, accepts them easily, and has quite a wide acquaintanceship among them. Peers have gone out of their way to indicate liking and respect for him. An anecdote he tells shows us both his and their feelings and actions. He had been absent during some class elections, and the following refers to what happened when his classmates had written his name on ballots to elect him:

"Well, I wasn't there—so I couldn't have signed the paper that I was willing to be an officer. After I got back and found they'd elected me, I wasn't going to take it. I didn't want it too badly, and anyway, I'd had it for one year. There's only four years and I thought there were quite a few other kids that would like to have it, so I shouldn't take it. One of the teachers talked to me when I decided not to sign —which would have been the same as resigning. She pointed out that the kids would be peeved who had worked so hard to get me elected. So I stayed in; but I just figure people have a better opinion of me than maybe they ought to have. Or it might be I'm too critical about myself."

Sociometric Interpretation Excerpt

Peers continue to accord him high social status in later years. In 1950 he is seen as being in the top decile for loyalty to the peer group and being responsible. He is also strongly regarded as having self-control, being honest and kindly. On the other hand, on the last sociometric record he wrote, he assigned slightly more negative votes to other people than is average for the group. He does seem able to evaluate others clearly, and does not hesitate to express negative as well as positive opinions. He had among the highest number of mutual choices of friends in the group, including six boys and one girl.

Essay (When I Am Twenty-Two)

After I get ready to go I'll get in my car and take off to town. I'll then have a game of billiards and then go to get my girl, if I have one, and go to a show or something of that order. After that I will go to some nightspot to eat and dance, possibly. Then I will take her home and later I will return home and retire.

Essay Interpretation Excerpt

Under this rather carefree attitude he maintains a Rational-Altruistic concept of what a person must act like to be a stable member of a community. From the evidence we know of him, and of the opinions peers have of him already, this can be considered as virtually a self-portrait:

Essay (A Good Kind of Person in Our Community)

. . . Is a Helpful Person. A person that is not a continual gossiper. This person should be willing to do his share of work and take his share in the community and do the best he can in it and everything he does. He shouldn't be the quitting type of individual; he should want to take responsibilities and opportunities that should come up in the community. He should not be an "old stick in the mud"; he should get out and take part in this world. He doesn't have to be wealthy, but have a good reputation and personality. He should take part in anything that benefits the community. He should be a person that pays no attention to slander or anything that doesn't do him or anyone else any good.

1950

Conference Excerpt

The community influences on Ralph's development were summarized in these words:

"School was the community institution from which Ralph gained the most. Always a good student for whom school work came easily, he found that teachers approved him for his good scholarship and for his dependability in clubs and other activities; while his age mates approved his athletic prowess and his general dependability for projects important to them.

"Ralph was not bound to the school. There were times when he spoke to his parents about dropping out. There were teachers he did not like and he could criticize them to their faces. Yet school remained for him a place for rewards for simply being himself. He did not need to exert himself. He seldom did homework, for example. He held the school in the hollow of his hand and yet it had a powerful influence on him. It was the one institution outside of home in which he was completely at home. All of his abilities were rewarded by the school. Consequently, he learned the values of the school—team play, punctuality, responsibility, if not intellectuality. And it is not surprising that he is planning to go on to college although his stated vocational aims at the ages of 15 and 17 were (1) large horse ranch owner and (2) mechanic.

"Church had no meaning for Ralph. His family never attended church and he usually spent Sunday mornings working with his father, since this was the one time of the week when his father was always free to work on their small farm.

"There seem to have been no young men in the community who had any unusual influence on Ralph, though he kept a cool and critical eye on them and was able to judge their strengths and weaknesses. On the Adult Guess Who Test he mentioned one community leader, two high school teachers, and several other stable men."

RALPH'S CHARACTER STRUCTURE

When Ralph was seventeen, he was asked by an interviewer what he would do if his family had to withdraw their financial support. His reply was, "Why, I'd get a job, I expect, and help the folks out till things got better again." This might sound like an ordinary response, if it were not that 90 per cent of his group saw in the question only the effect it would have on their own personal comfort and security. The actual "average" reply was something like "Get a job and support myself."

By contrast, Ralph took it for granted that if his folks couldn't support him, they would need his help. His spontaneous reaction was to assume responsibility, not because it would be "the thing to do" or because he knew he "ought to," but simply and directly as the natural thing to do. He did not consider it a sacrifice. He would work and turn over whatever money was needed, because he wanted to.

No one ever has or ever will accuse him of being a "do-gooder." He lives by his principles with little effort, and seldom thinks about them, except when an issue arises where action is necessary to support them. Most of the time, he is busy doing his job, or having a good time after his tasks have been finished. He does not "knock himself out" working; but he has always done a capable job at anything he undertook.

To illustrate his very human mixture of wishes, his 1949 story might be cited, to TAT Picture No. 1 (the boy with the violin):

"Well, this boy looks like he's been having to play the violin all the time. His mother and father have him do it, and he wants to go out and play or something. And he's just sitting there, wasting time. He knows he has to do it anyway. He has to practice, so he figures he might as well learn to play it now, since he has to do it. And since he has to learn to play he learns to like it and becomes a good musician later on."

Ralph has no more liking than the average boy for a new task; especially one that adults thrust on him. Unlike the average boy in his group, however, he soon discards his initial resistance. Here, as in school and work, he looks for the positive satisfactions to be found in the activity, whatever it is. Not surprisingly, he ends up enjoying himself, taking genuine pleasure in the use of his skills.

He has a functioning IQ level of 120, which is lower than his capacity of 130 only because he does not exert himself any further than is necessary to solve daily problems satisfactorily. He has a strongly practical, realistic outlook, which pervades even his mild fantasy. When he daydreams, it is almost always about real problems. He turns them over in his mind and figures out solutions which he later puts into effect.

He is keenly observant of how the world runs, without having to make any special effort; he reasons logically, and can usually predict quite accurately what will happen next, and how various people will behave. Ralph's powers of insight are not above average. Most of the time he is content to take people as they are, without trying to understand their private feelings and motives very deeply. His ability to empathize, while somewhat reduced by his disinclination to get too personally involved with any one individual, is still well above average.

Ralph is not superhumanly mature in his emotional reactions, but he is about as mature as could reasonably be expected of an adolescent. The effective realism Ralph shows, and the emotional spontaneity that accompanies it, illustrate a salient feature of the morally mature person. In Ralph's case, it would almost be misleading to speak of ego and superego as separate, conflicting parts of him. Rather, he has a strong, well-integrated ego, into which he has incorporated most, though not all, of the "superego" principles which he once irrationally derived from his parents' pronouncements of right and wrong.

He is self-critical, but not very self-punitive beyond an acceptance of deserved blame. He assigns praise and blame realistically, and without much regard for formal status or prestige.

Ralph's moral principles are clear, and of a piece. He is consistently responsible, whatever the specific situation, and he operates at the same high level in all areas of morality. While he has not yet thought much about the world beyond Prairie City, it seems safe to predict that his moral horizon will include everyone with whom he comes in contact, if not those in groups he has never met.

He is thoroughly self-directing by now; little swayed by others, whether peers, parents, or other adults. His autonomy of judgment and action has always been unusual. A case in point is the anecdote told by a teacher back in 1948, when Ralph was fifteen.

"One day in assembly Ralph came in late. Mr. Gates, our principal, had had a hard morning, I guess. Anyway, he lit into Ralph, and gave him quite a tongue lashing; used some pretty strong language before he was done. Well, Ralph just stood there and took it, though he turned red. But after assembly was over, Ralph went to Mr. Gates' office and told him he had no business using language like that, or bawling him out so hard for being late. Ralph was polite about it, and explained why he had been late, but he certainly spoke right up to Mr. Gates, and Mr. Gates agreed that Ralph was right."

It is scarcely surprising that in voting on Ralph's "moral courage," most adult judges checked the description: "He will stand up for what is right. Although he tries to avoid conflict with others, he will strongly resist either adults or children if he feels anyone is being mistreated."

Ralph's value system is thus part of himself. It consists of stable, general principles. He seldom reflects on them consciously, but he applies them rationally and firmly to daily events.

One consequence of his character has been his almost unsought but steady social mobility. His very active support and approval by people in Prairie City have been based quite as much on his sincerity and character, as on his ambition and ability. At latest report, he was back from Army service in Germany, and was enrolled in the state university's college of agriculture. The odds are that he will not marry until he has finished college, and that when he does, it will be a girl who possesses good character, good sense, and sociability in about the same proportions that he shows. He has dated other kinds of girls, but the only one he was ever half-way "serious" about had just these qualities.

RALPH'S FAMILY HISTORY

The Reed's live on a small farm just outside of town. Mr. Reed usually wears faded blue overalls and a faded blue shirt. In the winter he wears an old felt hat, in the summer a big yellow straw one. Ralph says, "Dad kids me when I get dressed up to go out on a date. He calls me a city slicker, especially like when I put on my blue suit for a school dance. He has a blue suit too but he hardly ever puts it on. He did the first time he went to a basketball game. Ma said he was squirming the whole time. He doesn't wear it any more to games." An interviewer described Mr. Reed as a "comfortable person." Another interviewer writes, "He has a knack for making you feel at home. He stands there smoking his pipe and telling you about the plants and he just makes you feel that he really likes you. He is a rather handsome man too, a kind of open and easy expression. He is tall and rather lean."

Mr. Reed said to an interviewer, "I always say to myself I'm a very lucky man. Sometimes when I read the paper at night about all those things that happen, I say to myself, 'Carl, you have everything a man could ask for.' I've got a swell wife and two swell kids. I've got a whole world right here on these 20 acres."

Mr. Reed is a firm but gentle man, warmly human, and respectful of the rights of his wife and children as human beings. He has, at the same time, considerable self-assurance and is the head of the family. The mother says, "The kids know when Pa says somethin' he means it. He don't tell 'em an awful lot, but when he does they listen."

Mr. Reed says, "I never ask Ralph to do nothin'. I pay him just like he was a hired man. I get paid for my work and he should get paid for his." In this connection it should be noted that the parents have seen to it that Ralph has used the money he earns to buy all his own clothes, and he saves most of the rest. Ralph says, "I've had my own savings account at the bank as far back as I can remember. One time I wanted to buy a cow, but Dad said no, one cow was enough."

In the course of Ralph's life he and his father have spent a great deal of time together working on the place. Mr. Reed says, "Ralph's a A-1 worker. He can do just about anythin' and anythin' he does, he does good. We all think a lot of him. He knows what's right. I've always been mighty proud of him, the way he's done in school and the way he gets along. Some people say he looks like me, Ma says so, but Ma's partial to us both." Ralph says, "Oh, sure, lots of times I have to work when I don't want to, but Dad always tries to fit the work into my schedule so I have plenty of time to do other things too. We usually talk it over and kind of plan ahead. It's pretty interesting working with Dad. He's like a magician with plants."

Ralph once said of his mother, "If Santa Claus were a woman, Ma would be a good Santa Claus." It is difficult to improve on this description of Mrs. Reed. She is a jolly person, high colored, and round.

Except for attending occasional basketball games and movies, Mrs. Reed's participation in the community has been virtually nil. Mr. Reed has always done the bulk of the necessary shopping. Mrs. Reed once told an interviewer: "I haven't been off the place in three months. By the time I'm through with what has to be done, I'm pretty much ready for bed. I'm up at five every day. I like to have a good breakfast ready on the table when Ralph's through milkin'. Pa's always up then too, likes to get started. Even Terry's up (younger sister), so we all pile into breakfast together. It's a bustle all right. There's nobody eats the same thing. Pa has fried eggs and bacon, Ralph fried eggs and a slab of ham, Terry a soft boiled egg, and you might know I get the stack of buckwheats. Pa says we're really at our best before the sun comes up."

An interviewer commented to Mrs. Reed on the amount of work she does in a day. Mrs. Reed said, "Shucks, this ain't work. It's them girls who work in factories have got the work." She paused a moment, rapped her knuckles on the kitchen table and said, "I shouldn't have said *ain't*. That's one thing I can't get straight. The kids always have to correct my grammar. Ralph started it first, now Terry's took it up."

In spite of the essentially acceptant attitude that characterizes Mrs. Reed, she puts considerable emphasis on middle-class values. For example she says, "Some of them boys just hang around the pool hall and smoke cigarettes. I think that's terrible. My kids always tell me where they're goin' to be before they go out, and when Terry is someplace and some boy wants to take her home, she calls up to see if it's okay with us first. It is usually okay, 'cause she's got a good head on her shoulders. But once I remember we didn't know nothin' 'bout the boy, so Pa went out and got her with the pickup. That's really what Terry wanted when she called, but the boy was listening and she couldn't say it. But we kinda guessed."

Also she says, "I'm a stickler on keepin' promises you make. I just don't think it's fair to people to go back on promises. Couple of weeks ago Terry made a date with Jesse Stevens for a dance. After she'd made the date Bob Polk called and wanted to take her and she wanted to go with Bob. But I told her she had to go with Jesse 'cause she had told him she would and he was plannin' on it. It wouldn't be fair." Like her husband, she has genuine respect for other people as individuals, and an interest in them. She, too, has fundamental self-assurance.

Mrs. Reed summarizes her attitude toward Ralph with the statement: "He never has done a wrong thing in his life." She is interested in her children and knows a good deal about their activities. A reader of the interviews is struck with her ability to quote Ralph, apparently quite accurately, relative to the latter's interests and doings. She goes on at length with such beginnings as, " 'Ma, you know . . . ,' 'Ma, I wish . . . ,' 'Oh, Ma, the only kids . . . ,' " etc., etc. She sometimes says with a broad grin as she quotes a gem particularly pleasing to her, "This is Ralph's way of puttin' it." Mrs. Reed has considerable confidence in Ralph. For example, on the subject of painting the new fence around the covered rhododendrons, she says, "Pa bought the paint and I know Ralph will get it painted. No tellin' when, but I know it'll get done."

Mrs. Reed respects Ralph's judgment. For example, she told an interviewer that Ralph had been going out quite a bit, staying up late several nights during the week; and she said that she had been a little bit concerned about it and had asked Ralph if he did not think his school work might suffer. "Ralph said to me, 'No, Ma, I won't drop behind,' so I didn't say no more about it. He knows what he's doin'." Mrs. Reed hardly ever ties Ralph down or censures him for his activities; rather, she has encouraged his peer participation. For example, Ralph reports, "My folks very seldom tell when I should be in. I can usually judge for myself." Mrs. Reed says, "I never have had much chance to get to know Ralph's friends, we live so far out. But the ones I know sure are nice boys. Sometimes he has a couple of kids here for the weekend. We have plenty of room and (with a twinkle) a special big chocolate cake then, too."

In later years Ralph and his younger sister, Terry, seem to get along very well together. At least there are several reports in the material of the brother and sister's doing things for each other, as in the above instance. There is also the report of their going on a double date to a school dance. In the early years they may not have been quite so compatible. There is, for example, Mrs. Reed's report: "They get along okay. Oh, once in a while they fight some—but if it's a case of anybody else, he'll sure stick up for her against them."

This is an orderly home of reasonably regular routine. Thus the mother says, "We usually eat dinner about six. But sometimes the kids are busy at school and don't get home by then. They let us know before if that's goin' to happen, and then we eat later. Nights when Ralph's got a game we eat at five." In answer to an interviewer's question as to whether the children sometimes fix their own supper, Mrs. Reed said, "No, we always try to eat together. Dinner is the only time we really have to sit down and talk things over."

Dinner time in the Reed home is truly a time for talking things over and reaching family decisions. The following scene is typical (although considerably condensed):

Ralph: Doug Leslie was telling me today that last Sunday their family went over to the State Park for a picnic. Why don't *we* do that this Sunday?

Terry: Why don't we? We don't have to work every Sunday. I'll fix up all the food.

Mr. Reed: Well, we've got a lot to do. And how can we all go in the pickup anyhow?

Ralph: Oh, phooey, the back's okay. What's the matter with the back? I'll bring Jim along and Terry can take Ruth. Oh, she'll probably want to bring along some boy.

Terry: Don't be so smarty-alecky. I'll bring Ruth. We can all fit in the back easy. But you two boys are not going to be playing with a football back there!

Mrs. Reed: Oh, you'll get all jostled around. When we get there your stomachs will feel like a bowl full of jelly and you won't be able to eat nothin'.

Ralph: Anything! You oughta try riding in the school bus sometimes. That's worse than the back of the pickup.

Terry: Sure.

Ralph: Aw, come on, it'll be a lot of fun.

Mr. Reed: You know, Ma, maybe they're right. Maybe we could do it. But if we do we're all goin' to have to work extra hard this week. We got to get the azaleas transplanted for one thing. The work's gotta come first.

Mrs. Reed: Well, I won't be the one who says no.

Next Monday morning Mrs. Reed reported: "We had a great old time. I'll say we did."

In connection with family discussions, Mrs. Reed's statement regarding Ralph is interesting. "If he's got somethin' on his mind, he'll come right out and tell it." The other members of the household seem to do just about the same thing. In this home, while control over impulse expression is fostered very definitely and consistently, harsh and guilt-producing restrictions are essentially absent. The home atmosphere in general is conducive to self-expression. Sex is accepted realistically. Thus, Mrs. Reed spoke freely with an interviewer about how she had explained menstruation to Terry, how she talked it over with her husband first, how Mr. Reed had talked with Ralph about the forthcoming birth of the colt on their neighbor's property, and how he had then taken Ralph actually to see the birth. Furthermore, no restriction is put on Ralph's dating. When he was sixteen years old he told an interviewer that he had been doing a good deal of dating recently "since I can have the pickup now in the evenings anytime I want." Nevertheless, as has been seen, for example, in Terry's telephoning, the parents make a conscientious effort to protect and guide the members of the family. Both parents are capable of taking a firm stand in maintaining the behavioral limitations that they have established from the very beginning.

From the very beginning the Reed children have known what their parents expect of them. They have learned that meeting these expectations brings them rewards: abundant approval and considerable freedom to express themselves within the broad limits that have been established and are consistently maintained.

IV

Personality and character

The Assessment of Character

As each person was studied and rated by the research team, he or
she was assessed on all five character-type dimensions, in order to determine what proportion of his character structure pertained to each
type. Each type was defined on a ten-point scale, intended to represent the full range to be found among sixteen-year-olds in the general
U.S. population. The detailed rating instructions are described in
the Appendix, pp. 220–236.

To assign a person a score on a given type, it was decided that there
must be evidence of behaviorally effective motivation of the kind
described for that type. For example, in their dreams most people
reveal some thoroughly amoral impulses—and sometimes in waking
fantasy. If these were never permitted to affect their behavior, however, in ways obvious or subtle, then no degree of amorality could
properly be ascribed to them. The character types were defined
mainly in terms of motivation, in order to describe *why* a person

behaved as he did; but it had to be motivation that resulted in actual behavior. (See Chapter I, p. 4.)

As Table 3 shows, the five character-type dimensions proved to be

TABLE 3.　INTERCORRELATIONS OF THE CHARACTER-TYPE SCALES

Type Arrays	E	C	I	R	Maximum "Explained" Variance (per cent)
A, Amoral	−.26	−.35	−.35	−.35	.52
E, Expedient		−.47	−.43	.15	.49
C, Conforming			−.01	−.31	.53
I, Irrational-Conscientious				−.18	.34
R, Rational-Altruistic					.27

distinctly different kinds of things. The low correlations among the types suggested that each of them was a rather unique kind, or component, of moral behavior. None of them could be adequately defined in terms of the others. Even the Amoral and Rational-Altruistic dimensions were definitely not polar opposites. Atomization of the character profiles into separately analyzed scales appeared inappropriate, however, for only the total profile represented the *configuration* of character which each individual displayed. Correlation of the single type scales with the personality variables demonstrated no regular relationships except for the Amoral and Rational-Altruistic scales.

As a way of taking configuration into account, it was decided not to take the absolute score on any one character-type scale, but rather to arrange the subjects in the order of the character type that was *dominant* in each person's profile, with allowance for profiles where two or more character dimensions had equal prominence.

The results of this process are illustrated by the profiles in Table 4. Each subject was assigned to a "type group" according to the predominant configuration in his profile. This use of a profile was a way of summing up the individual's character structure and identifying its dominant component or components. The intragroup variations were taken into account in the analyses. For example, none of the subjects represents a "pure" type. Those who received the highest ratings on A (Amoral) all showed evidence of one or another kind of moral conformity a fair amount of the time. There were no pure "psychopaths" in this group. Similarly, none of those rated highest on Rational-Altruistic were entirely free from less mature motives.

TABLE 4. THE CHARACTER-TYPE PROFILES

Type Group	Case Number	Maturity of Character	Character-Type Rating A	E	C	I	R
A	T-78	1	8	7	2	6	1
	T-25	1	7	5	5	4	1
	T-89	1	8	7	1	3	1
	T-42	1	7	5	3	5	1
	T-99	1	7	4	7	2	1
CEA	T-95	2	6	6	6	2	1
	T-55	2	4	5	6	3	1
	T-64	2	4	5	6	3	1
E	T-08	3	5	7	5	4	1
	T-52	3	4	10	5	3	2
	T-22	3	3	10	4	3	1
	T-76	3	6	7	5	2	1
IAE	T-16	4	5	5	2	7	1
	T-37	4	6	6	3	7	2
C	T-11	5	2	3	6	5	1
	T-17	5	2	3	7	7	1
	T-04	5	4	3	7	2	1
	T-57	5	1	1	8	6	3
	T-34	5	1	5	9	4	2
	T-88	5	1	3	9	6	1
	T-39	5	1	4	9	6	2
	T-49	5	1	4	7	6	4
I	T-79	6	1	3	6	9	1
	T-83	6	1	6	4	10	1
	T-28	6	2	3	5	10	2
Near-R	T-40	7	7	4	2	3	8
	T-60	7	4	7	6	3	6
	T-86	7	3	8	3	2	7
	T-50	7	1	8	4	6	6
	T-53	7	3	3	5	8	5
R	T-47	8	2	6	3	4	7
	T-51	8	1	5	4	2	9
	T-03	8	1	7	4	3	8
	T-06	8	1	6	3	4	9

The thirty-four children were grouped according to their dominant character-type patterns. These type groups were then ranked on an ascending scale. This was termed a scale of *Maturity of Character*. The groups were arranged in this order: Amoral, CEA, Expedient, IAE, Conforming, Irrational-Conscientious, High R Component, and Rational-Altruistic. ("CEA" represented children who received dominant and almost equal ratings on the Amoral, Expedient, and Conforming dimensions.) The order of the groups was automatically determined, for the most part. The main type groups were placed in their original order of A, E, C, I, and R. (C and I probably should have been assigned the same score value, in keeping with the original assumption of their maturational equivalence, instead of assigning a higher score to I.)

There were three intermediate groups, each of which showed a distinct type complex. These were interpolated according to the following reasoning: the CEA group was known to have a significant amount of Amoral motivation and behavior. Furthermore, since its members had, by the definition of the Conforming and Expedient elements, little internalized principle or control, it was decided to place them nearest the Amoral group. They should fall below the Expedient group, it seemed, because the Expedient children, by definition, made a more active effort to conform and did it more adequately than the CEA's with their sizable Amoral component.

The IAE group could have been placed next to the I group; but in view of the fact that their Amoral scores represented unprincipled, uncontrolled impulsiveness part of the time, and their E scores represented unprincipled, superficial "conformity" another part of the time, they appeared to belong somewhere down the line, closer to the A and E groups. Since they still showed a slight predominance of internally controlled, principled behavior, they were put just above the E group.

The remaining group consisted of subjects with a variety of type patterns, but with one thing in common. They all had a sizable secondary score for type-R behavior. Further, outside of the Rational-Altruistic group itself, they were the only members of the research population who received average or better scores on Rational-Altruism, even though they had as high or higher a score on one or another of the remaining type dimensions. It therefore seemed most logical to put them just below the R group, on the grounds that they resembled it most closely in their pattern of motives and behavior. One case, T-40, was included here because, although he had a rating of 8 on Rational-Altruism, he had a rating of 7 on Amorality, which brought his net maturity of character distinctly below that of the predominantly Rational group.

PERSONALITY FACTORS IN CHARACTER

The first method of studying the relationship of character structure to personality was to correlate the Maturity of Character scores, shown in Table 4, with the six personality vectors which had been derived from factor analysis of the personality ratings. The six vectors were defined as follows. (Detailed descriptions appear in the Appendix, pp. 243–248.)

P1, Moral Stability: The tendency to follow the established moral code, willingly and with genuine satisfaction.

P2, Ego Strength: A complex of capacities to react to events with accurate perception, appropriate emotions, and insightful, rational judgment; all proceeding from a well-integrated personality system. (This system permits autonomous behavior, and at the same time it includes a positive, ethical attitude toward other people.)

P3, Superego Strength: The degree to which behavior is directed by, or in accord with, a set of internalized moral principles—a conscience. These principles must be present within the person and they must also influence his behavior effectively.

P4, Spontaneity: The tendency to express feelings and wishes directly in action. (Positive feeling and empathy for other people are linked with this, it turned out.)

P5, Friendliness: A generalized attitude of warm liking for other people. Its polar opposite is a generalized attitude of hostility.

P6, Hostility-Guilt Complex: A complex of intense feelings of hostility, linked with strong feelings of guilt about inner impulses.

The correlations appear in Table 5. Correlations of the personality vectors with overall moral reputation at age seventeen, sociometrically ascribed by peers and by adults, are also given in Table 5. The peer and teacher ratings represent assessments of the subjects by the people who live with them every day.

For the research population as a whole, Moral Stability is highly related to Maturity of Character, to teacher-ascribed moral reputation, and a little less to peer reputation. This may seem mere tautology of definition until it is remembered that overt conformity to the moral code—which is what Moral Stability chiefly measures—on a priori grounds could as logically be expected to occur in people of the Con-

TABLE 5. CORRELATIONS OF PERSONALITY, CHARACTER, AND
MORAL REPUTATION

Personality Vector	Maturity of Character	Adult Reputation	Peer Reputation
Moral Stability	.84	.74	.63
Ego Strength	.77	.55	.69
Superego Strength	.68	.63	.53
Spontaneity	.24	.05	.16
Friendliness	.57	.13	.04
Hostility-Guilt	−.33	−.25	−.07

Levels of significance: $.44 < .01$; $.54 < .001$.

forming or Irrational-Conscientious type as in people of Rational-Altruistic character. The finding that Moral Stability and Maturity of Character correlate .84 indicates that consistency in overt morality is more dependably produced as one moves up the scale from Expedient, to Conforming, to Rational-Altruistic character structure.

In a similar manner, Ego Strength is highly correlated (.77) with Maturity of Character—partly a matter of circular definition, perhaps, though the correlation is nonetheless indicative that mature character does require rational judgment, emotional maturity, and psychological integration. (It may be of interest to note that teachers apparently give somewhat less weight to Ego Strength as a factor in morality than do either adolescents, themselves, or the research staff. Possibly these teachers, as a group, somewhat tend to stress conformity, per se, not always differentiating between unthinkingly imitative morality and intelligently purposeful morality.)

Superego Strength is related to reputation, as well as to Maturity of Character, although not to as high a degree; probably, because some strong superegos are blind to present reality while others are more flexibly attuned to the occasion. For the group as a whole, though, it appears that a firmly internalized body of moral convictions is a major component of good character; and as this declines in strength of influence, character proportionately declines in quality.

While the finding just noted is scarcely occasion for crying "Eureka," the relationship of Spontaneity to both character and reputation does contradict one ancient view of human nature, while affirming a different one. The fact that Spontaneity is *not* inversely related to morality seems evidence that "human nature" is not "innately evil." Contrariwise, as will be seen later, some people learn to have hostile or selfish impulses which lead to immoral behavior if spontaneously expressed; whereas some other people learn to have friendly, considerate, good-natured impulses which, if spontaneously expressed, lead to highly moral behavior. This fact is summed up in the lack of any linear relationship of Spontaneity, taken by itself, with moral character. Instead, as Table 6 shows, there is a curvilinear relationship between the two. A high degree of Spontaneity appears at the low end and at the high end of the character scale, with those of intermediate maturity of character showing a low degree of Spontaneity. Clearly, spontaneity can lead either to highly moral or highly immoral behavior, depending on the *nature* of the individual's feelings and motives.

The generalized attitude of Friendliness is significantly related to Maturity of Character. It is unrelated to morality as the teachers and age mates see it. The discrepancy reflects an element which is an integral part of genuine morality: a friendly, personal interest in others. The teachers and the adolescents, themselves, seem less inclined to give this much weight in assessing morality. Instead, they seem to look for overt conformity to the conventional rules of moral behavior, and be less concerned whether the rules are observed out of expediency, unthinking imitation, or active, ethical concern for others.

The existence of an inner complex of Hostility-and-Guilt is somewhat negatively related to Maturity of Character (at the 5-per-cent level of confidence, only). As might be expected from the pattern just discussed, the teachers and the adolescents apparently do not see this as a significant element in morality. Perhaps because it is an attitude that can be masked by overt behavior which conforms ritually to conventional moral rules, the effect of this attitude on the *quality* of morality may often be overlooked by youngsters, and also by teachers.

In summary, when the full range of morality is taken into account by analyzing the research sample as a whole, there are regular relationships between character and personality. It should be noted that both sets of measures were made by the same research staff, and therefore the relationship might only represent their opinions. To the extent that a similar pattern of relationship exists with teacher and peer appraisals, some wider validity may be implied.

PERSONALITY PATTERNS
IN THE CHARACTER-TYPE GROUPS

While systematic relationships are welcome when one is seeking some order in such complex behavioral phenomena, the analysis of grouped data may hide some of the most interesting and important patterns: those which occur differently within different individuals. Insofar as people of the different character types were expected to be qualitatively different in some ways in personality characteristics, it was desirable to examine the individual personality patterns within each character-type group. Since no statistical test of pattern differences was systematically applicable with these small subsamples, a qualitative analysis of the personality-score patterns was essayed.

In order to investigate the psychological pattern of each individual subject, in each character-type group, Table 6 was constructed. This was based on the standard scores computed for each subject on each of the six psychological vectors. For greater clarity, they are represented in Table 6 by plus and minus signs, to show varying intensity.

There are distinct personality patterns which characterize each type group, and which differentiate one group from another. If, instead of looking only at the separate components of each score pattern, one by one, its meaning as a pattern of interacting personality characteristics is examined, certain features stand out which characterize and differentiate the character-type groups. The following discussion of the type groups' personality patterns is an analysis of the data in Table 6, with occasional reference to the case data to describe particular ways in which the personality characteristics are expressed in individual instances.

The Amoral type

Four of the representatives of this type, T-78, T-25, T-89, T-42, have certain fundamental characteristics in common, judging from their psychological patterns. All these personality attributes are present at once. Theoretically, indeed, they must be, to create the Amoral pattern.

They have weak Ego Strength. This sums up a complex pattern which consists of: inaccurate perception of social situations, of other people, and of self; poor ability to set clear, realistic, attainable goals

TABLE 6.   SCORE PATTERNS OF THE CHARACTER-TYPE GROUPS
ON THE PERSONALITY VECTORS *

Type Group	Case Number	Moral Stability	Ego Strength	Superego Strength	Spontaneity	Friendliness	Hostility-Guilt†
A	T-78	− − −	− −		−	− − −	− −
	T-25	− − −	− −	− −	−	− − −	− − −
	T-89	− − −	− −	− − −	+ + +	− − −	− − −
	T-42	− − −	−		+ +	− −	− − −
	T-99	− −	− −	− − −	+ +	+	+ + +
CEA	T-95	− − −	− −	− − −	+ + +	− −	+
	T-55	− −	− −	− −	−	−	+
	T-64	− −	− − −	− − −	− −	−	+ + +
E	T-08	− − −	− −		+	− − −	− − −
	T-52	− −	−	− −		− − −	−
	T-22	−		−	− − −	− − −	+ +
	T-76	−	−	− − −	+	+ +	+ +
IAE	T-16	− − −	− − −	+	− − −	− − −	− − −
	T-37	−		+	+	− −	
C	T-11	− −	− −	− − −	−		− −
	T-17	− −	− −		+	− − −	− − −
	T-04	− −	− − −	− − −	+	+ + +	+ + +
	T-57	+ +	−	+	− −	+ + +	+ +
	T-34	+ +	−	−	−	+	+ +
	T-88	+ +	− −	+ +	− − −	+ + +	−
	T-39	+ +	−	+ +	−	−	− −
	T-49	+ + +	+ +	+ +	−	−	− −
	T-79	+ +	−	+ + +	− − −	− −	− −
I	T-83	+ +	−	+ + +	− − −	− −	+
	T-28	+ +	+	+ + +	− − −	−	+
High Secondary R	T-40	−	+ +	−	+ + +	+ + +	−
	T-60	+	+ + +	− −	+ + +	+ + +	+ + +
	T-86	+	+ + +	−	+ +	+ +	+ +
	T-50	+ + +	+ + +	+ + +	− −	−	− −
	T-53	+ + +	+ + +	+ + +	+ +	−	+
R	T-47	+ + +	+ + +	+	+ + +	+ +	+
	T-51	+ + +	+ + +	+ + +	+ + +	+ + +	+ + +
	T-03	+ + +	+ + +	+	+ +	+ +	+ + +
	T-06	+	+ + +	+ + +	+ +	+ +	+ +

* Symbol system—Standard score of less than 1.99: − − −; 2.00–2.49: − −; 2.50–2.99: −; 3.00–3.49: +; 3.50–3.99: + +; 4.00 or more: + + +.   Mean = 3; sigma = 0.5.

† Scale reversed: minus sign represents more than average Hostility-Guilt; plus sign, less than average.

of any kind; behavior which is ill-adapted to achieve whatever ends the person does have in mind; and poor control over impulses which will interfere with successful adaptation to the social world, even in the sense of achieving purely personal, selfish gratification.

They show hostile, immature emotionality. There is, moreover, a pattern of childishly inappropriate emotional lability which mobilizes excessive energy and imposes a severe strain on the individual's already weak self-control. The usual nature of these emotions is that of negativism and hostility. These subjects are unwilling to accept the self-restraints and positive precepts their society suggests. They are unwilling because they feel active, generalized hostility toward the world around them.

They have weak Superego Strength. They lack any integrated system of internalized moral principles which could act as an effective conscience to help them guide and control their behavior in a morally sound way.

Their behavior is characterized by blind impulsiveness. The combination of strong, hair-trigger emotionality, weak ego, and weak Superego Strength makes them blindly impulsive, either in general, or on frequent occasions when they are provoked beyond their power to resist.

They suffer from punitive but ineffectual guilt feelings, which are of little use in controlling their behavior. This in itself indicates sharp inner conflict and lack of positive, healthy self-regard or self-respect. What is more, it implies, as does their hostility, that the only pressures exerted on them as they developed have been harsh, negative sanctions, imposed so inconsistently as to be confusing. It requires experience of consistency of human relations to develop an adequately organized ego structure (see Chapter V). They lack that.

The consequence is that they are no more at peace with themselves than they are with the world, though they might defiantly deny it to any representative of the culture they so strongly reject.

To sum them up, they are poorly socialized, having little liking or regard for other people; highly unstable in their self-control; lacking in effective inner principles; and they are decidedly irrational. It is the combination of all these forces at once which makes them predominantly Amoral in their character structure. Indeed, this pattern might almost better be called Immoral, for these subjects.

T-99 represents a subpattern which more nearly deserves the term "amoral," rather than "immoral." He, too, is lacking in essential ego strength and superego strength. However, he is a friendly, well-meaning person. He simply has too poor a perception of the social world and too few inner guides to know what is right. He acts on impulse, therefore, getting into trouble more through thoughtlessness than intent. His weak integration, coupled with his friendliness, makes him highly and uncritically suggestible. This is a different pattern of Amoral character, which still shows about the same result of inadequate moral conformity (asocial by default), poor stability and self-control, and very little rationality.

The CEA type complex

As might be expected from the heavy Amoral component and the absence of internalized principles, these subjects are not very different from the Amoral group. Indeed, T-95 might properly be classified there, perhaps.

T-95, T-55, and T-64 are low in Ego Strength and Superego Strength. They are neither so strongly hostile as the type A's, nor do they feel much guilt. T-55 and T-64 are rather passive, low in morality as much from failure to act when they should as from acting wrongly. What direction there is in their lives comes from outside pressure, which is why they are rated up on Conforming motivation. They don't do it very well, but they frequently try to do what is expected, especially if some pressure is exerted on them.

The Expedient type

T-08 has a fairly significant amount of superego control, and is not a pure example of type E by any means. T-76 has A and C motives almost equal to his Expedient drive. T-22 and T-52 are the "purest" type representatives.

Nevertheless, they all share the same weak Ego Strength. This might seem surprising in view of the emphasis on egocentricity in this type's definition; but self-centeredness is no indication of a strong, autonomous ego. In fact, quite the contrary is true, for in their self-seeking these highly Expedient adolescents often fail to foresee the consequences of their behavior, even in terms of their own gratifications.

Taking T-22 and T-52 as the purest examples of the Expedient type, it appears that they have below-average accuracy and integration of ego perceptions and controls, and definitely ineffectual superego directives. T-22, who has no strong generalized hostility, feels little guilt. However, neither their rational nor irrational controls are adequate to enable them to meet normal expectations stably. T-22 might be termed more passive, T-52 more constricted than average. Since their superegos are even weaker than their ego structures, this represents an effort to hold themselves in, in order to "get along."

They take "the easy way out," in other words. Their almost exclusive expediency is thus not so much an active attempt to manipulate the people and events around them for personal gain as it is an effort to get as much personal gratification as possible by fitting in with their world when they have to, and avoiding as many social demands as possible which would require them to act in a positively socialized way.

Their constriction and relinquishment of direction to the social forces around them leads only to the absence of active immorality. This is not very highly desirable from a social and moral point of view. Furthermore, it requires them to suppress enough of their selfish spontaneous impulses to make them tense, restless, and uncomfortable with themselves. These subjects come the closest in the group to displaying the presumed motives of the "happy hedonist." They are would-be hedonists, without doubt; but it seems that the inescapable facts of social living make real happiness dependent on actively friendly, mutually warm relationships with other people. Since they have little conception of such relatedness, their efforts to grasp hedonistic pleasure result in empty satisfactions. They seek but do not find, for they are unable to recognize the human warmth and approval they vaguely but intensely want. They give up much of their spontaneity, yet get little in return. The self-defeating nature of insincere, expedient adaptation to society could scarcely be more clearly demonstrated.

The IAE type complex

The two boys who show this configuration reveal the inner conflict which could logically be predicted for anyone possessed of an active, controlling superego who is nevertheless unable to help acting in crudely impulsive ways much of the time. The strongest directive element in their make-up is their rather firm but primitive, harsh conscience. It must be a hangover from early years of parental dictation, for it has little to do with the things they would really like to do. They are covertly hostile, but are punished for it with marked feelings of guilt. They differ with respect to spontaneity, T-16 being severely repressed, T-37 mildly spontaneous. T-37, however, has relatively better ego integration and perceptiveness to guide him than T-16, who is very weak in this. Both are below average in Ego Strength, however. Thus, they are not "masters in their own houses." They react to impulse or to internalized, irrationally held moral principles in which they do not personally believe, in a sense. They don't care much for other people, and feel themselves to be quite bad. They are not conscious of much of their guilt, for they protect themselves against recognizing their basically low self-regard by consciously picturing themselves in more favorable but not very realistic terms. Even so, their inner conflict is too severe to be successfully ignored. They try hard, but don't find much real pleasure in life. This is more true of T-16, who has the deeper hostility and guilt, than of T-37.

The Conforming type

Before taking up the pure Conforming type, it might be useful to look at T-11 and T-17, who represent a rather pure form of the CI type complex, with little else in their make-up. These two girls show weak egos, weak-to-moderate superegos, and a passive constriction which holds in check their inner hostility. They can express few of their personal needs and wishes spontaneously, and derive little satisfaction from life. They feel strong, chronic guilt about their "bad impulses," even though they seldom actively express them.

Their superegos are almost entirely composed of negative "Don't's" which they have incorporated unquestioningly. They feel themselves to be a bad kind of person, just as they see little to like in others. They are unable to check the punitive voices of their conscience (almost a direct echo of harsh parental strictures, it seems) against the reality of daily life, in any rational, self-directing way. They are, in short, depressed, dull, unhappy, and quite unable to stand up to the world even to express their antagonism toward it.

T-04 is a case by himself: so weakly integrated, though friendly, that he cannot do much more than follow the directives of the stronger people around him.

The other member of this type group whose dynamics are not entirely representative is T-49. She is not a pure example in any case, having a respectable proportion of Rational-Altruistic motivation. She has both firm ego and superego; compartmentalized, though, for she has to repress a good deal of impulse which has irrational guilt attached to it. Her firm outward conformity operates in opposition to considerable inner hostility. Thus, she is almost as much type I as type C.

The purest Conformers are T-57, T-34, T-88, and T-39. They are all conformists to the moral code of the community. They have weak-to-moderate ego integration, moderate-to-strong superego direction, and tend to be on the passive side. Their conformity is therefore an outer-directed process. Except for T-39, who is mildly hostile in his underlying attitude and feels definitely guilty about it, they are friendly in their outlook and relatively at ease with themselves. Weak ego direction and willing conformity to outer pressures thus produce adequate morality in their behavior, reinforced by irrationally held internal moral principles which have been taken over without much question or examination from the people who run their world (their parents, chiefly).

The Irrational-Conscientious type

T-28, T-79, and T-83 are almost walking examples of the "Puritan conscience." More than by any other consideration, they are ruled by the dictates of their conscience, which consists of a firm, well-integrated body of moral rules. These rules which they follow so faithfully are much stronger than their ability to appraise present reality and figure out logical ways of behaving morally. In fact, their weak-to-moderate Ego Strength is not enough to enable them to test or question the rules they have internalized so uncritically.

They are necessarily constricted, for they have an appreciable degree of generalized hostility. This produces some guilt, but it is not intense since they are so utterly guided by their superego directives. They automatically behave in responsible, "loyal," honest, "kind" ways; but it is more by rote than by personal intent. They demand as much of others as of themselves in the way of conventional morality.

Nevertheless, their lack of any strong, positive concern for others as individuals, not to mention their repressed but definite hostility, makes them far too literal minded and rigid in their righteousness to be very easy to live with. In fact, they do not begin to approach the spontaneous, sincerely considerate behavior which marks the higher levels of morality. They are "pillars of the church and the community"; and often seem just about as warmly human as so many stone pillars. Needless to say, they demonstrate all the features of the person with an extremely compulsive personality structure, in psychoanalytic terms.

They do not really like people, and do not have any very positive or warm self-acceptance. They are unable to make discriminating judgments about the purpose of the moral rules which weigh on them so heavily, nor are they able to let circumstances alter cases, in order to preserve the spirit of the moral law. They take some cold satisfaction from rigorously observing the letter of the law. That is about the extent of their joy in living; not an enviable state nor a very attractive one to their acquaintances. Their peers respect them, but they don't like them.

The group with High Secondary R motivation

Although the type patterns and personality configurations of these adolescents are varied in many ways, they all have some striking features in common. T-50 is a partial exception. She is very much like T-49 in the Conforming type group. Both of them should perhaps have been given their highest ratings on the Irrational-Conscientious type. T-53 is also exceptional for Superego Strength; but otherwise like the group.

T-40, T-53, T-60, and T-86, whatever their differences, have in common a high degree of rationality, friendliness, and altruistic impulse. They have excellent Ego Strength, which includes the preceding characteristics and also includes high autonomy and good integration of most major drives. Except for mild conflict in the case of T-40, who is often impulsively self-indulgent in socially harmless ways, they are at peace with themselves and thoroughly spontaneous. If most of them do not have any remarkable level of moral conformity, it is the result of their deliberate decision to enjoy themselves in life; not at the expense of others, but also not with too much willingness to accept restrictions others might place on them. They are still more positively moral than otherwise, for they like people and would be unhappy to do them active harm. They are not lacking in inner principles. They are in control, though. They observe or ignore their principles according to their impulse; but, at the same time, according to the effects they foresee their behavior will have on other people. They seldom seriously fracture the moral code, but they feel free to ignore its more demanding rules when they don't feel like putting themselves out. They are not extremely moral, therefore, but others like them just as they like and enjoy themselves. They can be thoughtless, but they are as often considerate in a highly perceptive way.

Thus, their sizable component of Rational-Altruism is the mark of a strong, autonomous, reality-adapted ego which goes hand in hand with a good regard for people. Save for the quite similar T-49, these are the first people in the type sequence to show really sound, firm ego development and integration.

The Rational-Altruistic type

T-03, T-06, T-47, and T-51, without exception, show a personality configuration which is consistent, and unique in this population. They are the most morally effective adolescents in the study. They have the best ego development of all. They are well-integrated, emotionally mature, and highly rational in their choice of action.

They have firm, internalized moral principles which they frequently subject to critical inquiry and test to see if they work in practice. These principles are integrated into most of their thoughts and acts (compared to the rest of the population, at any rate). It scarcely seems accurate to describe them as having a separate, compartmentalized "superego." These adolescents act on rational moral principles rather than on "absolute" rules, because they have a high regard for people.

They are thoroughly spontaneous, which is a tribute to their intrinsic morality; for despite the fact that they decide issues for themselves, they are rather uniformly constructive and ethical in their behavior.

They have relatively few irrational guilt feelings, nor any reason to feel guilty. They conform to the moral precepts because they want to, and because—consciously, or unconsciously—they understand them. They enjoy life thoroughly and actively, having as healthy a respect for themselves as they do for other people. There is no false pride in this. They simply are well and accurately aware of their own natures and capacities. Since they are free from serious conflict, free from any irrational need to follow convention blindly for the sake of "security," they are free to use almost all their emotional energy. Inevitably, they channel most of this energy into socially constructive, highly moral actions. By nature, they could not do otherwise.

These adolescents have not achieved perfection. They are not entirely grown up yet. But they have the rare quality of being open to indefinite growth. They are already about as mature, emotionally and socially, as one of their years could be. They can scarcely help continuing to develop in wisdom, consideration, and knowledge of self and others, for it is in their very make-up to look life in the face, know it, and live by principles that bring the greatest good to themselves and to those they love.

THE CHARACTER TYPES AS A SCALE
OF PSYCHOSOCIAL MATURATION

Anyone familiar with the Freudian theory of personality development will recognize the close parallel of the present typology with that
theory of stages in psychosocial maturation (Rickman, 1951). When
one is dealing with adolescents or adults, the use of a genetic sequence
of stages to account for present behavior is, of course, an analogy.
It has some real truth in it, but it also involves an oversimplification
of the facts. To begin with, though, it may be useful to talk as if the
types really do correspond to developmental stages.

The *Amoral* type is a person with infantlike, inaccurate perceptions;
infantlike emotional lability; and infantlike inability to control himself in a way adequate to the demands of ordinary social living.
Since he has not accepted the basic premise of human society that
one must consider other people, he is infantlike in his lack of effectual
moral principles. He is contradictory, inconsistent, antagonistic, and
often openly hostile in his behavior.

The *Expedient* type is one who has come to terms with society in
a way; but his way is that of the young child who conforms in order
to avoid adult punishment or disapproval. He has no more accepted
the premise of active regard for others than the Amoral person. If
the punishments have been impressive enough, he may have internalized a few "Don't's"; but he has few or no positive moral directives within him. Like a child, he is short-sighted, does not look
ahead to foresee the long-range consequences of his behavior, even
though this omission may thwart the very purposes of self-gratification
he has in mind. He is not so well in control of himself, either, nor
so well-integrated, that he can always do the "smart thing" even if
intellectually he knows what it is. While he keeps his impulses in
check in order to get along without trouble, his inner emotional reactions are frequently as inappropriate as a child's, though they are
not the overwhelming elations and rages of the infant. He does not
always succeed in maintaining consistent adaptation even in his surface behavior, since at times his negativistic, basically hostile feelings
toward society break through his rather weak self-control.

The *Conforming* type is like a child who has come to accept the
dictates of his family and society in a placid, uncritical way. He goes
along passively with the social and moral rules in a rather literal
way. His acceptance is positive, if mild, for he has more liking than

resentment in his general outlook on the world. He is not capable of very complicated, rational thought, or at least has never learned to exercise it. He has intrinsically rather weak powers of self-direction, depending instead on the guidance of the people and the rules of the world he knows. He has incorporated many of these rules. He lives with and by them rather comfortably, for he does not have too many contrary impulses to occasion guilt or distrust of himself. Like the older child, he knows how to live peacefully in his familiar world, does not ask too many questions about its fundamental traditions, and more or less takes them for granted as absolutes. He lives in the heteronomous stage which Piaget ascribed to the years of middle childhood.

The *Irrational-Conscientious* type is as much like a child in his own way. He, too, lives by absolute rules. However, he has found himself forced to internalize them much more completely than the Conformer. He has a good deal of active hostility to be controlled, and since he accepts the dominance of society, he feels bound to control himself. His principles seem mainly to consist of "Don't's" (at least in the subjects in this study, and perhaps necessarily, in any such dynamic pattern). They are firmly organized, however, and rule his behavior. He is not emotionally capable of questioning his conscience or asking if it always serves a genuinely moral purpose. He does not have the freedom to perceive life whole, nor to act on rational assessment of particular situations, even if he wanted to. His superego is much stronger than the rest of his wishes and drives. It controls him, and there is not much he can do to modify or change it. In any case, it is not possible for him to seriously consider doing this. In his own way, he is no more autonomous than the Conformer. In a real sense his parents are still running his life almost completely, for he carries their injunctions around within him and heeds them constantly.

The *Rational-Altruistic* type is a continuously maturing person. He has not reached a level and stopped there for life. Instead, all his capacities are constantly and effectively at work to improve his own well-being and to promote the interests of his society, in which he takes a lively interest. He is in as full, rational control of himself as it is possible for a human to be. There is no particular age level which he represents, except that he is what is hoped for in the genuinely mature adult. As an adolescent, he does not have the wisdom of an adult; but he shows the certain promise of attaining it.

It might almost be said that he has no separate, dissociated superego. His conscience is an integral part of all the principles which he incorporates or develops; and he tests them out in action to make sure that they achieve that well-being of self and others which he actively desires.

PSYCHOLOGICAL TRENDS THAT RUN THROUGH THE CHARACTER-TYPE SEQUENCE

From Amoral to Rational there is evidence of increasing ego strength, including all the characteristics of rational, emotionally mature, integrated behavior.

There is a straight-line trend through the types, of increasing superego strength, in the broad sense of increasingly firm, internalized moral principles which act as an effective guide to behavior. There appear to be four stages or kinds of conscience within this sequence.

The first is the crude, harsh, punitive collection of "Don't's," which are repressive at best, and are internally inconsistent or impossible to follow, at worst. This is uniformly found in association with generalized inner hostility. The Amoral subjects show this kind of powerfully punitive but behaviorally ineffectual "conscience." It seems directly and literally to be the echo of scolding parental voices.

The second kind of conscience is a matter of rule conformity; not so heavily internalized, but bolstered by a ready willingness to do the expected thing as society defines it. It produces at best a passive kind of morality. It permits little initiative in meeting new or unfamiliar moral issues. It serves quite well to guarantee socialized behavior in a stable community committed to moral ends. However, it might be a dangerously weak system in times when a whole society faces a serious moral crisis.

The third kind of conscience consists of moral rules which are deeply internalized and rigidly adhered to. These rules are not accessible to rational investigation and testing. Originally derived by uncritical incorporation of parental dictates, usually including many harshly negative prohibitions, such a conscience tends to produce unvarying, rather stereotyped behavior. It also tends to generate a self-righteous dogmatism about what are called "principles," but are actually inflexible rules about acting in closely specified ways.

The fourth kind of conscience consists of firmly internalized moral principles which are continually open to rational experimentation in order to achieve the moral *purpose* inherent in the principle. This is not a discrete superego entity, operating in dissociated isolation from the effects of day-to-day experience. Instead, it is so intermingled and integrated with principles derived from rational assessment of experience, that to call it by a separate name would almost seem to do violence to the behavioral picture from which the term is abstracted.

In the case of the Rational-Altruistic person, it seems almost untrue to speak of a superego as a separate, distinct set of directives acting as an entity in the personality, distinct and cut off from the ego. Instead, it seems sensible to interpret the data to say that he has a firm body of ethical principles. It is too much to say of anyone that he has no irrationally held beliefs, but at least in relative terms the Rational-Altruistic person goes far in this direction. Instead of a dichotomized self with separate ego and superego, it very much looks as though he is a thoroughly well-integrated person. That is, many of his spontaneous (id) impulses are positively oriented in their very nature. He feels strongly that the best way to live is to give others as much consideration as himself, as often as possible. Finally, he checks each new situation alertly to see who is involved, how any given action will affect them, and governs his behavior accordingly, because he wants to. It is difficult to find in such a system any fixed, important body of compartmentalized principles which could be called a superego as sharply distinct from the ego.

It should be emphasized, of course, especially in considering the adolescents studied here, that by "rationality" is meant behavior which appears highly appropriate to the given situation, to presumably "expert" observation. It need not, and in these adolescents usually does not, necessarily imply conscious deliberation. Indeed, a mistake often made is to confuse conscious intellectualization about a social problem with genuinely rational response to it, whether consciously considered or not.

Making moral deliberation a conscious matter, if in consonance with the person's real underlying feelings and beliefs, undoubtedly improves the rational control he has over his own actions. Thus, this argument is by no means anti-intellectual; but it is definitely anti-"intellectualization" when this consists of rationalizations which are actually irrational devices to evade real issues. The truly rational person, that is to say, is one who *acts* with morality in the deepest sense. He may or may not talk about it. But talking "morally" is not necessarily related at all to moral action: "The Devil can quote Scripture."

The final theme which runs through the Maturity of Character scale (type sequence) could be summed up as *love*. The Amoral person feels unloved and is incapable of loving. The Expedient person is no more capable of genuine love and concern for others, no matter what counterfeit show he may put on; and he feels unloved himself. The average Conforming person tends to feel loved more than unloved, and to be able to love others; perhaps not with very keen perception of what others want and need, individually, but with a willingness to treat them considerately and affectionately. The Irrational-Conscientious person feels unloved and unloving; but has no choice except to act in conventionally "kind" and "considerate" ways. The essential lack of warmth is not overcome, however; and others sense this, whether or not they consciously recognize it. The overt "love" such a person shows, not unlike that of the Expedient person, is a matter of barter: "I will act as if I love you, if you will act as if you love me," with emphasis on the word "act." The Rational-Altruistic person feels, and is, lovable and loved. He is warmly, spontaneously loving. What is more, he is highly perceptive of others' needs and wishes, hence is able to be not just well-intentioned, but loving in a genuinely constructive way. Since he is at peace with himself and lives by his own resources, he need make no excessive demands on others. He can give love freely, without insisting it be returned as a precondition to his gift. He has his own deep human needs and would be deeply hurt by losing the love of someone near to him; but he is not a bargainer. What he gives, he gives because he genuinely wants to. It is a satisfaction in itself.

V

Family influences on personality and character

Certain characteristics of the adolescents' families had been measured three years earlier by another research group. The results were stored away, unexamined, until after the character conference had completed its study and rating of the individual adolescents. This made it possible to compare two sets of independent measures: one on the personalities and characters of the adolescents, the other on the family interaction patterns they experienced.

A factor analysis of the eight earlier ratings, plus two ratings on family characteristics by the character-research conference, yielded four dimensions of family dynamics (details are presented in the Appendix, pp. 255–258): Consistency of family life, Democracy vs. Autocracy of parental control, Mutual Trust and Approval among the child and his parents, and Leniency vs. Severity of parental discipline and punishment.

In order to compare the family data with the personality data, each child's standard score on each of the six personality dimensions was computed. Similarly, a standard score was derived for each family on each of the four family dimensions. It was thus possible to correlate the children's scores on the personality dimensions with the characteristics of their families.

TABLE 7. CORRELATIONS OF FAMILY AND PERSONALITY VECTORS

Variable	F2	F3	F4	P1	P2	P3	P4	P5	P6
F1, Consistency	−.01	.66	.37	.53	.56	.50	.05	.19	−.10
F2, Democracy		.53	−.65	.16	.43	−.07	.36	.33	−.40
F3, Mutual Trust			−.22	.60	.74	.33	.27	.44	−.40
F4, Severity				−.08	−.16	.26	−.38	−.38	.40
P1, Moral Stability					.73	.66	.11	.48	−.37
P2, Ego Strength						.48	.56	.43	−.33
P3, Superego Strength							−.24	.02	−.23
P4, Spontaneity								.39	−.28
P5, Friendliness									−.75
P6, Hostility-Guilt									

Levels of significance: .36 < .05; .44 < .01.

From Table 7, the significant correlations suggest the following relationships, presumably causal in nature, between family experience and personality:

Ego Strength seems largely produced by Trust (.73) and Consistency (.56).

Moral Stability also seems importantly influenced by Trust (.60) and Consistency (.53).

Superego Strength seems influenced by Consistency (.50) and perhaps Trust (.33).

Spontaneity seems influenced by Democracy (.36) and perhaps Trust (.27), plus a lack of Severity (−.38).

Friendliness seems most influenced by Trust (.44) and Democracy (.33).

The Hostility-Guilt Complex seems influenced by Severity (.40) combined with a lack of Trust (−.40) and of Democracy (−.40).

The pattern shown in Table 7 suggests that Mutual Trust among family members is rather closely related (.66) to Consistency in family life. These two family characteristics, working together, appear to be responsible for the development of healthy Ego Strength and Moral Stability. That is, a child's emotional maturity, personality integration, autonomy, rationality of behavior, and his willingness to adapt to society's expectations appear to be directly related to the degree of Consistency, Mutual Trust, and mutual approval he experiences within his family.

Superego Strength is not unrelated to Ego Strength, but insofar as it is a separate entity, it appears to be the product of a somewhat different pattern of these family forces. It seems mainly to come from a regular, consistent family life. Superego Strength is not at all the same thing as the Hostility-Guilt Complex; indeed, they correlate slightly negatively, $-.23$. Moreover, Superego Strength is unrelated to the generalized attitude of Friendliness. One might therefore think that Superego Strength would be associated with severe parental autocracy, but it is not. Judging from the case studies, the reason appears to be that while some children with strong, rigid superegos do tend to come from severe, autocratic families, there are other children who have equally strong internal principles but who test and apply them rationally. These latter children come from families that have been quite democratic and unsevere. Other data from the study suggest the existence of these two different kinds of strong superego, each of which has a different relationship with the Democratic-Autocratic family dimension. Spontaneity (P4) and Ego Strength (P1) are moderately related. Both characteristics appear to be favored by a lenient, democratic family atmosphere which actively promotes a self-accepting, good-natured spontaneity in the child.

Friendliness is significantly related to the degree of Mutual Trust and Affection within the family, whether or not there is stable Consistency in it. There are some friendly children who have weak egos and weak superegos. These come (in the present study, at least) from inconsistent, irregular families who follow a policy that might better be called "laissez-faire" than "democratic," though the parents show an uncritically acceptant attitude toward the children in a desultory, rather inattentive way.

The Hostility-Guilt Complex might readily be called a hostile but dependent, unresolved Oedipal complex upon examination of the variables that comprise it (see above). Not surprisingly, it tends to occur in children whose families are severe, autocratic, but unloving and inconsistent.

In general, insofar as these findings bear on present-day theory about personality development, they tend to corroborate that theory. These adolescents' personality characteristics proved to be significantly related to the emotional relationships and the disciplinary patterns which they experienced in living with their parents.

Since these personality characteristics appear to be major components of moral character (see Chapter IV), the evidence indicates that character is strongly—probably predominantly—shaped by family experience.

FAMILY CORRELATES OF MORAL MATURITY

The crucial test of the relationship between moral character and family background is the degree to which character, itself, is regularly related to family characteristics.   In order to make this test, two procedures were used.   The first was to correlate the Maturity of Character scores of the children with the scores of their families on the four family vectors.   The results are shown in Table 8.

TABLE 8.   CORRELATIONS OF THE FAMILY CHARACTERISTICS WITH
THE MATURITY OF CHARACTER SCALE

Family Vector	Child's Maturity of Character
F1, Consistency	.58
F2, Democracy-Autocracy	.26
F3, Mutual Trust and Approval	.64
F4, Leniency-Severity	−.16

Level of significance: .44 < .01.

Taking the group as a whole, it appears that stable, mature character is highly associated with those family traits which make up vector F3: parental trust and faith in the child, the child's readiness to share confidences with his parents, parental approval of the child and of his peer activities, and good interparental relations.

To almost as high a degree, sound character is related to those family traits comprising vector F1: consistency of parental control, regularity in the home, and common participation in activities by parents and children.

There is only a slight tendency for good character to be related to democratic family practices, rather than autocratic ones, *when this vector, F2, is taken by itself.*   However, as will be seen shortly, democratic direction of the child's life does have a systematically positive influence for good character *when it is combined with consistency and mutual trust.* Conversely, an autocratic home atmosphere prevents the development of anything better than rigid conformity, as will also be seen.

Leniency or Severity of parental control, F4, shows no significant relationship with good character—again, *when considered in isolation* from the other family characteristics. This is understandable, since it makes all the difference what kinds of moral behavior the parents treat leniently or severely, and how consistently they exercise their discipline. Yet in this instance, too, when this family characteristic is considered in combination with the other family vectors, its influence on character is not an unpredictable nor irrelevant one, as its low overall correlation might have suggested.

THE FAMILY PATTERNS
OF THE CHARACTER-TYPE GROUPS

In order to arrange the family scores so that their *pattern* in each case could be seen at a glance, and could be related to the character-type sequence, Table 9 was prepared. It is based on the rank of each child's family on each of the four family characteristics. For clarity, plus and minus signs have been substituted for the rank scores, according to the system explained in the footnote to the table. This is analogous to the method used in Table 6, Chapter IV, for the personality patterns of the children. Here, it shows how the child's family stands on each of the characteristics, relative to the other families in the study.

The general nature of the child's family experience can be reconstructed by looking at the total pattern of his family's four scores. It is necessary to view the whole pattern in each case, and to translate it into a living picture of the family, because each type of character structure can be, and often is, the expression of several somewhat different family patterns. These different patterns, nonetheless, tend to have a certain common nature within each character-type group, differentiated from the family patterns of the other type groups. For example, all the Amoral children's families are inconsistent and distrustful; but some are severe and autocratic, others are lenient and permissive. Yet this merely produces two somewhat different kinds of Amoral behavior.

TABLE 9.   THE FAMILY PATTERNS OF THE CHARACTER TYPES

Character Type	Case No.	I* Consistent-Inconsistent	II Democratic-Autocratic	III Trustful-Distrustful	IV† Lenient-Severe
A	78	− −	−	− − −	−
	25	− −	− −	−	− −
	89	− − −	+	− − −	+ +
	42	− −	−	− − −	− − −
	99	− − −	+	− − −	+ + +
CEA	95	−	− −	− − −	− − −
	55	− − −	+ + +	− − −	+ +
	64	+	− − −	+	− − −
E	08	+ + +	− − −	−	− − −
	52	−	+ +	+ +	+
	22	− −	+ + +	+	+ + +
	76	−	+ +	(+)	+ +
IAE	16	−	(−)	−	(+)
	37	− −	+ +	+ +	+ + +
C	11	− − −	− −	− −	− −
	17	− −	− − −	− − −	− −
	04	− − −	+	− −	+ + +
	57	+ +	−	+	− −
	34	+	− − −	− −	−
	88	(+)	− − −	− −	− −
	39	+ + +	− − −	+ +	− −
	49	+ +	− −	+ +	(−)
I	79	(−)	− −	− − −	− −
	83	+ +	(+)	(−)	− − −
	28	+ +	− −	+	− −
High R	40	+ + +	+ +	+ + +	+
	60	+ + +	+ + +	+ + +	+ +
	86	+ +	+ + +	+ +	+ + +
	50	+ + +	+ + +	+ + +	−
	53	+ +	+	+ +	+ +
R	47	− − −	−	−	+ + +
	51	+	+ +	+ + +	+
	03	+ + +	+ +	+ + +	+
	06	+	+ + +	+ + +	+ +

* Rank of 1–6: − − −; 7–12: − −; 13–16: −; 17: (−); 18: (+); 19–22: +; 23–28: + +; 29–34; + + +.

† Rank order reversed to make Leniency the positive end.

THE FAMILIES OF THE AMORAL CHILDREN

The most striking feature of these families is that, without exception, they are markedly inconsistent; and, except for the milder degree of T-25, they are highly mistrustful and disapproving of their children. These boys and girls have grown up knowing very little love, little emotional security, and little if any consistent discipline.

There is variation in the other two family characteristics, Democracy-Autocracy, and Leniency-Severity. These make sense, however, when each family is separately viewed. (The observations about the children's personalities are derived from Chapter IV.)

T-78's family has been mildly autocratic and mildly severe, while being extremely distrustful and decidedly inconsistent. It is not surprising to find him an intensely hostile boy with weak ego strength and very poor conformity to moral expectations, although he has strong guilt feelings and exercises sporadic control over his antagonistic impulses.

T-25 is a hostile, guilty girl whose poor ego integration is aided only by a generalized constriction and impulse suppression. She comes from severe, autocratic parents who distrust her somewhat but are inconsistent in their control.

T-89 is a very poorly integrated boy whose hostile or amoral impulses continually break out of control, although he feels very guilty about himself as a person. The ratings in Table 9 show his family to be lenient and mildly "democratic"; but extremely distrustful and extremely inconsistent. It seems a real misnomer to call it "democracy" here, where he is allowed to make decisions of his own only because his parents don't care enough to guide him, and pay only unpredictable attention to him, if any.

T-42, a much less destructive boy but still very childishly impulsive, was described in 1950 in these words: "What keeps him in hand is more the influence of early-introjected, punitive precepts than any great concern for others." That was written with no knowledge of these family ratings, which describe the family as mildly autocratic, extremely distrustful, inconsistent, but very severe in its punishment of transgressions. The two independent analyses appear to confirm each other.

T-99, the "different" Amoral boy, more the happy-go-lucky psychopath, comes from a family which has very little trust in him and is very inconsistent, but which gives him some voice in running his life and is extremely lenient in its discipline.

To sum up the forces that have shaped the Amoral person in this sample, he or she has experienced a chaotic, unloved existence. If his parents have been severe and autocratic, they have made him generally antagonistic, with only some crude "superego fragments" to make him feel guilty and to make· him exercise some intermittent self-restraint. If they have been lenient and "democratic," it is only in the sense of being too unconcerned to give him any steady guidance toward mature moral behavior.

The typical Amoral subject is a rejected child. His parents disapprove of him generally. The gratifications he can find through them are minimal. At the same time, their control is extremely inconsistent, though it may or may not be severe. It seems obvious that he could never, in this family environment, get any clear notion of moral principles. Not only do his parents not show any consistent moral principles, but they have given him abundant reason to feel that he cannot please them, no matter what he tries. So the Amoral person is amoral for three reasons:

1. He experiences nothing clear-cut or consistent in the moral sphere to internalize, from his parents' example.

2. Even if he did have something clear-cut to internalize there would be no real reward for internalizing it.

3. He has never been *consistently* punished for not observing his society's moral code.

Why is A impulsive? In view of the thorough-going disapproving attitude of his parents, and his concomitant inability to please them, the only avenue of gratification left to him is immediate impulse gratification, which he tries to find wherever he can. Sometimes he may be punished for impulse expression, but sometimes he can get away with it. The attempt to gain the satisfaction seems well worth the chance. With no experience of success in social relations at home, A goes out into the world with a general inability to cope with different reality situations, and a relatively strong tendency to find impulse gratification wherever he can.

A has been the long-term recipient of predominantly negative feelings from both parents. In addition, his relations with them were constantly frustrating because virtually nothing he did met with their consistent approval. In the attitudinal ratings he scores the very lowest on outer acceptance of mother and father. He has the most negative feeling toward mother, and extremely little positive feeling. He has, in short (except for T-99), little love for people; rather, he has an active hate for his family and for almost anyone else. Considering his background, he never had a chance to develop altruistic feelings, rationality, or personal stability, for these have not existed in his family world.

THE EXPEDIENT CHILDREN'S FAMILIES

The typical background of the child with predominantly Expedient character is exemplified by the families of T-52, T-22, and T-26. The pattern might be summed up as a *laissez-faire* home, where the parents give the child indiscriminate freedom to make his own decisions, approve of him, and are lenient in their discipline, but also are inconsistent in the moral and social pattern they set for him.

E has received no clear picture from his family life of rules of right and wrong. At home he *learns to do just about what he wants to do.* At the same time he learns to think in terms of "me." That is, he learns to do whatever is best for *him* to do, and nobody does anything to stop him. This could be put even more strongly: not only does nobody do anything to stop him, but he is rewarded by a *good deal of general parental support.* This general parental support, however, since it is combined with inconsistency, irregularity, and leniency, does not contain much real recognition or concern for the child as an individual. E's parents like him mildly, almost regardless of what he does, but in a detached way. They do not govern themselves in such a way as to train him in a firm moral code.

Thus, in the home, E has learned to do whatever brings him most gratification. In this atmosphere of inconsistency this is one of the few consistent principles he was able to develop. And it in no sense detracts from the support he receives from the family. Having experienced superficial success in the family, E goes out into the world with the orientation of considering himself and his own satisfactions first and foremost. However, because of the approval that has been bestowed on him at home, not only does he feel that he is important and able to cope with reality to his own advantage, but also he is sensitive to the approval of others. Unlike the Amoral person, his need for approval has been developed. In the outside world he strongly desires social rewards, partly because he lacks internal standards that would enable him to approve of himself. The family approval to which he is accustomed has come too easily and is too shallow. He now, without realizing it, sets out to get similar approval from the world; but it is admiration and applause he seeks, not the deep interpersonal relationships that require mutual sacrifices.

Accordingly, when he finds that the people in the outside world are not so lenient as his parents and do not bestow their approval so easily, he adapts his behavior sufficiently to their standards to increase the possibility of gaining satisfaction for himself, while at the same time maintaining their approval. E is out for himself—but he has had sufficient bolstering from his family to develop a fairly firm grasp of surface reality. He adapts himself in different situations in order to improve, wherever possible, on the superficial but pleasant support he early experienced in his family.

E's parents did not demand very much of E. They supported him without asking obedience or even love in return. He never had to learn to make sacrifices. It is not surprising to find he has low scores on outer acceptance of both parents' moral code. Nor is it surprising to find his general low intensity of feeling toward them, slightly more negative than positive. He can reject his parents when it suits his purposes, with a minimum of guilt or shame.

The notable exception to this pattern is T-08 and his family. In the first place, he is a very different kind of person from the other three: "At most times he is pushed by his punitive conscience into sullen immobility, but sometimes he acts as he really wants to, with thorough disregard for others." He probably should have been rated even more heavily than he was on the Conforming and Irrational-Conscientious dimensions. However, his morality is as low as the others', and when he conforms, it is from crude guilt or expediency, not for love of other people. His family background clearly foreshadowed such an orientation. It has been extremely consistent in an extremely severe, autocratic way, relieved only in that he and his parents are no more than mildly distrustful and disapproving of each other. This is very like the Conforming children's background, only more severe, even more consistent, and less trustful. While this complicates the picture of the Expedient group, it reveals no less clearly that a heavy-handed autocracy is as bad as an overlenient lack of guidance as a way of building character.

THE CONFORMERS' FAMILIES

First, there is a deviant subgroup composed of T-11, T-17, and T-04. The first two have had severely autocratic, inconsistent, and distrustful home experiences. In these respects, their family upbringing matches that of the Amoral children, rather than that of the more typical Conformers. What is more, their personality patterns match those of the Amoral children, rather than the pattern of the other Conforming children, except for their extremely depressed spontaneity scores. Thus, there is a close congruence between their family experience and their personalities. Perhaps it was simply a mistake, originally, to class them with the other Conformers as to character type. At most, they represent a quite different, and morally ineffectual kind of would-be Conformer.

T-04, whose personality and character were seen to be very much like T-99's, the good-natured Amoral boy, also has a family pattern which is almost identical with T-99's. He is ineffectual as a moral being, but was credited with somewhat more of a desire to conform than T-99. (He has low-average native intelligence, markedly depressed in its functioning by a chaotic upbringing.) His family has been extremely inconsistent, yet extremely lenient; distrustful, yet mildly "democratic." It is not surprising that he has the weakest ego structure in the whole population, and the weakest superego. His marked friendliness is all that accounts for what little morality he is able to show.

The more typical and effective Conformers have a common family history, in general: consistent, mostly very autocratic, with severe parental discipline. T-34 and T-88 have had distrustful, disapproving parents; the others tended to be trusted and approved.

What distinguishes the family experience of the Conformer who shows average or better morality, from that of the subjects with more inadequate character development, is the element of consistency in their home lives and in their parents' control over them. There is moderate-to-strong severity of discipline in all these families, but not extreme severity.

There is not much difference between the Conforming and Irrational-Conscientious groups in family background, any more than there is in their about-average level of morality. That is, these four family characteristics do not adequately distinguish between the forces which make for rule conformity and those which make for behavior dominated by rigid "moral principle."

(However, the Conformers' families are clearly differentiated from those of the children with more mature, rational, autonomous moral-character structure. The latter, who either are the Rational-Altruistic type, or have a strong Rational component, come from very trustful, democratic families which are consistent but also lenient, as will be seen.)

The typical Conforming person comes from a family which is regular in its rules and its way of life (rating highest of all when the trait scores on Regularity are examined separately). It is authoritarian and rather severe. There may be either mutual trust or distrust and disapproval. It seems that the consistent *authoritarianism* is what makes Conformers of the children. It provides them with stable moral behavior patterns, but ones which they must and do adopt uncritically, and which they thereafter apply without much adaptation to fit later circumstances. To put it another way, it trains these children to "do as others do" rather unquestioningly, all their lives, so long as the "others" are conventionally respectable people like their parents.

The Conforming children almost inevitably rate very high on acceptance of mother's and father's code; but they also tend to have positive feelings toward both parents, little hostility toward father, and only mild antagonism toward mother. In short, they like family life, as they know it. (This is relatively more true of T-39, T-49, and T-57 than of T-34 and T-88.)

THE FAMILIES OF THE IRRATIONAL-CONSCIENTIOUS CHILDREN

These three families are all severe to extremely severe in their discipline. In other respects, they differ somewhat. T-79's experience has been one of severe, very distrustfully autocratic parents who were about average in the consistency of their control. Not surprisingly, she is an anxious, "mousy" girl whose marked inner hostility is rigidly repressed by a punitive conscience which overpowers her relatively weak powers of self-direction (low ego strength). Her morality is stable, but blind and unthinking, hence only average in quality.

T-83's family is much more consistent, very severe in its punishments, but about average in mutual trust and in letting her share in decisions. There is a question whether the character-research staff would not rate the family as more distrustful and autocratic than did the 1947 research group. In any case, T-83 has not experienced the really positive approval and self-direction of the Rational-Altruistic children; although enough, perhaps, to explain why she is now firmly, if rigidly, guided by her own conscience.

T-28 comes from a consistent, severe, autocratic family which yet shows mild mutual trust, approval, and confidence. The source of her firmly directing conscience is evident in this family pattern, and so is her adequate, average ego strength.

Thus, these three girls are each somewhat different, while mainly conscience-ruled in a rather rigid way. The differences in their family experiences seem logically consistent with their respective personality characteristics.

THE FAMILIES OF THE CHILDREN WITH A NEAR-DOMINANT COMPONENT OF RATIONAL-ALTRUISM

From this point on in the character sequence (except for T-47), the families show an almost uniform overall pattern of positive scores. The only other partial exception is the T-50 family's "somewhat severe" score. The families which produce children with a near-dominant component of Rational-Altruism have these characteristics: they range from moderately positive to high in their consistency, regularity, and mutual participation. They are truly democratic, in the sense of permitting the child to explore his world and make his own decisions, because they trust him to do it wisely. They are lenient but consistent in their discipline; not in the way that the Expedient child's family is indiscriminately lenient.

THE RATIONAL-ALTRUISTIC CHILDREN'S FAMILIES

In view of the importance of this most mature kind of moral character as an ideal to aim for, it seemed worthwhile to examine these families in greater detail. Therefore, the families of T-1, T-53, and T-56 were studied by analyzing their relative standing on all ten of the original family traits, as compared with all the other children in the research population. The results are as follows.

R's home is characterized by more *common participation* among the members of the family than the home of any other character type. R is more likely to *share confidences* with his parents than any other child. R's parents are not only more *approving* of the child than any other parents but they are also more *approving of peer activities* in general. From the point of view of *interparental relations* the R home is the most harmonious.

The above characteristics are supplemented by above-average but not extreme regularity in the home routine. The parents are *trusting of the child,* and the general tone of the home is a *democratic one,* in which *leniency prevails over severity. Consistency* of parental control is an integral part of this picture, although not as extremely marked as in the "High Secondary R" homes.

The child who is raised in this home develops in a way that permits him to feel a good deal of positive feeling for his parents. Indeed, no child feels more *positively toward his mother* than the R child, and only one group (C) more *positively toward father*. The R child feels the *least negative toward mother*.

T-47 is the one marked exception. The behavioral data show him to be an emotionally mature, well-integrated, highly moral boy. Yet the data on the family in the mid-1940 interviews showed it to be a physically unkempt working-class home, in which little regularity or consistency was seen by the interviewer. This undoubtedly explains the pattern of family ratings. However, these ratings do not very well represent the *qualitative* summary on the family made in 1947: "His relationships with his family and his extended kin are mutually acceptant and supportive in a somewhat impersonal way, although without really warm affection."

The 1950 conference discussion pointed out that from the age of ten onward (Moral Ideology Test, etc.), T-47 had displayed the most positive and thoughtful set of moral values of any child in the entire T group; and that he specifically ascribed them to his mother, or "father and mother," as the person who would approve of such good conduct. Much other similar evidence makes it seem unlikely that the home was as chaotic as its surface noisiness and dirtiness had apparently implied to the earlier interviewers. However, they reported no *direct* evidence of the consistent, supportive guidance one would normally expect to find in the background of so stable and rational a boy.

In the light of these findings, it appears especially significant that T-47 was the one child in the study whom the 1950 conference rated as drawing a large part of his moral values from people outside his family. Considering this, together with the above-quoted 1947 description of the family, it may be that his parents and his large, readily accessible clan of aunts, uncles, and cousins gave him the basis for firm, self-respecting ego development, even if it was in a somewhat impersonal, matter-of-fact way. If he thereafter looked to the school, to friends, and to adults in town for cues to help him behave in a socially acceptable, ethical way, this is not inconsistent with the picture of his family as a supportive but rather off-hand group. Such an explanation also accords well with two other, independent appraisals of his adolescent behavior. The staff rated him very stable, mature, and rationally moral. His teachers rated him above average in character. His peers, as Chapter VI will show, similarly judged him to be a very warm, emotionally stable, morally courageous boy, although a little less than average in social dominance and only a moderately active participant in peer organizations.

This still makes T-47's upbringing an exceptional one for a Rational-Altruistic person. It may demonstrate that when a child is not actively blocked or seriously deprived in his emotional and social development within the family, but rather has dependably secure if not emotionally rich relationships with a number of close relatives, he can be free to explore the social world in a sensible, well-balanced way and develop a sound moral code. Such an explanation is possible, but it must be given the Scottish verdict "not proven." T-47 presents an unanswered question for later research to explore.

Why does the more typical Rational-Altruistic child develop his kind of character? The home is regular. Control is consistent. Control is not harsh, but it is not completely lenient either. The stage is therefore set for R's internalization of a consistent moral code. In return for doing this, he is rewarded with more approval than the child of any other character type, and he develops a great deal of positive feeling for his parents.

Having internalized the family code, R's code becomes increasingly rational as he is able to confide openly in his parents, discuss problems with them, and share in family decisions. As there is no harsh enforcement of rules in the home, R's morality has the possibility of becoming flexible and appropriate to the occasion in a rational way.

Thus the Rational-Altruistic child goes out into the world with the experience of social success in the family behind him. He can participate with other people without a great deal of personal anxiety. On top of this, his parents approve of his moving out into the world (approval of peer activities); and, on top of that, because his internalized morality is one that society approves and rewards, he receives even more bolstering. Accordingly, positive concern for people in general becomes a realistic possibility.

DIFFERENCES IN FAMILY EXPERIENCES AND IN CHARACTER AMONG CHILDREN OF THE SAME PARENTS

Thus far, the family has been viewed as though it were a unit, consistent through time in its main characteristics, as far as a given child is concerned. As the data have indicated, this is true, in the main, when each child's family experience is separately considered. However, there is one respect in which this is misleading—or it could be interpreted in a misleading way.

Different children of the same parents do not necessarily have the same kind of relationship or emotional experiences. One child's experience with his parents may be very different from that which a brother or sister has. It is a matter of everyday observation that there may be one "black sheep" among a set of otherwise respectable, moral children from the "same" family. The word "same" is in quotation marks for this reason: although, sociologically speaking, this family consists of the same members through the years, psychologically speaking it may be—and sometimes dramatically is—a very different world for each child as he or she grows up. Often, the differences are so subtle, or so unconscious on the part of all the family's members, that only a trained, detached observer could see them, closely observing day-to-day life in the family. These differences, nonetheless, can make family life greatly different for different children in the same family. The consequent differences in attitudes and behavior patterns in the end can amount to notable differences in character. In this research there was a brother-sister pair, very close together in age. Without identifying them further, it can be noted that they were rated different in dominant character type (C and IAE), and that the 1947 ratings were somewhat different in the kind of family relationships *each separately experienced*. The differences in family experiences were congruent with the character differences in the two children.

THE RELATIVE INFLUENCE OF MOTHER AND FATHER ON CHARACTER FORMATION IN THIS POPULATION

One of the results of the analysis of the entire group was the finding that many more of the personal and moral traits correlated significantly with the children's attitudes toward their mothers, and to a higher degree, than was true of their attitudes toward their fathers. Table 10 shows the marked difference. Table 11 summarizes the patterns in Table 10 by showing the relationship of attitudes toward the two parents with the personality vectors found by factor analysis of the original personality traits.

It would appear from these data that in the typical Prairie City family, the mother has more profound and influential an effect on the children's character and personality development than does the father.

The projective test records showed that most of the children reacted with considerably stronger emotion, whether positive or negative, to motherlike figures or stimuli, or to mother-child situations.

TABLE 10. CORRELATIONS OF PERSONAL AND MORAL TRAITS
WITH ATTITUDES TOWARD MOTHER AND FATHER

| | Attitudes | | | | | |
| | Toward Father* | | | Toward Mother | | |
Traits	7a	7b	7c	8a	8b	8c
3. Observation	...	44	...	...	60	...
4. Insight	...	53	...	...	55	...
5. Empathy	...	...	...	...	...	...
6. Locus of Concern	...	...	...	35	60	−35
7a. Outward Acceptance of Father's Code	...	50	...	61	...	...
7b. Positive Feeling toward Father	50	...	...	...	32	...
7c. Negative Feeling toward Father	...	...	...	...	...	...
8a. Outward Acceptance of Mother's Code	61	...	...	...	33	−43
8b. Positive Feeling toward Mother	...	32	...	33	...	−46
8c. Negative feeling toward Mother	...	...	...	−43	−46	...
9a1. Outward Feeling toward Same-Sex Peers	...	33	...	...	59	−42
9a2. Inner Feeling toward Same-Sex Peers	...	...	...	...	34	−52
9b1. Outward Feeling toward Opposite-Sex Peers	...	...	...	33	48	−36
9b2. Inner Feeling toward Opposite-Sex Peers	...	...	...	...	...	−38
11. Range of Moral Horizon	...	37	...	52	44	−35
12. Emotional Maturity	...	34	...	42	72	−40
13. Impulse-Behavior Identity	...	...	...	−35	40	...
14. Heteronomy-Autonomy	...	52	...	...	63	...
15a. Assignment of Responsibility	...	40	...	...	65	−39
15b. Rationality	...	44	...	...	61	−31
16a. Internal Consistency	...	47	...	46	67	−43
16b. Conformity to Moral Code	34	...	...	74	29	−38
17. Guilt about Outer Behavior	...	−38	...	...	...	...
18. Guilt about Inner Impulse	−44	−37	...	−42	−36	64
19. Accuracy of Self-Perception	...	58	...	...	66	−33
27. Emotional Stability	...	...	...	62	47	−36
28a. Absence of Overt Hostility	...	...	...	65	...	−51
28b. Absence of Covert Hostility	...	...	...	46	41	−76
30. Superego Strength	...	...	...	41	...	...
ME Moral Effectiveness	...	34	...	53	45	...

* Only significant correlations are shown; decimal points are omitted.
Levels of significance: .36 < .05; .44 < .01.

TABLE 11.   RELATIONSHIP OF PERSONALITY VECTORS TO ATTITUDES
TOWARD PARENTS

	Factor Loadings on			
Attitudes toward	P1, Moral Stability	P2, Ego Strength	P4, Sponta- neity	P6, Hostility- Guilt
Mother:				
Outward Acceptance	.81			
Positive Feeling		.47		
Negative Feeling				.73
Father:				
Outward Acceptance				−.47
Positive Feeling			.55	
Negative Feeling				

Their fathers, in most cases, seemed to be emotionally meaningful to them, but not as important as their mother to their sense of security— or in any other respect.

It may be pertinent here that in most of the relatively few instances when the field interviewers had personal contact with fathers, the fathers tended to refer questions about the children to the mothers for answering: "She knows more about that than I do."   Insofar as Prairie City can be taken as typical of Midwestern America, it seems that "the hand that rocks the cradle rules the world" is by no means an idle adage.   However, to call it a "matriarchy" seems of dubious validity.   Mother may set and enforce most of the specific rules, hour by hour during the day; but father is more often than not an active partner with her, and usually is looked to as such, in formulating general family policy and backing it up forcefully if her influence with the children is not enough to weather a crisis.   To be sure, this is not the old patriarchal family which still survives as an American legend. In some cases in this study it does seem that the father has defaulted from an active, responsible role in rearing the children, but these are the exceptional cases.

For the most part, there was little evidence in most cases that the father exerted as powerful an influence on emotional and moral development as did the mother.   Lest the cry of "Momism" be raised, it must be made clear that it was difficult to get first-hand data from or about the fathers of this group.   The research staff had to rely mainly on the evidence in the interviews and in the projective tests of the feelings and attitudes the child held toward the father. It may be that the ratings therefore were not based on a full and accurate picture of the child's feelings in this respect.

Even if it be true, as the evidence does tend to suggest, that the mothers of these "typical American children" have a stronger, more direct and lasting influence on the structure and content of their children's moral beliefs and actions, it should be pointed out that in most or all of these families, the father plays a vital role in supplying and maintaining the stability of the family group. This is not just an economic function. Without him, the mothers would feel seriously at a loss. In those families in the study where the father is separated or plays no dependable role, the children show serious confusion and conflict, not only internally but in their social and moral relations with their mothers, age mates, and neighbors. The case studies of these and the other, more stable families strongly suggest that however indirect the father's role in shaping his children's character may appear to be or may actually be, his active, dependable presence and contribution are vitally essential to the development of sound character and emotional health in his children.

On the whole, this type of family structure appears to be a workable and working arrangement. Its main shortcoming may lie, not in its direct effect on moral development, so much as in its deterrent effect on the psychosexual development of the boys and the girls, who need a present, active example of masculinity. Some of the boys in this group do tend to be mother-identified in a way which interferes with their learning an appropriately masculine role. Some of the girls have only a vague, unrealistic idea about the nature of men and how to behave toward them maturely. Insofar as this decreases the possibility of their learning to behave in a warm, mature, rational way with the opposite sex, this has a bearing on their moral character development. In such cases it may prevent them from learning to show the highest order of morality in a maturely heterosexual way. Average conformity is probably the ceiling, in these instances, in cross-sex interaction, and this constitutes an important segment of life.

MORALITY IS NOT A MATTER OF *WHICH* PARENT IS EMULATED, BUT WHAT *KIND* OF PARENT

As will be reported in more detail in Chapter VII, pp. 142–148, one of the assessments in the research was a rating on the proportionate effect on the child's character development of various people and influences. When the ratings were studied as to which *parent* was the chief source of values, and when these were compared with the child's main choice of parent to identify with, it turned out that for both boys and girls the sex of the parent with whom the child primarily identifies and/or from whom he receives the bulk of his moral values does not differentiate with respect to the development of a particular character type. For example, among the three highest boys in Maturity of Character (T-03, T-47, T-39) there are three different patterns:

1. T-03 is identified primarily with father, and the chief source of moral values is father.

2. T-47 is identified primarily with mother, and the chief source of moral values is mother.

3. T-39 is identified primarily with mother, but the chief source of moral values is father.

Among the four lowest boys in moral maturity (T-99, T-16, T-89, T-78) there are again three different patterns:

1. T-99 is identified primarily with father, and the chief source of moral values is about equally divided between mother and father.

2. T-89 and T-16 are identified primarily with mother, and the chief source of moral values is mother.

3. T-78 is identified primarily with father, and the chief source of moral values is father.

The most clear-cut Rational-Altruistic boy (T-03) exhibits the same pattern of primary identifications and sources of moral values as the clear-cut Amoral boys, T-78 and T-42. All three are primarily identified with father, as the chief source of moral values. Among the clear-cut Amoral boys, T-89 has a different pattern of identification (primarily with mother) and source of moral values (chiefly mother), from T-78 and T-42 (where primary identification is with father, and chief source of values is father).

The fact that all the girls (except T-52) are primarily identified with their mothers, and have mother as the chief source of moral values, indicates that these ratings in themselves do not differentiate with respect to Maturity of Character. Girls who receive the bulk of their morality from their mothers may be high on the character scale, or low, or anywhere between. They may be of any character type.

Apparently, whether a boy or girl acquires the major share of his moral perspective and motivation from his father or from his mother is not the crucial problem as far as the child's moral development is concerned. Rather, the crucial factor is the moral make-up of the person from whom the child learns his values. For example, the ratings indicate that both T-03 (Rational-Altruistic) and T-78 (Amoral-Impulsive) are primarily father-identified, and have their fathers as the chief source of moral values. In view of the fact that these boys are so different in their moral characters, the logical inference is that the two fathers are very different in character also. Actually, Mr. T-03 is a stable, trusted, respected person in the community. Mr. T-78 decidedly is not.

As for the girls, since they have all (except T-52) acquired the bulk of their morality from their mothers, the moral character of the individual mother appears to be the principal determining factor in each daughter's moral character. The family patterns shown in Table 8 seem adequately to account for the fundamental morality of the child by the dynamic patterns of family living which are initiated and circumscribed by the moral character of the parents.

For both boys and girls, it seems that moral values may be learned equally well—or equally badly—from either parent. The quality of the child's morality depends on the moral qualities of the parent whom he takes for his model. Since, in the majority of these families, both parents were closely similar in their moral values it may in many families make little difference which parent served as the primary model for the child's moral learning.

When father and mother agree, the crucial question once more becomes what kind of morality they show in their day-to-day treatment of their children. It is probably secondary, relatively speaking, what kind of morality they exhibit outside the home, insofar as their direct influence on the child is concerned. It is the way the child is directly treated by his parents which largely determines how he will treat other people in later life. In short, the child "does what we *do*, not what we say."

THREE KINDS OF PARENTAL "LOVE" AND THEIR EFFECT ON MORAL BEHAVIOR

The term "love" was not used in the definition of the family traits. However, it was implied by the ratings on trust in the child, approval of the child, and good interparental relations. It can be said with certainty, based on the case documents, that every family rated "distrustful" in Table 9 is an unloving family, from lesser to greater degree as the minus marks indicate.

The "trustful" families are, conversely, "loving"; but there are important distinctions to be made between different *qualities* of love. The parents of the children who have a lot of expedient motivation, uniformly reveal in the case documents a shallow, indiscriminate kind of affection, not based on active concern for the child as an individual nor on objective understanding of him and his needs.

The "trustful" families of the Conforming and Irrational-Conscientious children show, in the case documents, a deeper, more intense kind of love; but it is a rather blind, distinctly possessive kind of affection. It is, to an important degree, an attachment of the parent to qualities which he or she mentally projects into the child. It is not an objective awareness and love for the child as a distinct individual. Its possessiveness betrays that, and it also betrays the fact that the parents are at least partly "in love" with those qualities or those unfulfilled wishes which they have drawn from themselves and forced their children to adopt, whether or not these fit the child's temperament, hopes, and wishes.

We might reserve the term "love," in its richest sense, for the kind of affection shown by the families of the children with high or dominant Rational-Altruistic motivation. As both the score patterns and the case documents indicate, these parents understand what their children need and want, and love them for themselves, to use a familiar phrase. These parents are obviously people who are capable of such love, in general. They love each other in the same acceptant fashion as they love their children. They give each other, and their children a chance to be themselves, to have an effective voice in deciding how to act and what to do in day-to-day family life. Although the ratings were not designed to show it, the case evidence indicates that, relative to the rest of the population, these parents are secure, self-confident, emotionally mature people who have no need to irrationally project frustrated hopes onto their children, or otherwise treat them as objects for personal satisfaction rather than as individuals in their own right.

This is the concept of love advocated by Christian doctrine, as well as by other religions. It is also the kind of love advocated by psychologists and others who are interested in promoting mental and emotional health. As far as the present evidence goes, it appears to be an essential prerequisite for rearing children who will practice a meaningful, self-directed, loving kind of morality.

DISCIPLINE AND MORAL CHARACTER

Lack of discipline, in the sense of inconsistent parental control, produces only poor character, whether that discipline be lenient or severe. Severe, autocratic discipline, consistently applied, produces children who "toe the mark," but in a blind, unthinking way; and they usually end up feeling more hostile than friendly toward people in general, even if they do not allow themselves to act in an openly antagonistic manner.

By contrast, parental control which is at once consistent, trustful of the child, and allows him to practice making decisions together with the rest of his family—this produces mature, genuinely self-disciplined moral behavior. The parents who use this kind of discipline are rarely or never severe about it, and some of them are very lenient in their control without adverse effect on the child's behavior. This, in short, appears to be the best kind of discipline, and appears to be the only effective way to produce children of wholly mature, rational, self-disciplined morality.

In short, love and discipline are *both* essential, joint determinants of good character. From the present evidence, it appears that the only sure way to rear children with the best kind of character is by a combination of mature love and mature, permissive, but consistently guiding discipline. The fact is, these two kinds of parental behavior either occur together or neither occurs at all, in a mature form, in this population.

VI

Moral character and the peer group

Two major questions may be asked about the relationship between a person's character and his experiences with friends and acquaintances of his own age:

1. How is his character reflected in the way he behaves toward them, and in the way they judge him?

2. What effect, or what degree of influence, do his peer associations have on his character?

The peer group consists of children of roughly the same age and school grade *who feel and act together.* The term is here used to apply to all the children of a given age-grade level in Prairie City. This usage is reasonable in a place as small as Prairie City, where the children nearly all go to the same school after the fourth grade, and where the children do act together to a considerable degree. The 120 children of the T group in Prairie City can be called a loose-knit peer group, although a stricter usage would recognize some subgroups of

126

the T group as peer groups. For instance, the children of about the same age who go to the Lutheran Church are a peer group, and the farm children who come to high school are something of a peer group, as are the group of leading girls in the T group who formed a secret society. No doubt these smaller groups of youth who feel and act together are more influential in the formation of character than is the entire age group. However, since all of the T group know and react to each other, reputation ratings by the entire group have been used as the most stable measure of moral and social peer reputation.

To take up the question of causation first, any group of people with whom an individual associates intimately must have some effect on his moral character. At least, all that is known about human motives and human learning indicate that this is so. The question is *how*, and *how much?* As is indicated in the next chapter, the character conference concluded from intensive study of all the cases that both character structure and the value content of each adolescent's moral code came predominantly from the family. While there were many close similarities in values among large groups of the adolescents, in every case these values could be directly observed in the behavior of the individual's parents. It may be arbitrary, in a sense, to assume that the parallelism in the adolescents' moral codes came primarily from similarities in the parental codes. However, the assumption was made that the family influence is strongest, and that it deserves greater weight as a source, because it shapes the child's values before he ever gets in an age-mate group. Therefore, the peer group was credited with *originating* moral values for a child only when he showed values different from those of his parents (or other adult sources), but similar to the values some of his age mates displayed. This was not found to be the case, to any important degree, in this cross section of the youth of Prairie City.

There is some independent evidence which tends to corroborate this conclusion. It has been explained that the children's families had been rated by another research staff some years prior to this study. A set of independent measures of the children's behavior in the peer group was also obtained from the sociometric descriptions the children gave each other (see below). The results are of interest at this point, as concerns the shaping of character.

When the peer ratings on six characteristics of social interaction were correlated with the earlier ratings on the children's family backgrounds, the results were as shown in Table 12. The figures suggest that an adolescent's social and moral adjustment to his age mates is a reflection of the attitudes and behavior he earlier learned in his home.

TABLE 12.   RELATIONSHIP OF FAMILY CHARACTERISTICS TO ADOLESCENT
SOCIAL ADJUSTMENT

Peer Ratings

Family Characteristics	Warmth	Partic- ipation	Domi- nance	Impul- sivity	Emo- tional Sta- bility	Moral Cour- age
F1, Consistency	.42	.36	.42	−.08	.37	.36
F2, Democracy	.47	.49	.54	.50	.44	.51
F3, Mutual Trust and Approval	.69	.68	.68	.21	.60	.82
F4, Severity	−.35	−.44	−.32	−.29	−.28	−.49

Significance level: $.36 < .05$; $.44 < .01$.

Specifically, it is of interest that these social-interaction traits (which are moral as well as social in nature) are most highly related to the degree of mutual trust, approval (and, inferentially, affection) which the adolescent has experienced in his family. Indeed, if Moral Courage be taken as the most obviously "moral" trait, it is significantly the product of mutual trust between parents and child, and of democratic family procedures. It is related to familial consistency and regularity, to a lesser degree. Conversely, it is significantly hampered in its development by parental severity. (It is true that a correlation is not, per se, any indicator of causality; but it seems reasonable to assume, here, that the adolescent social behavior is the result of the pre-existing family conditions.)

The same pattern holds for all the other aspects of behavior in the peer group. It is not surprising that warmth in peer relations, for example, is highly related to the child's experience of mutual trust and approval in the family (and affectionate warmth, there, by implication). Nor is it surprising to find emotional stability, as peers see it, similarly related to familial trust and approval.

The correlations of mutual trust and of family democracy with dominance (leadership) could not have been so confidently predicted, if the question had been raised before these data were analyzed. Among other things, these correlations suggest that this adolescent group tends to pick warm, stable, morally courageous individuals as its chosen leaders. As a matter of fact, such a conclusion was reached by Hartmann in a separate study of the total T group, made while this research was in progress (Hartmann, 1949). The individuals these adolescents pick to lead them—or recognize as "natural leaders"—tend significantly to come from consistent, loving, democratic homes; and their parents use less than average severity in disciplining them.

The element of impulsivity is the only one not related consistently to any family trait except democracy. This was to be expected. A detailed inspection of the individual scores shows that when the adolescents rated this trait—as when the research staff rated for "impulse-behavior identity"—they gave high ratings to some of their Amoral age mates; but they also gave high ratings to some of their most mature, respected, and yet spontaneous acquaintances. In short, the definition of the trait prevents a straight-line relationship with either social or moral adjustment, although the trait describes an important aspect of behavior when considered along with the other traits.

In any event, these correlations between the family ratings and the peer ratings tend to confirm the conference's conclusion that moral character is shaped predominantly by the family, not *independently* formed or reformed to any great extent by experience in the peer group, in the ordinary case.

THE INFLUENCE OF THE PEER GROUP IN MAINTAINING AND REINFORCING MORAL VALUES

It is entirely another matter to suggest that the peer group exercises an active influence on its members to maintain and to develop, in age-appropriate ways, the values they have brought from home. The peer group rewards those individuals who exemplify positive social and moral values; and it can severely punish, by social rejection, those children who display antisocial or distasteful behavior.

This is not to say that adolescents are completely mature, accurate judges of the most important values, or of the morally best or worst individuals, in all cases. As will be seen, for a few years they can give their respect or their hearts to some "smooth operators," or to a happy-go-lucky though irresponsible youth. They can also condemn a few unfortunate children who suffer from social stigmata, rather than from real defects of character. On the whole, though, the adolescent *group's* judgment is sound, much more often than not, when compared with mature standards of conduct and of moral values. The evidence for this conclusion follows.

MORAL EFFECTIVENESS AND REPUTATION WITH PEERS

After the case conferences had ended, but before the Maturity of Character score was conceived, the research staff made a rating on the overall goodness of character of the subjects, and termed it Moral Effectiveness. Because it was found to correlate .84 with the Maturity of Character scale, and .85 with the Moral Stability measure, the Moral Effectiveness rating was ultimately dropped from the analysis to avoid redundancy. It may be taken as a close parallel, however, to the Maturity of Character scale and, since certain analyses of the peer ratings were made in terms of the Moral Effectiveness ratings, they are presented here, and in Table 13.

A series of five sociometric tests, given to the total T group during the period from age ten to age sixteen, provided data on individual moral reputation. These tests gave a reputation score on each of seven moral traits: Honesty, Responsibility, Kindness, Self-Control, Moral Courage, Loyalty, and Respect for the Integrity of Others. When the average of these scores at age sixteen was compared with the staff ratings for Moral Effectiveness, the product-moment correlation coefficient was .73.

This is a relatively high order of agreement, although it leaves room for an interesting amount of discrepancy, at least in a few cases. Three boys were rated considerably higher by their peers than by the staff. In character type, one is Expedient and two are Amoral. The Expedient boy, "Earl Eddy," is a "smooth operator" who was clever enough to make an average reputation among his age mates until age seventeen, although adults saw through him. (His peer reputation took a "nose dive" at seventeen, and stayed low thereafter. This was determined from a sociometric test given in 1950.) The Amoral boys were somewhat respected for their aggressive self-assertion which was mistaken by their peers for "moral courage."

A group of three girls, all of character type I, were rated higher by their peers than by the staff. These three girls show a rigid, upright morality which earned them a high local reputation but was not regarded as highly by the staff. On the other hand, several Rational-Altruistic boys and girls were rated somewhat higher by the staff than by their peers. These people happened to be quiet and late-maturing, so that they were slightly overlooked at that age by their peers.

The Moral Effectiveness rating was also compared with a score on peer status which reports the standing of the individual in the peer society, based on sociometric test items of the "whom would you invite to a party" and "who are your best friends" variety. This score is called the Index of Peer Characteristics by McGuire, its inventor (McGuire and Clark, 1952). It is weighted by the socioeconomic status of the people who name an individual. The correlation coefficient between Moral Effectiveness and the Index of Peer Characteristics was .47 at the age of sixteen in the T group. This is reliable at the 1-per-cent level, but not high enough to suggest a close, one-to-one relationship between moral character and acceptance by peers. When plotted on a scatter diagram, however, the data show that the correlation coefficient is chiefly reduced by a set of four cases who have high peer-status and low moral effectiveness scores. These are three boys and a girl. Two boys and a girl have Expedient character, and the other boy is of the Amoral type, with a considerable amount of Expedient motivation. The explanation seems clear: boys and girls with a strong Expedient component may put up a deceptive appearance of honesty and responsibility and friendliness, as their age mates see it, although this behavior is shallowly rooted in expediency.

Certain measures of social behavior were made from sociometric tests, given from age ten through age fourteen. These social traits were derived from items in the sociometric instruments which were selected and weighted to give a composite score for the appropriate trait. From this, a seven-point scale was derived for each trait, using the scores of the total T group. (It is indicative of the representative, cross-sectional nature of this research sample that by these peer measures, too, they show a fairly even distribution from the highest to the lowest scores in the total T group. See Table 15.)

Representative items have been selected to show how each measure was obtained and how the title of the social trait was chosen. The sample items are from the latest instruments (indicated by year) which contained the "purest" measure of a given trait, although the tests in the other years contained either identical or analogous items.

Warmth (1946 items)

Here are some people who:

A. Always like to be with other people . . . play with many children . . . make friends easily . . . are usually happy and cheerful.

B. Always want to be alone . . . sit and play by themselves . . . don't have many friends.

S. Are very kind . . . always think of the other fellow first . . . like to see other people happy . . . never hurt other people's feelings.

T. Are mean and unkind . . . always teasing somebody or picking on somebody . . . hurt people's feelings . . . always think of themselves first.

Participation (1946 items)

E. Good persons to have in our gang or club . . . keep secrets . . . stick by their friends . . . work hard for the good of any group they belong to.

H. Do not stick by their friends or their club . . . cannot keep secrets . . . won't help the rest of the gang or the club . . . are not proud of being in a gang or club.

Dominance (1947 items)

7. Who are the ones who are always trying to run things, always telling others what to do?

15. Who are the ones who let others tell them what to do, who let others boss them around?

19. Who are the ones you would like for leaders in work or play?

20. Who are the ones who can never think of interesting things to do?

Impulsivity (1947 items)

16. Who are the ones who are daring, who are not afraid to take chances, who never seem scared to do things?

10. Who are the ones who do not take chances, who seem a little scared to try new things?

17. Who are the ones who are always sort of wiggly, who seem restless, who just cannot be still?

18. Who are the ones who find it easy to sit still or who move about quietly without disturbing people?

Emotional Stability (1946 items)

K. Control their tempers even when angry . . . try to keep calm, even when things go wrong . . . finish an unpleasant job if they are sure it is important . . . have lots of self-control.

L. Get excited easily . . . lose their tempers and flare up when angry . . . act like babies . . . give up easily on a job . . . do not control themselves.

Moral Courage (1946, Form A)

25. . . . never lets his friends persuade him to do things that he believes are wrong.

26. . . . sometimes lets his friends persuade him to do something that he believes is wrong.

27. . . . does whatever his friends want him to do even though he believes it is wrong.

13. . . . always tells the truth, even if he gets into trouble because of it.

14. . . . sometimes lies to get out of trouble.

15. . . . always lies when it is to his advantage.

TABLE 13. MORAL EFFECTIVENESS AND PEER SOCIAL REPUTATION

Moral-Effectiveness Correlations

	Age 10	Age 11	Age 13(Feb.)	Age 13(March)
Warmth	.53	.55	.38	.60
Participation	.63	. . .	.42	.53
Dominance	.66	.64	.58	.62
Impulsivity	−.54	−.46	−.52	. . .
Emotional Stability	.64	.60	.70	.61
Moral Courage	.71	. . .	.58	.71

Significance level: .36 < .05; .44 < .01.

As is evident from the wording of these items, there are explicit moral connotations in all but those for dominance, and perhaps impulsivity. When these traits were correlated, year by year, with the Moral Effectiveness scores, it turned out that even impulsivity had a distinct moral connotation for these adolescents through age thirteen. As Table 13 shows, in each year from age ten to age thirteen (fourteen on some traits, as Table 15 shows), even so apparently non-moral a trait as dominance is strongly associated with goodness of moral behavior, as assessed at age sixteen by the research staff. It would appear, therefore, that from the age of ten on (to restrict the interpretation to the present data) the peer group assigns its liking, its respect, and its leadership roles with alert attention to the individual's moral behavior, with much the same definition of morality as was proposed in the research.

CHARACTER STRUCTURE AND PEER SOCIAL REPUTATION

In order to discover what relationship, if any, exists between character structure and sociomoral behavior as seen by the adolescents' friends and acquaintances, each of the six social traits was correlated with the Maturity of Character score. The results are shown in Table 14. Except for Impulsivity, which no longer correlates negatively with

TABLE 14.   MATURITY OF CHARACTER AND PEER REPUTATION

Peer Rating	Maturity of Character
Warmth	.57
Participation	.51
Dominance	.44
Impulsivity	.13
Emotional Stability	.61
Moral Courage	.67

Significance level: .44 < .01.

character by the time the children are 14, all the correlations are significant beyond the 1-per-cent level. Here, again, it appears that peer judgments and the research staff's judgments, made independently, tend to agree. (At age sixteen, the overall *moral* reputation ascribed by peers—the average of the ratings on seven moral traits—correlates .64 with the subjects' Maturity of Character scores.)

Since these social traits, by definition, are a mixture of moral and non-moral characteristics, these correlations—and the patterns shown in Table 15—are evidence that adolescents do recognize moral character as one of the most important factors in picking the peers they most respect, like, and follow. In order to see the specific values, both moral and non-moral, by which they choose to admire or reject members of their group, Table 15 will be analyzed for the individual patterns, amplified with observations from the personality data and the case material.

In the Amoral group, there is not one person who was seen by his peers as a consistent or dependable person, in either social or moral

TABLE 15. CHARACTER STRUCTURE AND PEER SOCIAL REPUTATION

Character Type	Case No.	Warmth (Age 13)	Participation (Age 13)	Dominance (Age 14)	Impulsivity (Age 14)	Emotional Stability (Age 13)	Moral Courage (Age 13)
A	T-78	+	− −	− −	+ +	+	− −
	T-25	− −	− −	−	−	− − −	− −
	T-89	− −	− − −	− − −	− − −	− −	−
	T-42	− −	− −	− −	+ + +	− − −	− − −
	T-99	+	+	+	+	− −	− −
CEA	T-95	− − −	− − −	−	+	− − −	− − −
	T-55	− − −	− − −	− − −	− − −	− −	−
	T-64	−	− − −	− − −	− − −	− −	− −
E	T-08	−		− −	− − −	− −	− −
	T-52	+	+ +	+ + +	+ + +	+	−
	T-22	+ + +	+ + +	+ + +	+ + +	+ +	+ + +
	T-76	+ +	+ +	+	+	+ +	+ +
IAE	T-16	− − −		− − −	+	−	−
	T-37	+ +	+	+ +	+ +	+ +	+ +
C	T-11	− − −	− −	− − −	+ + +	− − −	− −
	T-17	−	+	−	−	−	+
	T-04	− − −	−	− −	+	−	−
	T-57	− −	− −	− − −	− − −	+	−
	T-34	+ + +	+ + +	+	− −	+ + +	+ +
	T-88	− − −	− − −	− − −	+	− − −	− − −
	T-39	+ +	+	−	−	+ +	+ +
	T-49	+ + +	+ + +	+ + +	−	+ + +	+ + +
I	T-79	−	− −	−	−	−	− −
	T-83	+	− −	+	−	+ +	+
	T-28	−	− −	+	−	−	+ +
High Secondary R	T-40	+	+	+ +	+ +	+	+
	T-60	+ + +	+ + +	+ + +	+ + +	+	+ +
	T-86	+ +	+ +	+ +	+ +	+ +	+ + +
	T-50	+ + +	+ + +	+ + +	+	+ +	+ + +
	T-53	+ +	+	+ + +	+ + +	+	+
R	T-47	+ + +	+	−	−	+ + +	+ + +
	T-51	+ + +	+ +	− −	− −	+ +	+ + +
	T-03	+ + +	+ + +	+ +	+	+ +	+ + +
	T-06	+ + +	+ +	+ + +	+ +	+ +	+ +

Score of 1.0–2.0: − − −; 2.1–3.0: − −; 3.1–4.0: −; 4.1–5.0: +; 5.1–6.0: + +; 6.1–7.0: + + +.

terms.   T-78 was seen as a somewhat warm person, impulsive (though fairly stable), but lacking in willingness to participate, in moral courage, and in desirable leadership qualities.   The next three individuals were completely rejected, largely on moral grounds, it appears.   (T-89's very low impulsivity rating is undoubtedly due to the fact that he was passively quiet in school and around his age mates.   His violent outbursts of impulse were usually private, often "sneaky" ones.)   T-99, the happy-go-lucky but feckless boy, was mildly liked, but seen as unstable and lacking in moral courage.

The three CEA-type people were thoroughly condemned and rejected; again, mainly for the poor morality they displayed in the way they treated their age mates.

Of the Expedient group, T-08, who is sullen but passive in his grudging outward conformity to minimal social rules, was seen that way by his peers.   T-52 was seen as very impulsive and dominant ("bossy," as her peers put it).   She was viewed, nonetheless, as an active, welcome participant, fairly warm and stable, though rather lacking in moral courage.   Her active if expedient drive for recognition was a successful technique with her fellow teen-agers; and her advanced social skills outweighed her self-centered motives, in their eyes, during adolescence.

We now come to the first of two major discrepancies in the correlation.   "Earl Eddy," T-22, could practically do no wrong when he and his peers were in the early teens.   He was highly active, socially visible, and good at games and at dancing, well before most of the group had mastered these skills.   This is a vivid illustration of the way somewhat superficial values can sometimes outweigh the virtues of good character in the eyes of uncertain adolescents, until they have themselves achieved solid competence.   However, at the time T-22 was seventeen, he was still relying on his old techniques.   The group had mastered and outgrown these social and athletic skills as a primary basis for judging personal worth.   At that point, they dramatically lost respect for him.   He did not change, but the group outgrew his adolescent "techniques."

The evidence is not yet final in the case of T-76, whom they saw as a fine, likable boy at fourteen.   He was, and still is, a very likable *boy*, psychologically and socially.   It is questionable whether his age mates will continue to respect him as his lack of any real achievement drive or personal responsibility takes on a more serious aspect in the adult world.   In any case, here is another example of likable personality traits outweighing moral considerations in the adolescent group.

T-16, one of the IAE boys, was seen by peers for the uncooperative social isolate which he unhappily was, both socially and in psychological terms. Here, his poor morality was the decisive issue.

T-37, the other of the group, was almost a "pet" of the group at fourteen, and even much later. He will undoubtedly always be liked; though he, too, may lose some status with his friends as the years go by and he chronically shows more promise than fulfillment. Even during these school years, his friends "agreed" with the research staff that he had only average character, though they found him highly enjoyable, and though they mistook his mild rebellion against adults for "moral courage."

Of the Conforming group, two of the "sad sacks," T-11 and T-04, come from physically deprived, lower-lower class homes. They, along with T-57, were thoroughly rejected; but it was undoubtedly more on grounds of esthetic distastefulness and social ineptness than on moral grounds—although in the moral-reputation ratings their peers rated these children low. T-88 was rated low both in character and in social desirability. It may be remembered that her conformity was seen by the staff, too, as very childish and unthinking. Her adolescent peers undoubtedly felt unconsciously threatened by her living reminder of undeveloped (almost infantilized) childishness. This is a regressive tendency which most adolescents experience within themselves, from time to time, and which they must fight to overcome if they are to grow up as they want to do.

The Conformers whom the staff considered most mature of this group, T-34, T-39, T-49, were also liked and admired by their peers. Here, their good overt morality was expressed in attractive social behavior, so that these became merely two aspects of one consistent pattern. T-34 was rated very high on everything except impulsivity. This low score is the one indication that her peers sensed the essentially passive, uncritical nature of her conformity to the conventional rules she found about her. She was rated just above average, too, in dominance; in short, a happy, willing adherent to the established code of adolescent ethics. T-49, most highly regarded of all the Conformers, was likewise judged high in ego strength, with a respectable proportion of Rational-Altruistic motivation, by the staff.

The Irrational-Conscientious group, T-79, T-83, T-28, were regarded as almost dead-average by their peers. T-79 is, and was seen as, a mousy, uninfluential person. She was not strongly rejected but her classmates saw her (accurately) as too afraid to display much moral courage. T-83 was regarded as mildly warm, not consistently a supporter of her peers' activities, but stable, firm in her morality, and somewhat dominant. T-28 was seen as somewhat undesirable, socially; somewhat unstable and impulsive; yet on the dominating side and a strong defender of her own beliefs. These last two girls' social position was accurately seen by peers as that of representative and upholder of the adult moral code of parents and teachers. They were respected for it, but by no means popular.

From this point on in the table there is almost perfect agreement between character structure and peer social reputation. All the adolescents whom the conference judged to be highly or predominantly Rational-Altruistic in character type, were rated near or at the top by their peers in terms of the most desirable social behavior. Only T-40 was given moderate ratings; and as was seen in Chapter IV, he was judged to have a conflicted mixture of Rational and Amoral motivation.

The other two partial exceptions are T-47 and T-51. Peers regarded them as less than average in dominance, and in impulsivity; but considered them very warm, emotionally stable, and morally courageous.

It is interesting that peers rated the other seven Rational-Altruistic adolescents above average to top on impulsivity. This corresponds closely with the staff's ratings of these subjects as above average on spontaneity. It seems clear that the peer group recognized spontaneity as a highly desirable and morally positive trait in its members who were socially and morally mature, while condemning impulsiveness in its Amoral or childishly Conforming members.

Summing up the values which the adolescent group displayed in making their ratings, it appears evident that they combined moral values with social-skill values in judging one another. If we take the conference-derived character-type scale as the criterion of moral maturity, it seems that the adolescent group was "fooled" only by two or three of its Expedient members; and by seventeen they had already "caught on" to Earl Eddy's superficial "operating." They vigorously rejected two distastefully unkempt and socially inept lower-lower class Conformers (one of whom, indeed, was infantilized by his family to the point of appearing far below normal in intellect). Even here, the peer morality ratings of these children were not far different from the staff's. The group strongly rejected one other Conforming girl, whose character might be described as very weak, though not antisocial in content.

HOW THE PEER GROUP BUILDS MORAL CHARACTER

In the main, even with the inclusion of the discrepant cases, this adolescent group proved to like and to admire its members in terms of the same sociomoral characteristics which the conference staff defined as central to good moral character. On the basis of these findings, what is known in general about human learning can be invoked to explain how experience in the peer group is likely to influence character formation.

The peer group gives rewards and punishments to its members on account of their moral behavior. Those who are honest, responsible, loyal, kind, and self-controlled tend to be rewarded. It is not moral qualities alone, however, that determine whether a child will be rewarded or punished by his peer group. Operating in addition to the moral qualities are such non-moral qualities as diffuse geniality, and skill in games, which sometimes overshadow the moral qualities in determining the status of a child in the peer group. In general, though, the forming of stable, positive relationships within the peer group is indicative of sound character development, while inability to make friends may indicate the opposite. But there are exceptions to this rule of two kinds: first, there are some children who are not popular and not rewarded by the peer group who nevertheless have good moral character; and second, the moral standards of certain peer groups may be low ones as measured by sound social standards. For instance, the peer group may reward stealing from people outside the group, or irresponsibility and cruelty toward such people. This latter type of peer group is usually called a deviant group. It promotes moral behavior among the members of the group toward each other, but not toward people outside the group.

The peer group provides a basis for learning the major social loyalties. As the first social group which the child meets outside of his family, it tends to condition his attitude toward social groups in general. If he enjoys the peer group, he is likely to approach all groups with the expectation of liking them. Loyalty to nation, to community, and to a professional or working group probably depend upon the learning of loyalty to the smaller and more intimate groups of the family and the peer group.

The peer group helps a child build a rational foundation of moral behavior. By a rational foundation is meant a set of moral values and habits which are coherent and consistent with one another and which are subject to revision and redefinition on the basis of experience. For example, in the playing of games a child learns to respect the rules, which means that he learns the morality of the game. Then he learns to modify the rules of the game in agreement with his peers to make the game fit changing circumstances, such as the size of a playing field, the number of players, and the type of play equipment available. Thus he learns to respect rules, which is the essence of morality; but he also learns to modify rules on a rational basis. He learns a flexible, co-operative, rational morality which is essential for good citizenship in a changing democratic society (Piaget, 1948).

The whole business of making and modifying rules for games, for school and church and club activities, leads toward the Rational-Altruistic type of character. Without this experience, the child tends to remain on the Irrational-Conscientious or Conforming level of character, where his morality comes from his dependence upon his parents first, and then upon other moral authorities.

In general, the peer group presents a laboratory for the learning of moral behavior, in which the teaching by adult experts is kept down to a minimum, but where the learning experience is concrete and heavily reinforced by the rewards and punishments which the peer group dispenses.

TO WHAT EXTENT IS THE PEER GROUP A CAUSAL FORCE IN CHARACTER FORMATION?

As the evidence above indicates, it is questionable whether informal peer-group interaction is a force sufficiently strong to produce fundamental changes in character structure even after its influence has been operating through middle childhood and adolescence. Probably the guide lines of character formation are laid down in the family and are seldom disrupted by peer-group experience. This is partly because the family influences are earlier and more effective than the peer-group influences, and partly because the parents can influence what their child gets from the peer group, by controls they exert over his associations within the peer group.

Usually, then, peer forces can be seen acting to reinforce or crystallize behavioral tendencies already present. The peer group is less a causal force than a supporting force in the development of moral character. In the case of the Rational-Altruistic character, the experiences of middle childhood in the peer group seem to be testing and learning experiences which support the directions of growth already present.

The Rational-Altruistic motivation seems to require a combination of successful peer-group interaction, with family influences which are directed along cooperative and rational lines. On the other hand, the Irrational-Conscientious character may develop out of a rigid though supportive family with little or no peer group interaction.

This discussion emphasizing the primacy of the family influences in character development is not to be interpreted as indicating that the peer group is never a formative force in character development. On the contrary, particularly in the case of some children from chaotic, unloving families, it seems probable that the peer group might have been used, under the skillful guidance of interested adults, as a treatment agency to change their character. As it happens, this was not done for any child in this research sample; but this kind of human influence is a *possible* way of shaping or reshaping character toward mature, rational morality, even in cases of severely deprived or severely antisocial children (Bettelheim, 1950; Redl and Wineman, 1951, 1952).

VII

Sources of moral values in the social environment

An assumption was made at the outset of the study that the child *learns* his moral values and his moral behavior from the people with whom he grows up. There is evidence for this assumption in the data already reported; and, of course, this assumption is in accord with all that is known from the many studies of child development and personality development.

The chief question therefore became, precisely which people or which social influences have produced a given child's moral value system, and in what relative proportions have the various influences had their effect? In order to estimate this, we devised a set of ratings on "Sources of Moral Values," among which we divided ten points according to how much effect each source seemed to have had on the child's values. (The detailed rating instructions are given in the Appendix, pp. 224–227.) Eight possible sources were postulated:

Rating
Number   Source

20a	Mother
20b	Father
20c	Parental Surrogates (adults acting *in loco parentis,* in daily charge of the child)
20d	Older Brothers or Sisters
20e	Peers
20f	Institutions (school, church, etc.)
20g	Figures Vicariously Experienced (heroes, heroines, villains, etc. in movies, books, radio, newspapers, magazines, comic books, etc. Television had not yet come to Prairie City at the time of this study.)
20h	Other Adults in the Community (neighbors, relatives outside the immediate family, and any other adults in Prairie City whom the child knows.)

This set of ratings was based mainly on two kinds of information. First, and most important, all that was known about a child's parents, friends, relatives, et al.—chiefly from the observational and interview material gathered through the years—was examined in order to determine what values each of them held and displayed in his or her behavior. The child's values, as deduced from all the data on him, were then compared with those of each person or group who might have influenced the formation of his values. Where there was correspondence between the *behaviorally effective* values of the child and of a particular source, that source was credited with the appropriate number of points to indicate its relative influence.

The second kind of information was derived from the child's projective-test records. Here, specific evidence was sought which would show toward what people the child felt the deepest similarity, in his own (largely unconscious) thinking; to whom he felt most deeply attracted; and whom he tried most to be like—whether or not his feelings for a given person were mixed positive and negative feelings or unmixed attraction. This most often gave evidence which was useful in differentiating between the mother and the father as a moral model, although other people were sometimes introduced by the child in his stories or responses. In any case, such evidence was taken only as a supplement to the direct comparison of the child's values with the observed values of the parents, peers, and other people. In a different regard, the projectives were also valuable. They gave a penetrating picture of the values which the child, himself, held and which most powerfully directed his moral behavior. Observational, interview, and sociometric data were equally important in this respect, of course.

Two additional assumptions were made. It was assumed, first, that the family, and particularly the parents, were the most likely source of major values. This assumption had this explicit influence on the ratings: whenever an important feature of the child's moral code matched that of one or both parents, that parent—or both, jointly, if they both held the same value—was credited as the source of that aspect of the child's code. If further investigation showed that the child's teachers or peers exhibited a similar moral attitude or practice, the parents were nonetheless assumed to be the primary source of that value, for that child. In a sense, therefore, there was an explicit bias in favor of crediting the parents as the main source of the child's values, *if there was no evidence to the contrary.* However, whenever the child showed a belief or practice which was different from that of his parents or family members, the most probable outside source was sought and credited as the originator of that much of the child's value system.

The other assumption was that these ratings should represent the sources of values which had *most immediately and directly* shaped the child's values. This is not to say that extrafamily influences are not important in the development and maintenance of moral character. If, as the present investigation indicates, the parents exercise the major direct influence, these ratings simply state that the great majority of children—perhaps all—learn their moral value system chiefly in and through their family; indeed, predominantly from their parents. The importance of teachers, church leaders, peers, and other people in the child's world, as *reinforcers* of his home-derived values, is another matter. This is not shown in the present set of ratings on the *direct* sources of values, but will be discussed later in this chapter.

Table 16 shows the relative weight given in each case to each possible source of moral values. This was done one case at a time, of course. In the end, it appears that one or both parents contributed the greatest part of the child's moral values, in all cases. There is a formal exception in only one case, that of T-52. She lived for some years with an older relative who acted *in loco parentis.* During that period in early life, neither T-52's father or mother was on the scene. That parent surrogate was credited as the major source of T-52's value system. (It may be recalled that T-52 was judged to be predominantly of the Expedient character type. Her early experience of a somewhat disrupted home may not be irrelevant to her character.)

The only other case where no more than half of the child's values were estimated to come from his parents was T-47. Appreciable

TABLE 16. DIRECT SOURCES OF THE CHILD'S MORAL VALUES

Case No.	Mother (20a)	Father (20b)	Parent Surro- gates (20c)	Sib- lings (20d)	Peers (20e)	Insti- tutions (20f)	Vicar. Exp. (20g)	Other Adult (20h)
T-3	3.4	5.0	0.0	0.0	1.1	0.5	0.0	0.0
T-4	4.4	1.8	0.0	3.1	0.0	0.0	0.0	0.7
T-6	5.8	2.4	0.0	0.0	1.1	0.7	0.0	0.0
T-8	5.4	2.6	0.0	0.0	0.0	0.0	0.0	2.0
T-11	7.8	1.2	0.0	1.0	0.0	0.0	0.0	0.0
T-16	7.3	1.8	0.9	0.0	0.0	0.0	0.0	0.0
T-17	7.8	1.0	1.0	0.0	0.0	0.1	0.1	0.0
T-22	4.9	2.2	0.0	1.9	1.0	0.0	0.0	0.0
T-25	7.8	1.6	0.2	0.0	0.0	0.4	0.0	0.0
T-28	5.9	2.3	0.0	0.0	0.0	1.3	0.0	0.5
T-34	4.5	2.5	0.0	0.0	1.0	1.0	0.8	0.2
T-37	5.0	3.0	0.0	1.0	1.0	0.0	0.0	0.0
T-39	4.2	5.4	0.0	0.0	0.0	0.0	0.0	0.4
T-40	3.6	6.2	0.0	0.0	0.2	0.0	0.0	0.0
T-42	3.6	5.2	0.0	0.0	0.0	0.0	0.0	1.2
T-47	3.1	2.0	0.3	0.0	1.4	1.6	0.0	1.6
T-49	6.8	2.2	0.0	0.1	0.6	0.3	0.0	0.0
T-50	6.4	1.6	0.0	0.0	2.0	0.0	0.0	0.0
T-51	4.4	2.3	2.1	0.0	0.2	0.0	0.0	1.0
T-52	2.8	0.0	6.4	0.0	0.8	0.0	0.0	0.0
T-53	5.6	2.4	0.0	0.4	1.4	0.2	0.0	0.0
T-55	6.5	1.2	0.0	1.1	1.2	0.0	0.0	0.0
T-57	6.3	2.5	0.0	1.0	0.0	0.2	0.0	0.0
T-60	5.4	2.3	0.0	0.6	1.6	0.0	0.0	0.1
T-64	5.6	1.8	0.0	2.6	0.0	0.0	0.0	0.0
T-76	5.0	3.0	0.0	1.0	1.0	0.0	0.0	0.0
T-78	2.5	6.8	0.0	0.0	0.7	0.0	0.0	0.0
T-79	6.9	1.9	0.2	0.2	0.0	0.8	0.0	0.0
T-83	5.6	2.8	0.0	0.0	0.0	1.6	0.0	0.0
T-86	3.4	4.4	0.0	1.1	1.1	0.0	0.0	0.0
T-88	5.3	2.0	0.3	2.0	0.4	0.0	0.0	0.0
T-89	4.4	2.2	0.5	1.1	0.0	0.0	0.9	0.9
T-95	3.4	5.2	0.0	0.0	1.4	0.0	0.0	0.0
T-99	3.5	3.4	0.1	1.4	0.6	0.0	0.0	1.0

parts of his values were judged to come from peers, from community institutions (chiefly the school), and from adults outside the family. It was noted in Chapter V that although he was assessed high in Rational-Altruistic motivation, his family background was the one exception to the pattern found for all the other children who were high in Rational-Altruism. Since those family ratings were made independently from the "source of value" ratings, it is of interest that these present ratings credit extrafamily influences as the source of half of his value system. This suggests a genuine exception to the general rule of family dominance in value formation.

Other cases like this are known, from studies of social mobility. Indeed, non-moral social values in the case of mobile people are known to differ quite radically, often, from the values of the mobile ones' parents. From the fact that only one of these thirty-four children shows a marked difference from his parents in *moral* values— although several of the group have shown definite signs of social mobility during adolescence—it might be speculated that moral values are apt to be more deeply and permanently held than non-moral features such as social manners, etiquette, and similar outward symbols, which change with social mobility.*

As for other sources of moral values, it appears that older brothers and sisters contributed at least 10 per cent of the child's values (to put it in simplified, quantitative terms) in over a third of the cases. This is after all allowance has been made for direct parental influence. In all but one of these twelve cases, a curious fact appears: these children were rated from low-average to very low in ego strength, in the psychological side of the study. This almost suggests that brothers and sisters may have a noticeable influence on a child's moral values and character only when the parents have failed to give the child a solid basis for good personality and character development. Certainly, in all but one of these cases, older siblings have apparently played the role of moral model to the child mainly because the parents defaulted from that role in some respects.

In fourteen of the cases, the child's age mates were credited with providing 10 per cent or more of his values (or having a 10 per cent

---

* We can only report, in keeping with this unproven hypothesis, some impressions gained from projective personality testing of some nine to ten thousand adults in the business world over the past twelve years. Many of these men have been socially mobile; but, as far as the evidence goes, it is this writer's impression that there is relatively greater permanence of moral values, as distinct from social customs and esthetic tastes. However, this remains a subject to be investigated much more explicitly (Peck and Parsons, 1956; Peck and Thompson, 1954).

share in the formation of his total value system). There is no simple relationship here to psychological qualities or character structure. Some of the weak-ego children appear in this group; but so do some of the most mature, Rational-Altruistic children. It seems possible that there are two different processes at work here.

There is one group composed of predominantly Amoral or Expedient children, all with below-average ego strength and (with one moderate exception) below-average superego strength. There are T-22, T-37, T-52, T-55, T-76, and T-95. It seems that in their cases peers have contributed significantly to their value systems partly by parental default, and partly because these children are much more suggestible than the rest of the population. Hence, they may be much more apt to "go along with the crowd" in the sense of uncritically adopting their age mates' standards. This may be all to the good, in some cases, from a moral point of view.

At the other pole are T-3, T-6, T-47, T-50, T-53, T-60, and T-86. They all have a large or dominant proportion of the Rational-Altruistic element in their character structure. These children have taken some of their values from their peers as a matter of rational choice; and they may even have improved on their home-derived moral code by doing this. At least, such an explanation is in keeping with what is known of their behavior and their relatively mature kind of morality.

It is of interest, too, that only one child of the Conforming or Irrational-Internalized groups was seen to draw a noticeable part of her values from her age mates. This is T-34, a good-natured, thoroughgoing Conformer who is somewhat below average in both ego strength and superego strength.

This discussion, of course, argues from the relatively slight clues in the value-source pattern, in a way that cannot be decisively tested by quantitative methods. However, this pattern suggests something that tends to be confirmed by the family-background data in Chapter V: the children who are chiefly of the Conforming character type conform mainly to the rules which their parents strictly lay down. They are not, as the case material shows, chameleonlike conformers in the sense that they bend to every breeze of opinion or of shifting moral values in their age-mate group. Indeed, in terms of inner psychodynamics, it is not always easy to see the distinction between children of the *Conforming* and the *Irrational-Conscientious* character types, although it seems to be a meaningful and descriptive distinction, as concerns the motivation patterns in moral behavior. In any case, what slight evidence Table 16 contains tends to confirm the relatively fixed, unchangeable nature of the rule systems these Conforming and

Irrational-Conscientious children have taken over from their parents.

As for the other sources of values, Table 16 indicates that a parent surrogate was influential in four cases, because of special family circumstances.   Other adults were seen contributing some values in six cases; these were chiefly neighbors, or in one case, an employer. Institutions (school, church, youth clubs) were credited with "10 per cent" or more direct influence on the child's values in only four cases. It is especially noteworthy that in no case was there evidence of any appreciable effect from the movies, radio, or reading.   T-84, a Conforming girl, showed some influence from the popular stereotypes of proper, popular behavior as given in movies and movie magazines. T-89 showed some effect of his reading of novels.   But in neither case did this noticeably alter the general tenor of the child's value system.

On the whole, the general trend of these "source of values" ratings are confirmed by the other kinds of data, independently derived. Indeed, if the evidence in Chapters V and VI were not confirmatory, these ratings would have to be questioned, for they could have represented only preconceived opinion on the part of the research staff.

So far, only direct influences have been discussed.   Some forces which lie outside this immediate sphere also deserve attention.

SOCIAL CLASS AND MORAL CHARACTER IN THIS POPULATION

In order to determine whether character was systematically related to the social-class background of the children, Table 17 was drawn up.   No generalization can be drawn about the class-typical moral behavior and character structure at any social level from such a small sample.   Table 17 does definitely indicate, however, that every character type appears in both the Lower-Middle and Upper-Lower class groups, in a random fashion.   Whatever the differences in values between these classes, the distribution of *character types* in Table 17 suggests that the class differences have no highly predictable effect on character structure, although *reputation* varies significantly by class, in favor of the higher-status children.   The individual differences of the families would appear to be the decisive factor, with the possible exception that the lower-lower class may produce a disproportionate number of children with poor character.

Thus, in this sample, there was a very limited relation between character and social status, with the children of the lowest social status somewhat less effective morally than the other children.   Since the

TABLE 17. DISTRIBUTION OF CHARACTER TYPES AND REPUTATION
BY SOCIAL CLASS

Social Class	Case	Maturity of Character	Character Type	Reputation D Scores*	
				Peer	Adult
Upper-Middle	1†	4	IAE	20.6	19.4
Lower-Middle	2	8	R	22.6	22.9
	3	7	ER	26.7	24.4
	4	6	I	22.5	25.3
	5	7	AR	22.8	18.9
	6	5	C	24.1	24.0
	7	3	E	23.3	20.3
	8	3	E	22.8	17.8
	9	1	A	19.6	16.4
	10	2	CEA	16.0	14.6
Upper-Lower	11	8	R	24.4	24.4
	12	3	E	16.7	16.9
	13	4	IAE	20.2	20.4
	14	5	C	21.8	17.9
	15	1	A	17.4	15.7
	16	5	C	21.4	22.3
	17	5	C	19.2	22.1
	18	1	A	15.3	17.0
	19	8	R	20.8	21.7
	20	8	R	22.6	20.1
	21	7	IR	25.0	24.1
	22	5	C	17.0	22.9
	23	7	ER	21.6	20.4
	24	2	CEA	12.3	no data
	25	6	I	23.9	23.8
	26	6	I	22.9	25.2
	27	7	ER	21.0	17.3
	28	5	C	15.2	17.6
	29	1	A	16.2	16.9
Lower-Lower	30	5	C	15.3	21.0
	31	5	C	12.0	14.5
	32	3	E	21.3	16.4
	33	2	CEA	12.5	16.3
	34	1	A	17.4	19.8

* D scores: mean = 20; sigma = 4. Derived from the score distributions of the entire T Group, at age sixteen.

† Case numbers are changed to prevent possible identification by knowledge of an individual's social-class position.

ratings on character were made on the basis of a variety of information, by the character conference staff, they are probably less subject to "halo" effect than ratings on character given by adults and by other children in Prairie City.   On the basis of such "local" ratings, in an earlier study of moral reputation, there was a greater relationship between socioeconomic status and moral reputation, expressed by a coefficient of correlation of .52 (Havighurst and Taba, 1949, p. 48).

MORAL CHARACTER AND CHURCH EXPERIENCE

The churches of Prairie City may also be compared, concerning their relation to the moral maturity of youth.   When this is done for the thirty-four individuals in the study, no relationships appear.   There is a scattering of Catholics, Methodists, Lutherans, Baptists, and Presbyterians.   The top six people are all different in religious denomination, including one who has only a nominal church relationship.   The bottom six have all five major denominations represented, including two mixed Catholic-Protestant marriages.   It is true, however, that the church ties are very tenuous for the youth in the lowest group on Maturity of Character.   With one exception, neither these children nor their families have attended church or participated regularly in religious observance.   In the exceptional case, the family is active in church, but the child has refused to go to church or Sunday school.

While no single religious denomination stands out as closely related to high or low moral maturity, it is nevertheless true that the children who rank high tend to come from families that are actively religious, and the boys and girls themselves have attended Sunday school and church services fairly regularly.   This parallels the finding in the earlier study, in which it was found that the youth who were rated by their pastors as "actively religious" tended to rank above the average of the total group in moral reputation.   In the present study, the two young people who were most active as leaders in the young people's work of their churches ranked together at the top of the middle third in moral maturity.   They both were strongest in the Irrational-Conscientious component of character.

THE SCHOOL AS A CHARACTER-FORMING AGENCY

The school stands for character. To some extent it teaches character explicitly. Does it influence character formation? When the thirty-four subjects were scored according to the decile in which they fell, within the total 1933 group, on school achievement (derived from their average course grades during the latest year they attended school), this array correlated .70 with the Maturity of Character scale. The reasons for this might be as follows, although they can only be speculated. Those with poor moral character possess precisely those qualities of instability, antagonism to the social system, and inability to concentrate or to assimilate knowledge rationally, which are apt to make them poor achievers in school, regardless of their native intelligence.

Moving up the scale, the middle group possess adequate stability and reasonable, if rather passive, conformity to school expectations. Some of them, of course, work very hard indeed; and some of them have very good intellectual endowment. Their low-average ability to make rational appraisals of problems may operate better in subject-matter learning than in the more complex, less closely directed problems of interpersonal living.

The subjects at the upper end of the maturity scale tend to have superior intelligence. What is more, they are able to use it effectively. In addition, they have an active incentive to do well in anything they undertake, not to mention their desire to live up to the expectations of their families.

There may also be a direct effect of moral character on school grades. It is not uncommon for teachers unconsciously or consciously to reward with good grades those children who behave well, and to punish with perhaps unduly severe grades those whose behavior is undesirable.

Doubtless both effects operate, so that assessments of moral character taken on a large group might be nearly as good a predictor of school achievement as group intelligence tests. This is probably not a very practical undertaking, but in a broader sense it appears that moral character has almost as much to do with sheer school achievement, in one way or another, as intellectual capacity; a finding which may be no news to educators, but seems worthy of attention.

All of the children who dropped out of school before graduating from high school were in the lower half of the moral-maturity scale.

Here, too, the results are similar to those obtained in the earlier Prairie City study, where the highest correlation coefficient (.74) with moral reputation was obtained for school success, among a variety of measures of personal qualities.

Although there is this high statistical relationship between morality and scholastic success, this does not demonstrate a cause-effect relationship, nor does it tell the direction of such cause-effect relation as may exist. That is, the children of good moral character may do well in school, they may learn moral character to some extent from the school, or there may be no causal relationship between the school and moral character.

This much can be said with some assurance, however. The school is a laboratory for the learning of moral and intellectual characteristics. A positive correlation should be expected to prevail among these two sets of traits, because of their observed tendency to reinforce one another. A youth who is responsible, loyal, and honest in school is rewarded by better school grades than he would get otherwise. Being rewarded, he will tend to become more responsible, loyal, and honest, at least in the school situation. The relation is even somewhat higher between school grades and moral maturity (.70) than it is between intelligence and moral maturity (.57).

From this kind of reasoning it is not at once clear whether the school encourages the most desirable kind of moral motivation—Rational-Altruism. It might be encouraging a Conforming or an Irrational-Conscientious motivation pattern. The kinds of school program that might be expected to help the youth develop a Rational-Altruistic type of moral motivation need to be explored.

INFLUENCE OF PEOPLE OUTSIDE THE FAMILY ON MORAL EFFECTIVENESS

People outside the immediate family may influence the moral character of a child through their personal relations with him. He may learn from what they say and from how they behave—although more from their example than from their precept. In the intensive case studies a number of clear-cut examples were found of a relationship between an adult or an older youth and one of the children in the research group. In most cases these relationships were apparently quite similar in their general character to family relationships between the boys and girls and older brothers or sisters or aunts or uncles. The older person spent a good deal of time with the younger one, played with him, worked with him, advised him, and generally served as a model.

The relationship appeared to be present about equally often in cases of high and low morality. For example, one of the "low" boys had a close relation to a young man who was his employer. The employer was not himself a moral success in any sense, and his influence could hardly have helped the boy much, beyond giving him the assurance that someone respected and liked him. One of the "high" girls had a long-standing relationship with a young neighbor woman who was like an older sister to her. This young woman was an ordinary, wholesome person, who probably served as a model to the girl as she grew up. Thus it seems not to have been the presence or absence of a close relationship with an adult, but rather the quality of the adult that mattered as far as character building is concerned.

This matter was more systematically investigated with the aid of the Adult Guess-Who Test, in which each subject was asked to write the names of adults in the community who fitted thumbnail descriptions of people who were community-minded or were friendly to younger people, or trustworthy, good-looking, or carefully dressed. The names of people written by the boys and girls tell which adults may possibly have served as models to the youth of the community.

The morally mature subjects tended to name several teachers, a small number of "community leaders," and a larger number of solid, reputable people who were living in their neighborhood. The "low" group gave a more scattered response, including a few teachers and community leaders, but also several young adults who were generally considered to be of questionable character or to be somewhat shiftless. One of the low group, a boy, mentioned mostly women, thus showing that he probably had no substantial male persons to serve as models for him. It was a striking fact that clergymen were almost never mentioned by boys or girls, regardless of their rank on the moral maturity scale.*

In this connection the question of cause-effect sequence may be raised again. Did these youth make a connection with an older adult and then use that person as a model for character development; or did they choose older people as models who were already somewhat like themselves in moral character? Probably both elements were present, making it a circular process.

---

* Results of use of the Adult Guess-Who Test with another group of boys and girls are quite similar to these. They are described in Havighurst and Taba, *Adolescent Character and Personality,* pp. 73–80.

Thus it appears probable that adults in the community, and especially young adults who are teachers, club leaders, employers, and neighbors did have some influence on the character development of these boys and girls. It is less probable that people who came vicariously into the lives of the boys and girls of the study group had much character-building influence on them. Such people as movie stars, professional athletes, historical and fictional characters appear to have had very little influence on these youth. There was a period in their lives, from about age ten to about age fifteen, when such people were mentioned in the essay "The Person I'd Like to Be Like," but these distant and "glamorous" characters were superseded in the essays by attractive, visible young adults of the community, or by composite, imaginary persons. The great heroes of history seem to have had little or no influence on the youth of Prairie City. They practically never named such people as "The Person I'd Like to Be Like." They seldom mentioned reading about such people—indeed they seldom read books, aside from school-assigned books, after the age of fourteen.

VIII

The consistency
of moral character
through time

As the children were studied from age ten through seventeen, each tended to show a stable, predictable pattern of moral character. Many of their overt actions changed, of course, as they grew older, learned new social and intellectual skills, and developed through puberty. However, each child appeared to maintain very persistently his deeply held feelings and attitudes toward life, and the modes of reacting which we call his character structure.

RATING EVIDENCE ON THE CONSISTENCY
OF CHARACTER

The first kind of evidence on the consistency of moral character and moral behavior through time, consists of certain ratings which were made on all the cases. Simultaneously with this study of character, a study of "developmental task achievement" was being conducted, which has not been mentioned until now. This was simply a different set of measurements applied to the subjects of our study. (The "developmental tasks" on which the children were rated are defined in Havighurst's *Human Development and Education.* Some results of our study are described in Chapters 19 and 20 of that book.)

The significant and convenient feature of these ratings is the fact that each child was rated on each task as he was meeting it at ten years of age, at thirteen, and at sixteen. In short, these are longitudinal ratings running from age ten through age sixteen. Table 18 shows the correlations of the ten-year-old ratings with those for the same children at thirteen and sixteen, and between their thirteen- and sixteen-year standings.

TABLE 18.   CORRELATIONS OF MORAL VALUES AND OTHER DEVELOPMENTAL
TASKS BETWEEN AGES TEN, THIRTEEN, AND SIXTEEN

Age Levels	Conscience and Moral Values	Emotional Independence	Sex Role	Age Mates	Intellectual Skills	Average, r
r, 10–16	.78	.79	.42	.71	.78	.70
r, 10–13	.80	.83	.61	.75	.92	.78
r, 13–16	.98	.95	.84	.94	.91	.92

Of chief interest is the first column, which concerns the task of developing a conscience and a set of effective moral values. (This is closely similar to the Moral Effectiveness rating, which was made only for the children at age sixteen.) As can be seen, there is a very marked tendency for the level of morality at age ten to be about the same at age thirteen and sixteen. Even more pronounced is the evidence of the .98 correlation that moral character changes little or none from thirteen to sixteen.

The figures for the other developmental tasks provide supplementary confirmation of the enduring nature of personality and character. Except for Sex-Role Adjustment, which shifts noticeably (and understandably) between ten and sixteen but still tends to be more constant than not, each child's degree of success in meeting life's problems at ten years forecasts about the same degree of success (or failure) at thirteen. Even more notable is the very close similarity between his relative success at thirteen and his relative success at sixteen, in all the various aspects of life. This is true even though the specific skills and expectations change markedly across these three age levels.

In other words, a child who has good moral values for a ten-year-old can be expected to behave morally at age thirteen, by standards appropriate for thirteen-year-olds. And if he displays a well-developed conscience at thirteen he is almost certain to show equally good morality at sixteen. On the other hand, a child with poor or ineffective values at ten can be expected to be relatively no better at thirteen or at sixteen. One with just average morality at ten is likely to be just average at thirteen; and if he is just average at thirteen, he is almost certain to be no better and no worse than that at sixteen.

In short, the ratings and the actual case histories both suggest that whatever pattern of moral behavior and character structure a child shows at ten years of age, he is far more likely than not to display into late adolescence; and, our belief is, for the rest of his life. Both the case records and the ratings which were based on them show that there is *room* for change in later life; but, like the other studies cited later in this chapter, they suggest that prolonged, deep-going influences would be necessary to effect such a change, and that such influences are not likely to occur in the average person's life.

HOW CONSISTENCY SEEMS TO BE DEVELOPED

Studying these children from ten to seventeen, with reported data going back into their early years in most cases, revealed a characteristic personality and character pattern which was largely laid down by age ten and changed little thereafter. Earlier data tended to fall in the same line in each case, wherever it could be obtained.

Briefly, this suggests that the child of each character type starts very early to develop along that type path, and that growth simply makes him more and more that kind of person. Since the family influence is usually continuously the same, whether in a stable or confused pattern, this is understandable. The Amoral child, for example, never got far beyond the point of being Amoral. As he grew, he may have developed a few more socialized, superficial adaptations; but mostly he became a bigger and stronger Amoral person.

Similarly, the Expedient child learned more and better ways of being Expedient. He did not move firmly into a Conforming or superego-ruled pattern at any time; nor did the Conforming or the Irrational-Conscientious children evidence a predominantly Expedient character structure which later changed markedly to their final Conforming or Irrational-Conscientious pattern.

The Rational-Altruistic child showed definite signs of behaving by rational, altruistic principle—appropriate, of course, to the powers of understanding and judgment of a child his age—at least as far back as ten or eleven. Prior to that, he was mostly Conforming or Irrational-Conscientious, but with a warm feeling for people and a flexible reasonableness—like that of his parents—which foreshadowed the ultimate emergence of his Rational-Altruistic pattern.

This is not to say that many or most of the children did not show any effort to mature beyond a childish level of morality, or did not regress to less mature levels under stress. Indeed, the first four or five years of school, in particular, were marked by active experimentation in many cases, as the children tried one means and another for winning an accepted place in the world outside the home. In the end, they almost all wound up with a character and personality structure that could have been predicted from the nature of their parents' rearing of them; but this was decidedly not a passive, "rubber-stamp" process, unmarked by children's efforts to break away or change this pattern.

It is largely, though not wholly, speculation to consider the early founding and etiology of the several character-type groups. If we assume that all infants lack character, it is clear that they can scarcely be other than Amoral. Similarly, at progressively later ages, the child of one to two years is unlikely to have internalized much of a conscience as yet, hence no child at this age is likely to be much beyond the Expedient level of morality, when he does behave morally. By four, five, or six, if the child is going to develop some moral principles, he probably now has their rudiments and might be considered able to demonstrate a Conforming or Irrational-Conscientious pattern with reasonable stability, if the home fosters such a pattern. It is perhaps only at this level, and later, that a child can begin to show an organized, effective pattern of moral behavior that could reasonably be called Rational-Altruistic.

However, a basic foundation of generalized expectancies, attitudes, and habits may well be laid down almost from birth, in such a way that the general outlines of later character could almost be foretold from a study of the parents' early treatment of the child. The parents, we found, tended to be just as consistently what they were, through the years, as did the children—particularly, in their relationship toward a given child. Insofar as this is true, it follows that the child who was Amoral at ten or eighteen had usually experienced from the start a chaotic, unloving home, and that it kept on being this way. Whereas children from different families had the incentive and the guidance to outgrow their amorality as they passed beyond infancy, the Amoral child had neither the help nor the incentive to want to attain a better degree or kind of morality.

Even choosing a dramatic example such as "Arthur Adams," the Amoral boy in Chapter III, is to oversimplify the facts greatly by labeling him solely "Amoral." He did experience at least some normal satisfactions, and he did learn to want desperately the affection of other people, even when he simultaneously felt hatred toward them. So Arthur did develop some Expedient morality, even some Conforming and some Irrational-Conscientious motives for behaving ethically. These presumably developed during his early childhood and were refined into somewhat acceptable behavior patterns by his early school years. He fluctuated markedly as later events affected him deeply. His parents' divorce when he was ten apparently broke his more matured self-controls so that he erupted with open, childlike hostility for the next five to six years, only gradually reshaping a barely adequate adaptation to the moral demands of his society. Thus, while Arthur's character may have had a dominant element of amorality from the start, and though he maintained a very low level of moral character relative to his age mates at each age level, he did not suffer this fate gladly nor without continual struggles to do better, however ineffectual they proved on the whole.

To take another example, "Catherine Cranek," the Conforming girl of Chapter III, had a firm, authoritarian but approving family world from the outset. Thus, as soon as she could respond obediently to parental control, she probably began to be a person who actively wanted to do just what Momma said, even as a very little girl. She could not have developed an integrated, self-sustained pattern of conformity before the age of three or four at the earliest, we might guess. Once she could do it, though, she adopted this character pattern very firmly, on the whole. Even she rebelled inwardly at times; sometimes even outwardly, in a half-hearted way, during later childhood and adolescence. It seems that it was the continuing weight of the family influence that kept putting her back into the Conforming pattern, though, just as Arthur's family experiences kept depriving and upsetting him all the way through adolescence.

To take "Ralph Reed," the Rational-Altruistic boy of Chapter III as the third example, there is some retrospective evidence in the data which indicates that he had a warm, loving, reasonably permissive and rationally ordered experience from his early years. Insofar as his warm friendliness and his ability to think clearly, without undue inner conflict, are salient elements of his Rational-Altruism in adolescence, it might not be wrong to say that the groundwork for these feelings and behaviors was laid down very early in his life, and consistently maintained as he grew from infancy, through boyhood, to adolescence. Certainly, he could not have been very rational by adult standards, at four, six or seven; but by ten he was already showing clear signs of being one of the most purposefully and reasonedly ethical children in his age group, by standards appropriate to that age. Ralph was and is no inhuman paragon of virtue. Even as Arthur and Catherine sometimes reached out for more mature, self-directing morality, Ralph sometimes backslid mildly. His consistency, like theirs, might better be considered an average of all his feelings and behavior rather than a totally fixed, unchanging pattern. Nonetheless, at each age he was accorded and earned a top position in his age group, in moral terms, just as Arthur hit bottom shortly after ten, and stayed there through eighteen. Similarly, Catherine ranked well above average, though not outstanding, in the quality and maturity of her moral behavior as the years went by.

This matter of consistency despite growth changes is one of the many paradoxes which our language creates. It is difficult to express in one and the same breath that children develop through changing stages and also run true to type, without generating confusion. What seems to happen is this: the entire age group develops and changes through the years, but each individual child tends to maintain about the same generalized attitudes, and also the same standing relative to the total population in terms of the quality and age-appropriate maturity of his character structure and moral behavior. Thus, a predominantly Expedient child may acquire somewhat better socialized habits of moral behavior as he grows older, by comparison with his own childhood behavior, even if he is still powered largely by Expedient motives. However, the rest of his age mates are simultaneously developing increased discrimination, considerateness, and self-control in their moral behavior. Thus, they maintain their relative superiority to him at each successive age level, in terms of their behavior; and if they have the family backing to do so, they can develop more mature character structure while he remains fixated at the level of Expedient character.

POSSIBLE INFLUENCES FOR CHARACTER CHANGE

Had a child in this study entered a deeply emotionalized relationship with a kind of person new to his experience, on the order of emotional intensity of the parent-child relationship, basic changes in his character might have occurred. However, in no case studied did such an influence intervene. In view of the usual course of life in an American community, such consistency in the major influences in the child's life is probably the general rule, with exceptions rather rare.

One such influence for deep-seated change might be the child's experiencing intensive psychotherapy, in the case of an unadjusted boy or girl. There is, however, no professional psychotherapist in or near Prairie City. It is by no means agreed, in any case, that even major psychotherapy produces change in basic character structure very often, however important its effects may be in helping the person to adjust more satisfactorily to himself and to his society in his daily behavior.

More generally, it seldom seems to happen that a child of ten—or even younger, perhaps—who is living with his parents, forms as deeply penetrating or profoundly influential relatedness with anyone outside his home. There were a few children in this study who acquired step-parents when they were eight or older. Changes in some of their feelings and their adjustment did occur; changes which they felt keenly, for better or worse. Still, even such a new influence, probably as effectual as the child was likely to encounter, seemed on the whole to bring out and intensify his or her already-existing feelings, more than it produced change in those deepest-held habits and attitudes which constitute the child's "personality" or "character structure."

Such observations are in line with the results of a large-scale, eight-year study reported by Edwin Powers and Helen Witmer. The title of their report indicates the nature of their research: *An Experiment in the Prevention of Delinquency.*

The Powers-Witmer book is a report on a long-continued effort to influence and change moral character. They report only limited success, even with the intensive program of case-work counseling they undertook. (It must be noted, though, that their staff and their program were seriously disrupted by the advent of World War II.)

Most to the point, perhaps, is an observation in Dr. Gordon Allport's foreword:

> It is important to note that in very few cases was a counselor able to provide full and sufficient emotional anchorage for a boy whose own parents rejected him. Every youngster, at least until the age of adolescence, needs a rooted sense of security and love in his home. Neither the school nor the social agency can supply the lack nor fully repair the ravages if this condition is missing. When a basic security in the home exists, then, it is found, counselors can do much to make up for other, less serious, parental inadequacies.

In this present study of character in Prairie City, an effort was made to discover the nature and structure of character over the entire range of morality. It appears that the conditions which are reported by the Gluecks (Glueck and Glueck, 1950), and by Powers and Witmer, as forming and shaping character at the delinquent end of the scale apply with equal force at every level of morality. That is, the influence of the child's home is so paramount that it is difficult to find later-exerted forces which may have much effect in changing it.

At the bottom of the scale we, too, have found the moral character of the actual or near-delinquent to be relatively fixed under almost all circumstances likely to occur. This permanence of character structure seems just as true at the middle and upper levels of the scale. The evidence on ego strength and superego strength indicates that it would probably be just as hard to break down the firm morality of the Rational-Altruistic children as it would be to make a basic improvement in the moral character of the Amoral children.

There is no evidence to suggest any "predestination" in this phenomenon. From all that could be found, moral character is formed by the child's family experiences, not genetically inherent. However, by the age of ten—indeed, perhaps much earlier—whatever character the child has, he is likely to have for life, in most cases. For practical purposes, this suggests that the only realistic, efficient way of really insuring good character is to somehow work with parents, before and soon after the child is born. If this sounds impractical, it is important to note that the methods of didactic teaching, "reform" schools, and preaching, used by themselves, are apt to have little practical effect. At their best, such methods seem to be mildly ameliorative, and discouraging results can be expected more often than not.

This is no more than a statement of the *probability* that no marked change will occur, *under usual circumstances*. It is not to say that change *cannot* occur. In his foreword to *An Experiment in the Pre-*

vention of Delinquency, Dr. Allport says of Dr. Richard Clarke Cabot, the founder of that study:

Granted that genuine reformation of criminals is a rare phenomenon, he had none the less observed that in all cases known to him, "there has been at least one necessary condition: *that someone should come to know and to understand the man in so intimate and friendly a way that he comes to a better understanding of himself and to a truer comprehension of the world he lives in.*"

This is practically a verbatim rendering of two of the elements postulated here as basic to morality: friendly, positive concern for others (altruism), and rationality. The element of stability is perhaps implied by the reference to "reformation."

Elsewhere in his foreword, Dr. Allport remarks: "[Certain results of the study] may mean that a warm-hearted unprofessional approach —consistently maintained for a long period of time—will in fact accomplish more than a professional approach lacking equal warmth."

These observations parallel the conclusions drawn in Chapter V, from the study of the parental methods which produce the most mature kind of moral character. As was seen there, the steady, attractive example of wise and loving parents was the one—indeed, the only—influence which produced children with Rational-Altruistic morality. While consistent, relatively autocratic, though affectionate, parents produced Conforming children of good morality, perhaps it takes an extra, intensive application of understanding and liking to compensate for the affectionally deprived experiences of children with inadequate morality. Thus, it may require a significantly Rational-Altruistic adult to rehabilitate a serious delinquent, whereas a solidly moral Conformer might make an effective leader for youth of more normal, acceptable morality.

Such speculations go beyond the scope of this study, of course; but they concern matters of importance to the planning and conduct of child education and parent education, where character development is a major issue. The present study can do little more than raise some questions and perhaps suggest some leads for more extensive and definitive study in this field.

IX

Summary

THE NATURE OF CHARACTER

The questions posed at the outset of the study now appear answerable, for the most part. There does seem to be such a thing as individual character: a persisting pattern of attitudes and motives which produce a rather predictable kind and quality of moral behavior. To be sure, there are some inconsistencies within the moral behavior of just about everyone. Some individuals are markedly inconsistent—now considerate, now callously selfish; responsible here, irresponsible there. Such a pattern has its own kind of "consistency," though. It is an enduring, predictable kind of pattern that sets the person off from other people of different character.

As it turns out, adolescents, their teachers, and professional research people, all find it both meaningful and valid to describe and assess an individual in terms of a general pattern that can be called his moral character. There is a significantly high degree of agreement among these disparate judges when the same individuals are assessed, even when the dimensions are not defined in exactly identical terms

164

for the different sets of judges. When age mates and teachers provide appraisals on such moral traits as honesty, responsibility, self-control, kindliness, and the like, and an average on all traits is struck for each individual subject, that appraisal correlates highly with psychologists' and sociologists' assessment of the same subjects on a scale of *inner* maturity of character.

The pattern of motives and typical actions each individual shows by age ten, moreover, tends to persist through adolescence. (The likelihood seems very strong that character is even more stably persistent, in most people, in the adult years, although this was not tested in the present study.) This persistence is observable in two ways. The adequacy of an individual's moral motives and behavior, relative to his own age group, tends to stay at about the same *relative* level as he develops through later childhood and adolescence. While almost all children learn to exercise some increasing degree of self-control, for example, from ten to sixteen, the ones who have *relatively* best self-control at ten are likely to have the best self-control in their age group at sixteen, in terms of the behavioral norms of sixteen-year-olds. There are exceptional cases, to be sure, but not many.

Quite apart from the matter of relative standing, it has been found that most individuals tend to maintain *the same attitudes and motives* through the years, in major aspects of morality. The child who is deeply friendly and affectionate at ten, for instance, is most likely to show the same warm, trustful feelings for people at sixteen and seventeen. Conversely, the child who is deeply cowed, submissive, and yet covertly resentful toward people at ten is most apt to show just about the same reaction pattern at seventeen, even allowing for all the pressures and encouragement to become more independent as adolescence progresses.

In short, if character be defined in terms of powerful, emotion-laden attitudes, as well as action patterns that tend to become habituated, the evidence indicates that there is indeed such a thing as individual character, and that it tends to persist through the years. Numerous details of attitude and behavior normally do change during the course of adolescent development, and allowance must be made for these maturational changes; but once such allowance is made for the changes "everybody" undergoes, it is remarkable how little alteration there is in the basic motive pattern of most adolescents. Indeed, in the majority of cases there seems to be very little alteration in basic character structure, regardless of developmental changes in the surface details of behavior.

Judging from the present research, it appears possible and useful to define "basic character" in a series of five types, arranged on an ascending scale of psychological and moral maturity:

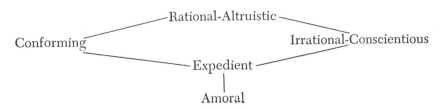

These "types" are merely a descriptive device. It was found, as anticipated, that no one was entirely of one type. All the subjects proved to be complex mixtures of motives. Nonetheless, when the *dominant* type in each individual's profile was used to classify him at the appropriate point on the ascending scale of Maturity of Character, it turned out that the subjects who fell in each type group showed some highly significant psychological features in common, and equally important differences from the subjects of the types above and below them on the scale.

THE PSYCHOGENESIS OF CHARACTER

"Character" can be regarded as a special aspect of personality; or, otherwise stated, as a function of certain personality characteristics. In this research, six aspects of personality were found to be relevant: Moral Stability, Ego Strength, Superego Strength, Spontaneity, Friendliness, and a Hostility-Guilt Complex. *Moral Stability* is composed of such things as overt conformity to the expectations of mother, age mates of the opposite sex, and the community at large; stable, controlled overt behavior of a pleasantly toned kind; and a wide range of moral horizon. It is more a descriptive than an explanatory, motivational dimension. *Ego Strength* subsumes the perceptual capacities of intelligence, observation, and insight; realism in appraising self and others. It also includes psychological autonomy, maturity of emotional reaction, and internal consistency—or integration—of the personality system. *Superego Strength* measures the degree to which behavior is effectively guided in accord with a set of inner moral principles, whatever those principles may be. *Spontaneity* includes spontaneity, as such, and also such characteristics as empathy, a lack of guilt about overt behavior, and good feelings for father and for same-sex peers. *Friendliness* is a measure of a generalized, inner attitude toward other people. The *Hostility-Guilt Complex* consists of hostile feelings toward mother and toward opposite-sex peers, overt rejection of father's standards, and chronic guilt feelings about one's inner impulses.

In general, moral stability, ego strength, and superego strength all correlated very significantly with the Maturity of Character scale, and with moral reputation attributed by both teachers and age mates. Spontaneity showed a curvilinear relationship with character. Spontaneity tended to be highest among subjects of either very good or very poor character; it was lowest among the Irrational-Conscientious, the Conformers, and even the Expedient adolescents, in the middle range. Friendliness was significantly related to the Maturity of Character scale, although not to moral reputation with age mates and teachers. The Hostility-Guilt Complex was negatively related to good character.

The adolescents who showed the most notably Amoral tendencies had a distinctive personality pattern: extremely low in moral stability, ego strength, and superego strength, and, with one exception, an actively hostile attitude. Several were extremely spontaneous; but others were actually somewhat constricted and restrained. All of the highly Amoral subjects, except the one friendly "moral weakling," had intense cases of the hostility-guilt conflict, although the subjects with composite profiles of equal Conforming-Expedient-Amoral scores were more free of this complex. All in all, the poor character of these people could easily be understood. They hate life. They have chaotic perceptions, extreme, inappropriate emotionality, ineffective superegos, and generally disorganized, internally contradictory, often impulse-ridden personalities. They have neither the internal incentive nor the capacity to conduct themselves in a stably ethical manner. The one partial exception was a boy who "meant well" but was too passively dependent on others' good will, and too inadequate in his personality, to conduct his own life dependably.

These adolescents with a large Amoral component in their characters might be described in neo-analytic terms as heavily fixated at the early "oral" stage of psychosocial development. They demonstrate a profound lack of what Erikson has called "basic trust" (Erikson, 1950), and also lack the perceptual and judgmental ego powers which are necessary to achieve what both Erikson and Piaget have referred to as "psychological autonomy." It is not much use appealing to their "reason," for they are largely incapable of ruling their own behavior according to intelligent reasoning. They are very much at the mercy, too often, of violent hungers, hates, and other passions which can overwhelm what "good sense" they may at other times demonstrate.

Remedial treatment for such children requires firm outside control and guidance, at the start, as Bettelheim (Bettelheim, 1950) and Redl (Redl and Wineman, 1952) have empirically demonstrated.

The subjects with dominant or near-dominant Expedient motives show low to very low moral stability and below-average to very weak ego strength. They range from a little above average to very weak in superego strength, and also in spontaneity. These self-centered "operators" are by no means just gaily impulsive. On the contrary, with the exception of two rather passively self-indulgent boys, these adolescents show a good deal of strained self-control. Except for one of the boys just mentioned, all the Expedient subjects are actively hostile in their underlying attitude toward life, most of them to an extreme degree.

The unspoken attitude of these children might be summed up as "you have to look out for yourself; if you don't, nobody else is going to look out for you." Psychogenetically, their orientation is not much past the late "oral" stage. They are self-centeredly preoccupied with *getting*. At the same time, they show a chronic sense of frustration; they never get "enough," or not enough to make them view the world as a trustworthy, rewarding place. They have developed sufficient ego identity and enough realism to recognize the need to go along with society's rules, when they have to, but they have not internalized these rules very much; not to the point where any of them could be said to have strong moral convictions or principles. They are more autonomous than the Amoral subjects, but not any more than the Conformers. Some of them show a little more initiative, in Erikson's sense; but even here they tend to be driven from within by irrational hungers that ordinary acquisitions or human response cannot satisfy. All in all, the subjects at this level show a narcissistic, childlike orientation toward life that years of experience through childhood and adolescence have not appreciably altered.

The modal pattern in the Conforming group is one of definite moral stability which is produced much more by habituated superego dictates than by reasoned use of ego powers. Indeed, these subjects tend to have below-average ego strength. They show a built-in, restrictive inner control, however, which keeps them firmly in line with the conventions of their world. Some of them are very friendly and good natured in their general attitude; some distinctly are not. In either case, how they feel personally, influences their behavior much less than what they believe others expect of them—and, indeed, what they rather blindly expect of themselves, in terms of the social rules they have unquestioningly incorporated. Even at seventeen, these are "good children" of the unthinkingly submissive kind, little more developed in their psychological autonomy or use of reason than in middle childhood. They have mastered and passed the developmental tasks of the "anal" stage—except, perhaps, for their underdeveloped autonomy—but they have not met and resolved the issues of the "genital" stage. They may consciously rebel, sometimes, at direct dictation by adults; but they need and seek to be surrounded by a familiar world that reinforces their belief in the rightness of the authoritative "answers" that have been trained into them without their own participating thought.

The Irrational-Conscientious subjects show only differences of degree, in the characteristics measured, from the Conformers. They, too, have relatively undeveloped ego powers, but they have even more powerful, dominant superegos. They are covertly hostile, but too restrained to allow themselves to show it in any way that would violate the moral conventions they have learned to observe.

The most highly Rational-Altruistic group tend to show the highest degree of moral stability of all, but not by unreasoning imitation or habituation. They have highly developed ego powers which they use to probe and solve ethical problems. Often, their reasoning is not made conscious nor is it always verbalized; but that does not necessarily decrease the quality of their judgment. They have moderate to strong superego principles. These are not compartmentalized from their reasoning, however, and they do not blindly dictate stereotyped behavior. These principles of conscience are held open to examination and redirection, to suit changing circumstances.

As an integral part of their personalities, too, these subjects show a very decided friendliness of outlook, and notably lack the hostility-guilt complex. They can therefore afford to be thoroughly spontaneous, and they are. The nature of their impulses is in comfortable accord with their ethical principles and with the ethical needs of society.

Of all the adolescents studied, only these last are still growing, psychologically, and still open to further growth. The other three-quarters of the research population appear to be fixated at immature levels of development, and in the ordinary course of events may remain permanently "stuck" with childlike ways of viewing and meeting life. The quarter, or so, who show a significant degree of rational altruism are almost the only ones who are able to question life intelligently, question their own preconceptions, and thus be able to grow in moral wisdom and meet unforeseen situations with effective morality.

They show the characters of Freud's "genital" type; and of Erikson's person who has firm identity, good capacity for human intimacy, and a creative, generative orientation. They likewise fit Fromm's "productive orientation," and Reisman's "autonomous character."

Some central threads run through the character-type sequence. From Amoral to Rational there is *increasing ego strength*, including all the characteristics of rational, emotionally mature, integrated personality functioning. A second theme is that of *increasing strength of conscience*, in the sense of increasingly firm, increasingly internalized moral principles which act as an effective guide to behavior.

There appear to be four qualitatively different kinds of conscience, however. The first, most primitive, and least effectual consists of a collection of harsh, crude "Don't's." At best, these act in an unthinkingly repressive way. At worst, they are so internally inconsistent or so excessively frustrating that they are impossible to follow. This kind of superego appears in the Amoral and Expedient groups, with traces in some of the more cowed, childish Conformers.

The second kind of conscience is largely a matter of rule conformity, with the main weight of authority still residing in the people around one. Its one central principle is a willing, sometimes anxious desire to do whatever the "respected others" require. Most of the subjects who show this kind of conscience are not simply passive moral "chameleons," however. They do possess a body of internalized rules for action which they could not easily discard nor dramatically alter without feelings of guilt. The preponderant element in their moral control system, nonetheless, seems to be the desire to do "what people I respect want me to do." They find a good deal of needed reassurance in their acceptance by the "respected other," and experienced shame when found wanting. This pattern is very like the "conventional" type of authoritarian personality described in the California studies (Adorno et al., 1950). This kind of superego might be described as one which has been incorporated from outside authority figures, but without severing the "umbilical cord," so to speak. The rules are believed in, with personal conviction, but final recourse is usually sought to the approval and support of those authority figures, or their later surrogates.

The third kind of conscience consists of a firmly organized body of internalized moral rules which maintain their own autonomy. They are not much affected by what other people may say; but neither do they permit themselves to be questioned or tested by rational inquiry. Together, they form the tyrannical neurotic superego first described by Freud. This kind of conscience is largely walled-off from influence by ego functions.

The fourth kind of conscience is the one found in the Rational-Altruistic subjects. It is a firm set of internalized moral *principles* which are accessible to rational questioning and testing. Such a conscience is not a compartmentalized fragment of the personality. On the contrary, it tends to interact rather freely both with the ego functions and with the impulse life. It is probably inevitable that such a conscience was found to occur only within a personality where the "id" impulses were basically positive, constructive, and friendly, for the most part. This most mature form of conscience is not a discrete entity, functioning in isolation from day-to-day experience. Instead, it changes and deepens in wisdom as new experiences are encountered.

Another theme that shows developmental evolution through the character-type sequence is one that might be called *the capacity to love*. The Amoral and Expedient subjects essentially feel unloved, and they are almost incapable of unselfish affection for others. To them, other people are at best a potential source of gratification for their own selfish desires. However, they don't really trust other people. Indeed, they have come to expect others to be as selfish, unpredictable, and hostile as themselves. This does not seem to be a case of projection, so much as it is an over-generalization from the kinds of people who affected them most profoundly—their families —and who actually were just about what the Amoral and Expedient adolescents expect everyone to be.

The Conformers, in many cases, feel loved and give love to others. Overawed by "the system" and by rules for living, their capacity to perceive what another individual really wants or needs is not very highly developed; but their intentions are genuinely good. Some Conformers, on the other hand, feel unloved and unloving. Their conventionality is more actuated by a generalized fear of social punishment than by the hope of social reward from other people.

The Irrational-Conscientious subjects, at least in this research sample, feel quite unloved and covertly hostile toward others. They lack any real warmth, even though they may dutifully obey the rules that call for "kind" or "considerate" behavior. Their actions at such times show much more devotion to the letter of the law than to its spirit.

The Rational-Altruistic person feels, and is, both well-loved and loving, warmly and spontaneously so. Being accurate in his perceptions and realistic in his judgment, he is able to express his liking for others in ways that effectively advance their well-being. It was neither expected nor found that any subject acts in this way all the time; but by contrast with almost all the other types, those with considerable Rational Altruism are the only ones who regularly show *both* good intentions and thoughtful, accurate judgment in their treatment of other people. Moral dilemmas often involve the necessity for choosing one good moral consequence at the expense of some other, lesser, but nonetheless good consequence. When faced with such a dilemma the Rational Altruist is concerned about the real effects of each possible action, not with abstract verbal labels such as "truth," "honesty," or "loyalty."

He may not always be able to suppress personal desire sufficiently to bring about effects which are maximally good for other people, but he seldom tries to justify himself by hypocritical talk of high principles or by self-righteous rationalization. Most of the time he is straightforwardly and honestly aware of what he is doing, and what effects it will have. He has a great degree of self-acceptance. This enables him to critize specific shortcomings he may demonstrate without fearing so intense and general a sense of guilt or moral worthlessness that he cannot stand to risk any self-criticism. In the same manner, and perhaps for some of the same reasons, he is able to love other people intelligently. That is, he can see specific shortcomings in another person without reducing his overall feeling of respect and affection for that person. He does not "love" blindly a projection of his own wishful imaginings onto another person. When he loves another, it is with a realistic perception of what that person is like, and the qualities he finds lovable are real qualities of that other person, not wishful creations of his own mind. Alone among the types, therefore, such a person is capable of mature, unselfish, realistic love. If he cannot be ruled at all times by this, nonetheless the very capacity to do it makes him qualitatively different from the less mature people. Their "love" is largely a hunger to receive, and their "generosity" is usually either a ritualized effort to win social esteem or an effort to win vicarious satisfaction through another's fulfillment, without knowing if their own wish is really identical with the wish or need of the other person. The Rational-Altruistic orientation is the only one that combines ethical desire with ethical intelligence and thus insures that real love will be effectively expressed.

A basic, qualitative difference exists between the psychological maturation pattern of children who are becoming rationally altruistic in their character pattern, and those who remain fixated in more primitive patterns. It is customary to point out the maturation of reasoning powers and of measures for self-control. However, in pointing out that a great many selfish, primitive "id" impulses remain active in all of us throughout life, Freud and some of his followers either minimized or overlooked the fact that in people whose psychological development is healthy there is not only a maturing of ego and superego functions: there is also a maturing of at least some part of the *impulse life* into desires which are inherently socialized and ethical by nature.

Some of the only half-matured adolescents in the study were nonetheless capable of genuinely unselfish impulses, of genuinely unselfish love. They sometimes did generous or helpful things with no thought of reward, simply because they cared about the other person. At such times, it was not a case of having to repress, control, or "sacrifice" a selfish impulse in order to carry out an unselfish deed. Such behavior was not limited to the Rational-Altruistic group, alone, although they showed it most consistently and most frequently of all.

In short, *the id grows up, too,* in the healthily developing person. It would be folly to ignore that this process never reaches full completion in the best of men. Darkly violent or greedy or animalistic urges rise in the relatively most matured people, whether in this study or among the healthiest adults. Such primitive, powerful impulses can only be wrestled down or harmlessly diverted, at best. But among the Rational-Altruistic subjects, especially, the only way to interpret accurately their positive, considerate impulses may be to recognize that a successful, ethical process of child rearing produces something that can only be called maturation of the id, to some degree. This kind of development occurs little, if any, among the predominantly Amoral and Expedient groups. It seems to be a minor, rather infrequent feature in the development of the Conforming and Irrational-Conscientious groups. Even among those who come closest to the standard of Rational Altruism, many powerfully selfish impulses exist alternately or side by side with the socialized impulses. The degree of socialization of impulse is modest, indeed, in childhood and grows only gradually during adolescence, even in those cases where it appears strongly enough to be worthy of note. In the most Rational-Altruistic adolescents, however, there is evidence of a continuing openness to experience, a continuing tendency to grow, which makes it seem most likely that they will continue to mature in their basic impulses throughout adult life, just as they look most apt to mature steadily in wisdom.

This phenomenon, if it is as real as it has seemed in this research, deserves and requires a great deal more precise definition and more detailed, systematic study, preferably longitudinal in nature. This kind of maturation, indeed, would seem to provide the only solid, trustworthy foundation for dependably ethical behavior in the absence of social controls or a rigidly dominant superego, neither of which is as effective or desirable a way to maintain morality. As yet, there is very little scientific research, and even a lack of vocabulary, in this important area of healthy development. In part, no doubt, this is because this phenomenon does not occur to any noteworthy degree in the development of severely psychopathic, neurotic, or psychotic people. By nature, it may only occur in very healthily developing people. By this standard, it would not notably occur in more than a minority of the population, and these are the people least likely to come to the attention of most professional people who are interested in the inner dynamics of human nature. As in so many other instances, such reflections point to a great need for much more extensive study of the nature of *healthy* human beings—mentally, morally, socially healthy—and the nature of the developmental process in healthy people. It seems to be qualitatively different, at least in some important respects, from the developmental process in unhealthy people.

CHARACTER AND THE CULTURE

The content and the organization of moral values are largely set by the culture. Not only the specific rules, but the definition of what classes of attitude and action have moral aspects are a large and important part of the behavior pattern we call "culture." To achieve an adequately complete analysis of moral behavior, and its sources, would require a detailed and extensive analysis of the concepts, the symbols, the communication processes, the institutionalized educative processes, and the specific content of the moral code embodied in the culture (Warner, 1959).

The present study did not undertake this kind of analysis in a systematic way. Rather than pretend to "measure" macroscopic culture patterns too intricate to truly measure in the available time, this research focused on the microscopic structure of individual character and on some measurable details of the face-to-face interactions of people in their immediate, intimate groups. These interactions both represent and transmit the culture, of course; but no generalized analysis was made, of the kind a cultural anthropologist would make. Certain aspects of the culture of Prairie City are reported elsewhere

(Warner et al., 1949*a*; Hollingshead, 1949). Separate but relevant data have been reported in West's study of Plainsville (Kardiner, 1945), the Lynds' study of Middletown (Lynd, 1937), and many other scientific and popular reports on the mores of America. Fromm (1955), Reisman (1950), Brinton (1959), Nicolson (1956), and numerous others have put the matter in historical perspective. In this study, that broad tapestry was taken largely as given, discussed in detail in some of the case studies, but subjected to no formal analysis. That part of the story remains to be told in other places, in a somewhat different style. Its omission here does not mean that it was viewed as an unimportant aspect of the problem of human morality, nor as an aspect unsuited to scientific inquiry. Its omission simply followed from the restrictive fact that with normally limited time, staff, and budget, a choice had to be made as to the focus of the research. The present focus was chosen, and thereafter absorbed the available resources.

FAMILY INFLUENCES ON CHARACTER FORMATION

Character, as defined in this study, appears to be predominantly shaped by the intimate, emotionally powerful relationship between child and parents, within the family. Forces outside the family are not negligible nor irrelevant in their *indirect* effect on character formation, but it looks as though these forces operate mainly as they shape and guide parents' behavior, and as they reward or otherwise reinforce child behavior that follows the socially approved parts of the parents' behavior.

Four aspects of family interaction were assessed: mutual trust and approval, consistency of family life, democratic control, and severity of parental punishment. A score was derived for each family, on each of these dimensions. When these were correlated with the child's six personality ratings, it turned out that there were highly significant relationships between family experience and the adolescent's personality. Ego Strength and Moral Stability proved to be closely associated with (probably produced by) Mutual Trust, and Consistency in the family. Superego Strength was most highly related to Consistency. Friendliness was most closely related to familial Trust, and Democracy. The Hostility-Guilt Complex, conversely, was associated with Severity of discipline, a lack of Trust and a lack of Democracy.

The Maturity of Character scale correlated separately to a significant degree with Mutual Trust and with Consistency. Democracy and parental Severity did not correlate directly but proved significant in character formation when considered in combination with the other factors.

Taking the subjects in groups according to dominant character type revealed a clear-cut pattern of family experience for each of the major types. The Amoral adolescents had familial relationships that were chaotically inconsistent and so lacking in mutual trust or affection as to deserve to be called actively rejecting. Several of these families were autocratic and severe in their punishment of the child. The rest were lenient and rather *laissez faire* in their discipline.

Most of the Expedient subjects were reared with a good deal of lenient, indiscriminate freedom by parents who tended to approve of them, but in an unthinking and inconsistent way. One different family pattern was found in this group: a highly consistent, highly severe and autocratic control by mistrustful parents. Consistency without love, or "love" without consistency appear to be equally ineffective ways to produce adequate character.

The most representative Conformers came from consistent, autocratic families where punishment was severe. Some experienced parental trust and love, some did not. The firm, authoritarian consistency of their rearing seems to have stamped them into a permanent mold of conventionalized conformity.

A subgroup of Conformers, who were very weak in ego strength, in superego strength, and (almost inevitably) in moral stability, turned out to have family experiences that closely resembled those of the Amoral children: chaotically inconsistent and mistrustful to the point of rejection. Two such families were autocratic and severe; one was lenient and somewhat *laissez faire* in disciplining the child. These adolescents were almost identical to the Amoral group, too, in their personality patterns. Perhaps they were misclassified as Conformers, although they showed a beaten-down anxiety to comply that set them apart. Perhaps other characteristics than those measured in this study would distinguish them from the Amoral ones. Their family experience, certainly, was very little different in the respects measured here.

The Irrational-Conscientious subjects all came from very severe families which otherwise differed somewhat. One was deeply mistrustful and unaffectionate, autocratic and about average in consistency. Another was much more consistent and about average in trustfulness and democracy of control. Another was very consistent, very autocratic but moderately trustful and approving. The average to high consistency, coupled with extreme severity, seems to be the source of these subjects' strong, rigid superegos that largely dominate their behavior.

With one partly puzzling exception, described in Chapter V, there was a distinctive common pattern of family experience which was unique to the subjects with a major component of Rational Altruism. Their rearing was consistent, strongly trustful and loving ("approval" does not do justice to the evidence in the case materials), highly democratic, and lenient in its punishments. Apparently, to have sincerely purposeful altruism of attitude, it is necessary to experience love and approval from parents who are consistent in their standards and in their guidance, but who do not punish severely. (Severe punishment may almost always be a direct or disguised expression of hostility on the parents' part, and thus may counteract the beneficial effect of parents' more loving moods.) Further, in order to be intelligently and effectively ethical it appears necessary to add to this pattern the element of democracy: the opportunity to experiment in making decisions, and to develop and trade ideas, unafraid, with parents and other family members.

The most democratic of these families, relative to the total population, were by no means "child-centered" in the manner caricatured as "progressive." The parents unmistakably and firmly reserved the right to make final decisions, whenever they felt it necessary. They had an attitude, though, of expecting and encouraging the child to learn to make an increasing number of decisions each year, on more issues, as his judgment became competent on such issues. The only families in the study that approached the "child-centered" model were those of several Expedient subjects.

More important than the finding of some general regularities among the families of the crudely classified character-type groups, is the fact that when each adolescent is considered by himself, his personality and character are linked with the nature of his family experience in an almost inexorably logical way. With only one possible exception in the whole research population, each adolescent is just about the kind of person that would be predicted from a knowledge of the way his parents treated him. Indeed, it seems reasonable to say that, to an almost startling degree, each child learns to feel and act, psychologically and morally, as just the kind of person his father and mother have been in their relationships with him.

Comparing the data in Tables 6 and 9, it appears that disorganized parents breed a disorganized child with weak ego functions. Hostile, rejecting parents create a child who is hostile and rejecting of others.

Undisciplined, uncaring parents create a child who has little incentive to internalize an effective conscience, and who has very poor models from whom to learn any organized moral principles.

Parents who are lazily and uncritically glad to let their child run loose to rear himself betray a childish self-centeredness that is mirrored in a child who is selfishly expedient. He is anxious enough for further approval to make him responsive to social expectations, but his capacities for self-discipline and self-restraint are too weak to generate very dependable moral behavior. Such parental "indulgence" may be obvious or subtle, but it is discernible and its effect is predictably poor character.

Contrariwise, harshly autocratic but consistent parents create a child who is overtly submissive during youth and apt to take over the role of a rigid rule-transmitter upon embarking on parenthood himself. He comes to have an unquestioning conviction that "the rules"—eventually, almost any "respectable" rules—are unquestionably right. Self-restraining authoritarians themselves, such parents rear a child with a repressive, spontaneity-killing superego that overshadows his underdeveloped ego powers. During childhood and youth, the child's overt compliance and submissiveness may seem the opposite of the parents' dominating assertiveness; but even by late adolescence, most such children show a restless urge to break free and set up their own families where *they* can be "boss." This replication of the parental style does not obtain in all cases; but the replication of the authoritarian, conforming value system does seem to apply in all such cases.

The only kind of adolescent who shows a capacity for mature love for others, effectively expressed, is the child of parents who showed *him* maturely unselfish love in a kindly yet reasoned, predictably consistent way. Organized and perceptive in their behavior, these parents create a child who has sturdy, maturing ego powers and a well-organized set of firm, positively phrased moral principles.

The general conclusion seems inescapable that a child's character is the direct product, almost a direct reproduction, of the way his parents treat him. As they are to him, so he is to all others.

There is a complication in the fact that few parents really treat all their children alike. If there are any immaturities, any insistent, unfulfilled wishes or intense, repressed feelings in a parent, these very often emerge in the form of highly polarized attitudes toward different children. One child becomes the embodiment of sternly self-denying achievement drive, whereas another child becomes the object of (self-) indulgent delight, underdisciplined. One child may be the warmly loved apple of the parent's eye while another child becomes the habitual target of parental wrath. The mechanism at work here is projection onto different children of different aspects of the parent's personality and wishes. This occurs minimally, it seems, with psychologically mature, healthy parents. It occurs increasingly with increasingly immature parents. For such reasons, the family ratings in the present study were carefully defined to represent the family *as-the-subject-experienced-it*, not necessarily as other children in the family experienced it. There is thus no necessary paradox in accounting for children of the same biological parents who develop different character structures. It is well, also, to recognize that adults who act one way in a social or work setting may show very different characteristics in the intimate interchanges of family life. Perhaps the maturity of personality and character of one's children is the acid test of one's own completeness of maturity; for maturity is far easier to display outside the family than in it, it seems. The depth of feelings and perhaps the temptations of superior power make parenthood the prime evoker of immaturities in the parent, if any exist. The prediction of the character of an adult's child without intimate knowledge of the parent's total personality, the actual home relationships, or preferably both, can thus be a chancy undertaking. Some of the "best families" turn out moral weaklings or criminals, as is well known. Some outwardly poor-looking families produce some children with fine character, as is equally well known. To use a cliche, appearances can be deceptive.

Data such as the present, do not of course prove whether character is learned, or is somehow genetically inherited, thus transmitting the similarities from generation to generation. The most sensible explanation, however, seems to be that character is learned. Perhaps the best evidence comes from the work of people like Bettelheim (1950), and Redl and Wineman (1952) with children who show almost incredibly malformed personality and character. Like Freud, Rogers (1951), Axline (1947), and many other therapists, they have demonstrated that it is possible to *teach* such children to have greatly different, dramatically improved personalities and characters. It requires exhaustively long, patient, intensive treatment, but the fact that it can be done at all would seem to argue for the learning theory of character development.

Specifically, this pattern of character teaching, from parent to child, is strongly reminiscent of the concepts of Harry Stack Sullivan (1953). The most powerful, most persistent attitudes, perceptual sets, and reaction patterns of adolescents appear to be those they have learned in the first ten years of life through their emotionally paramount, moment-by-moment interactions with their fathers and mothers. "There's no place like home" is sheer, unsentimental fact in a child's world.

This explanation of character formation is similar, too, to the cross-cultural findings of Whiting and Child (1953), "We have strong tentative evidence for the importance, as a variable in socialization, of a distinct process of socialization through identification" (p. 260).

Some of the specific patterns of character formation closely resemble those reported by Sears, Maccoby, and Levin (1957), "Mothers who love and accept their children, and who use love-oriented techniques of discipline rather than material or physical techniques, produce relatively more children with high conscience" (p. 389).

Harlow (1958) has presented not just cross-cultural but cross-species evidence which strongly indicates that satisfactory "mothering" of even infant monkeys, and even if only by a mother surrogate, is essential to the development of the capacity for giving affection, or indeed for any kind of normal social responsiveness thereafter. Modern psychobiology would seem to be vindicating one of Freud's conceptions, about the paramount importance in personality formation of the earliest months and years of life, especially life with mother.

From quite another line of approach, the present study found that in most families the mother has had a more profound, direct influence on the child's character and personality than has the father. This does not seem to be a case of Philip Wylie's "Momism," deliberately fostered by maternal intent. In part, this may be a rather universal effect of the literal absence of the father from home much of the time. As much or more, perhaps, it is due to the cultural assignment of child rearing more and more exclusively to the mother. There appears to be no generally deleterious effects of this matriarchal pattern on the development of character, per se; but there are some visible defects in these adolescents' capacity to understand, empathize with, and develop solid emotional intimacy with members of the opposite sex. They do not look at all different in this from other American adolescents, but perhaps this problem really is endemic in our present culture. Further research on this would seem indicated.

The major determinants of character in the parent-child interaction appear to be love and discipline; but both terms require much more careful definition than they are ordinarily given. Three greatly different kinds of parental attitude were found which ordinarily are lumped together as "love." One kind, shown by the parents of several Expedient children, was a shallow, indiscriminate affection that treated the child more like a pet than like a human individual. Indeed, there was a good deal of manipulatory use of the child to elicit affection and other enjoyable sensations for the parents' pleasure. These parents quite sincerely regarded themselves as unusually affectionate and "loving." Some not-very-hidden actions that one could only call seductive were visible in some of these parents' behavior.

A less seductive, more responsible attitude was the "love" shown by the parents of some of the Conformers. It was deeper, but it was rather blind and distinctly possessive. Much of it was the parent's attraction to qualities which he or she projected onto the child, or with which he or she blindly identified, in the child. It did not reflect a recognition of the child as an individual. On the contrary, the child was treated as a creature to be trained to habituated obedience to parental wishes. Some of these parents talked quite fluently about the child's "individuality," but when it came time to act, there was no mistaking the blind, though strong connectedness between parent and child.

In keeping with a good deal of current literature, the term love might best be reserved for the attitude shown by the parents of the Rational-Altruistic children. They showed a warm affection but at the same time they demonstrated a realistic awareness of what a given child really needed most at a given time. They did not mistake a child's every whim for an essential need. On the other hand, they gave the children many chances to develop their individuality in age-appropriate ways. They did not want their children to be puppylike pets, but to grow and be happy in their own ways. None of them was notably self-sacrificing; yet perhaps the crux of this kind of love lies in the fact that "doing for" the children did not strike these parents as "sacrifice." They simply enjoyed doing it, and they did not mistake their own likes and dislikes for their children's wishes.

Similarly, a remarkable diversity of parental behavior went by the name of "discipline." Anything from a brutal beating, to ineffectual verbal nagging unbacked by action, to rigorously enforced conformity to every parental dictate (and lots of them), to a clearly reasoned, light-handed guidance of a child along a well-explained path, with allowance for non-dangerous, experimental side excursions—all these were called "discipline" by somebody. They were not equal, needless to say, in their effect on character.

Lack of discipline, or inconsistent parental control, produced only poor character. Severe, autocratic discipline, consistently applied, produced adolescents who were passively conforming to direction and convention in an unthinking, unautonomous way.

On the other hand, parental control which was at once consistent, trustful, averse to severe punishment, and giving some limited but growing practice in decision making—this kind of discipline produced mature, *self-disciplined* adolescents.

Mature parental love and rational discipline thus appear to be inter-related, perhaps overlapping phenomena. Such love and such discipline are *both* essential, joint determinants of good character. In fact, in this research, either both these kinds of parental behavior occurred together or neither occurred in any mature form.

CHARACTER AND THE PEER GROUP

The peer group appears to be less an originator than a reinforcer of moral values and behavior patterns developed in the family. Adolescents, as a whole, prove to admire, respect, and reward very much the same moral behavior as do the "respectable" members of adult society: their parents, their teachers, and the social scientists working on the study. In fact, the patterns of family experience prove to be prognostic of adjustment and acceptance in the adolescent society to a highly significant degree. In particular, the degree of trustful, approving treatment a child has received at home is highly correlated with his peer-group reputation for such things as warmth, social participation, social dominance, emotional stability, and especially moral courage.

It seems particularly significant as a reflection of adolescent values, that these same aspects of adolescent reputation were found to correlate significantly with the Maturity of Character scale. To sum up the implications of this in simple form, it appears that these adolescents tend to like and admire age mates in direct proportion to their *moral* maturity, at least to a significant degree. They are sometimes misled for a few years by the surface skillfulness of some Expedient "operators," but by late adolescence that kind of superficial "sophistication" loses its appeal, in most cases, and most of them suffer a drop in reputation and popularity. Although, as the history of the Hollywood star system attests, adults as well as adolescents sometimes evince a permanent "soft spot" for some "charming psychopaths" whose off-screen behavior is often far from charming or moral.

Adolescents sometimes give an athletic star or a precocious social light in their group a higher moral reputation than his behavior warrants. They sometimes rate down quiet or late-maturing boys or girls whose character may be excellent. Since such invalid appraisals occur in adult society, it is hardly surprising to find them among adolescents. The surprising thing, perhaps, is the quite high degree of overall agreement between the adolescent group's assessment of the moral character of its members and the assessment of these same youths both by their teachers and by the research staff. Whatever disagreements occur in the case of some Expedient youths, and a few Conforming ones who win high peer repute, on one thing the research staff and the adolescents were in unanimous agreement. Both gave highest rank to those of Rational-Altruistic character. They were accorded the highest moral reputation. What is more, their peers showed them the highest regard for their warmth, sociability, emotional stability, and in most cases, for their social-leadership abilities.

The qualitative data in the case studies indicated that the peer group provided the area of greatest opportunity for independent thought and rational testing of moral behavior and its consequences. There is a degree of equalitarian democracy among adolescents that does not exist within families, and that does not exist within the schools, churches, or any other adult-run organizations. This opportunity is used to some degree by most adolescents; but to a really major degree only by the Rational-Altruists, it appears. The Expedient, Conforming, and Irrational-Conscientious youth mostly keep repeating and reinforcing their habituated patterns of behavior. They, too, however, tend to broaden their loyalties to much wider groups, beyond the family; and they turn to their peers, more and more, as the arbiters of moral propriety rather than to adults. Nonetheless, their essential lack of autonomy, their dependence on the authority of group convention or rigid rules that were earlier swallowed wholesale, remains evident. They grow up, but they do not necessarily mature in their inner character, even with the democratizing influence of the peer group.

The peer group *could* have been used by wise adults as an aid in helping some of the disturbed and disturbing children, especially in the Amoral group. Age mates are more acceptable models and guides than adults to most adolescents, and especially to the hostile, rebellious ones. This did not occur, in fact, during this group's adolescent years; but it remains as a potentially powerful aid in character education.

COMMUNITY INFLUENCES ON CHARACTER

The direct sources of both the structure and content of character appear overwhelmingly to be the face-to-face relationships the child experiences in the family; and predominantly, the relationship with the parents. Other sources assume major significance only if the parents default from their role. Even siblings seem to have little effect, in most cases, except probably to reflect and reinforce parental values.

At the same time, it must be recognized that the parents draw their values from *their* familial experience, daily reinforced by the culture around them. For almost all parents except those of the Amoral children, the dominant moral code of the community is an ever-present, potent influence. The mores preached and upheld by church, by school, by the law, by the powerful voice of "the neighbors," are a constant reminder for parents to observe, to teach, and to require of their children.

The conventional virtues of Prairie City, *if* intelligently interpreted, and *if* applied as ethical principles rather than rigid rules, would insure highly ethical behavior in most situations. If much of Prairie City's actual behavior falls considerably short of the ideal, it is not because the ideal is not known. It is because irrational, immature emotional drives often overpower the ethical judgment of the majority of people. To help keep this in bounds and to bolster the voice of moral judgment, the institutions and the communication media of Prairie City keep up a constant barrage of both overt and covert exhortation and stories "with a moral." The effect of this could not be measured directly, in the present study, but it is unquestionably important to the maintenance of adequate morality, probably for the majority of people.

The much-debated effect of movies, comic books, and similar media, as far as could be told, did little to change the kind of character structure or specific values any given child had learned from his family experiences. Such media did offer vicarious gratification of otherwise repressed wishes, for some children; but the emphasis should decidedly be put on *vicarious*. Undoubtedly, *if* a child of highly unstable character, given a how-to-do-it manual of sadism in the form of a bad "comic" book, were pressed by immediate circumstances to feel violently hostile, he might find this the last straw that breaks his self-restraint. Such cases have been reported; but none even approaching this were observed in Prairie City. Perhaps all such media have their chief impact on children insofar as they unwittingly betray an officially denied but effectively "leaked" element of sadism, sexual pornography, and the like, among adults in our society. Ironically, the front pages of the average "family" newspaper are daily crowded with lovingly detailed though properly "horrified" tales of murder, sexual assault or perversity, sadistic torture, civic corruption, individual dishonesty, drunken irresponsibility, and other assorted moral sicknesses. An observant child could scarcely be blamed—or contradicted!—for concluding that the majority of adults find such immoralities fascinatingly attractive, even if they are supposed to be put down in one's own behavior. The typical comic books and movies available in Prairie City during the study were bland fare compared to most urban newspapers, such as the ones regularly read in Prairie City.

None of these media, in any case, showed much effect on the children's values in the sense that they altered or contravened values learned earlier from the parents. As with adults (Warner and Henry, 1948), these media seemed to have their greatest effect as "safety valves" for the fantasied solution of problems that remained insoluble in fact. In most instances, they actually had the added function of repeating and reinforcing the conventional morals of middle class America.

Social class as a factor in character formation proved to have largely random effects, except possibly at the lower-lower level. The sample is both too small to generalize from in this way, and too skewed away from the general class distribution in the U.S. to be representative. There may have been a disproportionately high percentage of children of poor character in the lower-lower class. Otherwise, all types and qualities of character were found at all levels up to the upper-middle class. More recent evidence from the Kansas City Studies of Adult Life (Peck, 1959) indicate that there probably are some significant class differences in personality factors related to character, improving with increasing status; but that is outside the bounds of the present study.

Church affiliation, per se, and even church attendance was no guarantee of well-developed character; but that is scarcely unreasonable. It is true that most of the children with good character came from actively religious families. Even though there are exceptions, this indicates a favorable influence of religious activity in many cases.

The Prairie City schools seem less to shape character than to crystallize and throw into sharper contrast the punishments for undesirable behavior and the rewards for proper behavior. Even more extremely, the schools tend to discriminate widely, and rather persistently, between those individual children who show inadequate character and those who show good character. While the children's behavior undoubtedly justifies many of these distinctions, it was surprising to find how highly character maturity was correlated with school grades. It may have been an accident of sampling, in that the children of best character tended to have higher intelligence, in this sample. This might be more than would hold true in larger samples; although in view of the requirement for rational thought at the highest levels of the character scale, this might not necessarily be an artifact. In any event, it is amply evident that school teachers reward Rational-Altruistic, Irrational-Conscientious, and effective Conforming behavior and (literally) mark down children of Expedient and Amoral character.

It appears, in summary, that the basic qualities of personality structure and of interpersonal attitude are predominantly created by the child's experiences with his parents. This is not to say that no other people, during his lifetime, could affect or change his character development. It is *possible* to exercise a curative (or destructive) influence even after the child has borne the impress of his family experience for years. What the present data say—as is suggested by other studies, such as those cited in Chapter VIII—is that such later influences seldom are intensively enough and personally enough exerted, in this typical American community, to make any noteworthy change in the character of its children, for good or for ill. This is not to say that change *cannot* occur. It is simply to say that it *does not* occur, in most cases. Judging from the literature, from the public press, and from professional experience, it appears that this observation probably holds true for most American communities.

Influence on character formation from outside the family could come from the peer group; from adult-directed institutions such as the school, the church, and youth groups; from media such as radio, television, movies, books, magazines, and comic books; and from the example of adults in the community.

The informal peer society tends to reproduce the moral atmosphere set up by the parents. It is a vital testing and training ground in the details and the specific skills which implement those adult-derived sociomoral values; but, by itself, it seems seldom to alter those values. Indeed, this fact should be reassuring to worried parents who are not sure "what Johnny is doing" with his childhood and adolescent friends. The likelihood seems strong that if his parents have given him a reasonably loving, emotionally secure, consistently but not severely disciplined upbringing, Johnny is behaving as his parents would want, whether or not they are around. What is more, the kinds of friends he is most likely to pick will themselves tend strongly to approve him for behavior his parents would think good, and to punish him in very effective ways if he violates the code which the children share with their parents.

Conversely, of course, a hostile, unhappy youth is apt to pick, and be picked by, acquaintances who themselves have questionable morality. However, if these "birds of a feather flock together"—as they usually do—nine times out of ten it is because they had family experiences which were similar. The similarity may not be an obvious one. It may cut across social lines. However, it is apt to be a deep similarity in the emotional climate of the families: loving or hostile, democratic or autocratic, consistent or chaotic. Hence, moral behavior and friendship cliques in adolescence are alike reflections of the way Johnny's parents have reared him.

This is probably most true in a stable community like Prairie City, where there is omnipresent pressure from a commonly held code of ethics to encourage and enforce the maintenance of morality; even if, in some cases, it is not much more than an outward show of conformity.

Except possibly for the Rational-Altruistic children, who come from families with a "built-in" kind of mature, rational morality, it appears that the existence and active influence of a stable community moral code is an essential and potent influence on the children's learning of adequate morality. This influence is partly direct, via institutional teaching and individual adult example. Mostly, though, it seems to exert its influence indirectly by maintaining active social pressure on the parents to behave, and to rear their children, according to generally approved moral standards.

The importance of the moral milieu might be more evident in circumstances where there is a breakdown or reversal in the moral code of the community, such as happened in Germany when the Nazis seized power. One can only speculate, of course, but if we project the various character types into such a setting, perhaps something like the following would happen.

The Amoral people would continue to behave antisocially, undoubtedly; indeed, some of them might rise to power under a Nazi-like regime. The Expedient people would probably adapt readily to the new code of sanctioned cruelty to scapegoat groups, of disloyalty to parents or friends who held out against the new regime, and similar, immoral parts of the new "moral" code. Perhaps some of the Conformers might hold to their old ethical code; but if community leaders fostered the new code or demonstrated "blindness" to its immoral aspects, probably many of the Conforming group would soon accept the new way of life. Besides the Rational-Altruists, the Irrational-Conscientious group would be most likely to hold their old values, out of firm conviction if not out of enlightened, rational morality. Of all the types, though, only the Rational-Altruistic people would seem certain to actively oppose the new immorality, and to make an effort to ameliorate the plight of victims of the new ideology.

Such speculation goes far beyond the scope of our present data, of course. It does seem to touch on a crucial issue, nonetheless, relevant to the talked-of breakdown in moral controls in the large modern metropolis, as well as to broader social breakdowns in time of wide-spread societal disruptions. Much more extensive research would clearly be needed, to determine what effects such broad upheavals have on moral behavior, and to what degree they affect the morality of people with the different kinds of character structure.

The chief purpose in even introducing this issue is to make it clear that while this quantitative study of the *direct, immediate* forces in character formation showed relatively little influence from extrafamily sources, there was substantial qualitative evidence for the importance of a stable community moral code. The fact that it was not, perhaps could not, be quantitatively represented is not to say that the indirect influence of the church, the school, the government, the press, and other media is inconsequential or dispensable as a force for the maintenance of sound morality in both children and adults.

Some implications
and prospects

CHARACTER EDUCATION

Since character structure, and even specific, detailed ways of acting, appear largely learned by emulation of the attitudes and behavior of those few people who are emotionally essential to the growing child, it seems evident that moral preaching which is not backed by consonant behavior is largely a waste of time and effort. Indeed, it may often be worse than useless, if it teaches children to say one thing and do another, either through mental confusion or through conscious hypocrisy.

Children do as we do, not as we say. Their character tends to be an accurate reflection of the way their parents act toward them, no matter what contrary pretenses some parents try to present to society. There is no way for parents to explain away or to give away this responsibility; it is a simple, inexorable fact.

School and church personnel should not expect to work many "miracles" of character reformation—and certainly not by dealing with children en masse. It is possible to salvage even severely maldeveloped children, but it takes extremely intensive, long, personalized treatment. In a real sense, an adult who hopes to improve a child with immature character can only expect to do it by taking on the security-giving functions as well as the guiding functions ordinarily performed by the parents. To do this effectively requires unusual wisdom, unusual personal maturity, and sometimes almost superhuman patience. It also requires a strong, personal *caring about* the child, albeit of an unsentimental kind. In short, in teaching character as in teaching intellectual knowledge, no one can teach what he does not know. In character education, this includes much more than intellectual knowledge, alone; it requires that the "teacher" of character personally possess genuinely mature feelings, attitudes, and ethical behavior, or no success can be expected.

This fact can be uncomfortable, even embarrassing, for teachers, church workers, and social workers, just as it can be for many parents. Good intentions or wishful thinking will regularly be exposed as empty, unworkable pretenses, if they are not backed by genuinely good character on the adult's part. It is easy to see: children will not improve under anything but genuinely understanding, truly ethical treatment. Of course, even the best of treatment cannot have much effect in many practical situations where destructive influences far outweigh the limited ameliorative efforts. No simple formula can justly be applied to assess the "genuine maturity" of the "teacher's" character or his character-education methods. A careful, objective study of the undertaking, over numerous cases, is the only fair basis for appraisal.

Another clear implication is that parents cannot reasonably expect to turn over very much of the character training of their children to other people, whether in school, church, or youth organizations. By the very nature of character formation, no one other than parents can ordinarily have one-tenth of their influence; and if the parents are continually reinforcing their own influence by their day-to-day treatment of the child, other adults can have little expectation of outweighing the parents' influence. Dramatic exceptions to this rule are known, to be sure; but they are dramatic precisely because they are so rare and so hard to achieve. No such exceptions occurred in the Prairie City group, during the study.

If extrafamilial institutions are to foster good character in any degree, an examination of workable and unworkable methods of character training may be long overdue. The first and most crucial question for schools and churches, especially, is what *type* of character they want to achieve in the children they serve.   Doubtless most schools and many churches would agree on the Rational-Altruistic pattern as the most desirable one; yet this is not what many teachers and many preachers really foster.   Many of these, and perhaps most adults, treat children in a manner that, at best, fosters Conforming or Irrational-Conscientious character.   This must be what such adults really *want*, too, judging by their persistent behavior.   They may not be aware of what they are doing; although many are perfectly well aware.   Some of them might be shocked if they could see the later, less happy consequences of what they do with children; but most of them have never learned to put such facts together and take the long-term view.

It is temptingly easy and insidiously gratifying to "mold" children, or to "whip them into line" by exercising one's superior status and authority as an adult.   It is often personally inconvenient to allow children time to debate alternatives, and it may be personally frustrating if their choice contradicts one's own preferences.   If there is any selfish, sensitive "pride" at stake, it is very hard for most adults to refrain from controlling children in an autocratic manner.   Then, too, like any dictatorship, it looks "more efficient"—to the dictator, at least.   However, the effect on character is to arrest the development of rational judgment and to create such resentments as prevent the growth of genuinely altruistic impulses.   For thousands of years, the long-term effects have been ignored and sacrificed to short-term adult advantages, most of the time.   Probably it is no accident that there are relatively few people who are, or ever will become, psychologically and ethically mature.

Specifically, it appears that if character is really as important to us Americans as we say it is, then there should be rigorous, alert recruiting and selection of teachers and other youth leaders on grounds of *maturity of personality and character*.   Their own natures are going to influence children much more than any verbal information they convey.   At present, often nothing but lip service is given to this idea, or "character" is defined as the absence of certain conventional "vices" such as smoking, drinking, or consorting with the opposite sex after working hours.   It might cost a little more money to appraise personality and character, as well as school grades, with the best assessment methods now available; but if we are not willing to spend a little money on character training, we cannot reasonably complain of the expensive consequences in organized crime, civic corruption, penal costs, relief costs for deserted children, and the like.

Some of the ancient methods of character development, or reformation, are grossly illogical and destructive in their effects. The whole idea of penal "treatment" flies in the face of human nature. Severe punishment breeds hatred; hatred breeds either antisocial behavior or a grudging, resentful conformity to convention which has no real ethical intent in it. It is a matter of record that the "punishment" theory of crime prevention simply does not work; and it worked no better with Prairie City children.

The *only* method that works in favor of mature, dependable character is first to give people—whether children or adults—reason to feel an *incentive* to behave ethically; and then guide them intelligently, patiently, and with growing freedom to make and test their own decisions. This way works; *none* of the other methods of child rearing, or of reformation, breeds more than unthinking, rigid compliance at best—and many methods breed savagely hostile revenge behavior.

In school, church, or scout work it is fatal to the development of mature character to enjoin behavior solely on the weight of authority, or because "it says so, here." Even in church, when the issues are ones of human ethics, or interpersonal morality, it is always possible to explain the *reasons* for ethical principles in terms of entirely observable cause and effect. Truly, convention and tradition usually persist because they continue to have functional value; but they are too notoriously susceptible to blind, foolish, or immorally expedient application to be used literally and uncritically. *Even if tradition is right*, to teach children to obey it simply *because* it is tradition, or an "authority," is to cripple their capacity to become truly mature and intelligently self-governing in their moral behavior.

This is a familiar idea in American educational philosophy, but it is honored far more in theory than in practice. Most of the recent critics of our schools, quite ignorant of the facts, have assumed that John Dewey's observation about this same fact of human learning has "taken over our schools." In fact, the average American school is run in a highly, if sometimes subtly, authoritarian manner, from principal down to pupils. Perhaps because it requires much more mental effort of the teacher to encourage pupils to think for themselves, and yet guide them sensibly, the pragmatic approach to facts, ideas, and skills has never yet succeeded in displacing rote memorization of assigned subjects, in an assigned order, for unstated, unquestionable reasons, in most schoolrooms. Even most college students, for example, show panic unless given specific assignments, at a pace and in an order decided by the instructor. Their most recurrent question is not "what do I need to know" but, quite literally, "what do *you* want us to do?" Twelve or fourteen years of conditioning in the public schools have made anxiously dependent conformers of them, even though they actively resent being "told," at the very same time.

Certainly, this is not to advocate "child-centered" schools. Only a few silly people ever achieved that caricature of education. Children need to be guarded from their own ignorance and restrained when their self-restraint is yet inadequate. They need to be taught a great many more facts about human nature than are presently part of any public school curriculum. Perhaps as much as they are taught how to reason about numbers and words, they need explicit teaching of that most complex of all intellectual skills: understanding human behavior. Nobody learns to reason intelligently and objectively about their own or other's behavior merely by "growing up." The knowledge and the skills required are far harder to achieve than those required even in mathematics or the natural sciences. The subject matter is much more complex, by nature, and objectivity is far harder to achieve. Only such skill suffices, however, when one is called upon to act ethically in our complex, changing human society.

In these many ways, adults who purport to develop children's characters must be "ahead" of them: in knowledge and in judgment, as well as in maturity of attitude. Yet a great difference remains between the purposes, attitudes, and actions of the adult who wants to control children for authoritarian purposes, and the adult who judiciously measures out control mixed with gradually increasing freedom, in a deliberate effort to help and to allow children to grow up into mature, wisely self-guiding people, whose moral behavior is internally motivated and foresightedly intelligent. *If* this kind of maturity of character is what we want for our children, the ways to get there may be hard but they are clearly marked.

The chief obstacle to progress in this direction probably lies in a different fact: a good many Americans either do not really want children to become independently responsible beings, or they will not tolerate the frequent frustrations of selfish impulse which are required to treat a child in an ethical manner. This is true of a good many teachers and preachers, just as it is true of many millions of American parents. The millennium in human ethics will not come by wishing; it is a far-distant goal that must be arduously worked for, on a personal scale, day to day. Whether increasing knowledge of what builds character will increase the actual motivation of enough people to bring about really significant improvement is a question only the future can answer.

As for a positive program for schools to use in developing good character, Cronbach (1954) has summarized it succinctly:

First, the school builds emotional readiness by making the pupil secure. Second, it reinforces his desire "to be good." Third, it teaches him to see ethical conflicts as problems to be solved intelligently. Then, while this growth is continuing, the school provides opportunities to deal with such conflicts and gain experience in solving them. Any school program presents some occasions for ethical learning. The fifth aspect of building character is to translate the experiences into conscious generalizations. The verbal summary may be brief and simple with young children; with older ones there will be occasions for discussing complex dilemmas. Out of this thinking they will create properly complex philosophies of life.

Special thought needs to be given to covering the range of important problems. For example, a program where students always interact with the teacher, having no occasion to work in groups, will confront them with none of the problems of settlement of disputes or delegation of responsibility. Therefore extracurricular activities and student government are of special value because they introduce problems the school subjects do not.

A person who learns to reason about his conduct and learns what he holds most dear can adapt his character to new strains and new uncertainties. We would disagree with James's view that character is "set like plaster at thirty." Character begins to set almost at the time of birth. Some of the underlying fears and pleasures are firmly set before school entrance, and the later structure of character does grow around this framework. But a person can acquire new understandings and attachment to new ideals throughout his life, if at his core he likes the world, feels that the world likes him, and believes in the power of his own intelligence.

SOME SPECULATIONS ABOUT CHARACTER IN MODERN SOCIETY

There is no shortage of commentators on modern society, and its ethics. John Dewey (1948), Sigmund Freud (1953), Carl Jung (1933), Anatol Rapaport (1954), Erich Fromm (1955), David Reisman (1954), William H. Whyte (1956)—these and hundreds more have pointed, often with alarm, at the all too irrational, at least semidestructive modes of conduct which distinguish "civilized" man. There have been both delightful discussions and angry arguments over whether the ethical situation is getting better or worse. Most of the time the plaint seems to be that things are getting worse, although there is a lack of objective facts about representative samples of even the previous generation. Apart from speculation based on literary research, there probably is no way to make a valid test of such assertions.

We have quite enough problems inherited from that past, however, to occupy our attention and our grave concern. Now that we have learned how to sterilize the earth of all life with almost ludicrous ease, it looks as though the rapid development of a much more ethical habit of conduct would have a newly urgent survival value. This, of course, has the disadvantage of being a merely rational argument. It has been daily repeated for at least four thousand years of recorded history, to little avail, because the great majority of people never have been effectively capable of rational behavior. What is more, they have not really *wanted* to practice the golden rule. However shortsighted it may be shown to be, most men throughout history have acted on the mistaken assumption that selfish grasping for security or money or power or prestige, without an overnice concern for anyone else, would bring them happiness.

Barring new evidence to the contrary, the safest guess appears to be that there are just about as many knaves today as there have been in earlier generations, although the pressures for social control of behavior have become greatly strengthened in some Western societies, at least some of the time. There seems no way to prove it with any precision of figures, but it seems likely that there are probably no more and no fewer blindly conforming "sheep" among modern men than among our grandsires. Public education has done an amazing job of making a larger proportion of men somewhat more informed. But education can scarcely be blamed if it has not worked the miracle of transforming the motives and attitudes required if people are to *reason* with that information, and *act* more rationally than their forebears.

Moreover, until just a few years ago, the idea was rarely given any serious consideration that *learning to reason about human behavior* is as feasible and certainly just as important as learning to reason about numbers, machinery, or dollars. A little of it is now taught to some college students. A rare high school includes a little of it, although under risk of attack for "wasting time," as though this were not the most arduous of intellectual skills to master.

The idea of giving any formal place to the phenomena and laws of human behavior in the curricula of elementary schools as yet seems to strike most people as bizarre. If only because of tradition-bred familiarity, it seems more "sensible" to spend years studying the geography of foreign lands, the construction of sentences, and the mysteries of the multiplication table, rather than spend some time each day teaching children how to understand and how to reason about the behavior of themselves and others. They *must* cope with human behavior, all day, every day. They care passionately about making sense of it. Yet we leave them mystified, confused, and ignorantly inept at it.

This seems to be one aspect of character training in which public education could easily do a much better job, if we simply made the decision to start doing it.   There is no need to give it any fancy titles. It would probably be better not to call it "psychology," if that would risk surrounding it with a spurious air of polysyllabic mystery.   The content, however, would be some of the facts and principles of human behavior which are now only obtainable in college psychology courses, and not always there.   This is not at all a brand new idea.   Ojemann (1956) and people in a few other places have been getting such training under way at the elementary school level, in appropriate ways and amounts.   An appropriate book for children at this level is represented by Phillips and DeVault's *Psychology*.   Little spread of this practice is yet noticeable, however.

Perhaps one of the chief obstacles is simple but profound ignorance. At a guess, 90 per cent of the American population probably has no knowledge that human behavior has as lawful, if complex, regularities and predictabilities as the phenomena of arithmetic, or house construction, or budget balancing.   Indeed, a great many educated people who are aware that such lawfulness exists, seem to be deathly afraid that, given any liberty, psychologists and other social scientists would misuse their knowledge to brainwash or regiment everybody else.   Such tirades and misquotations as mar some of the pages of Whyte's "The Organization Man" make it appear that the scholars of human behavior are either weak or unscrupulous enough to want to turn humanity (all the rest, that is) into zombies, or at least into stupidly complacent sheep.

It may be hoped that this study will indicate, if nothing else, that social scientists are no more enamored of the "organization man" than is Mr. Whyte; that the most desirable kind of character structure they can conceive of is that of the free-thinking individual.   "Adjustment," by this standard, is a far cry from herd conformity.   Indeed, the Rational-Altruist not infrequently finds himself differing with the popular rules, when the rules would do violence to ethical principle in the acutal circumstances at issue.

Apart from this misunderstanding, there is a great deal of agreement between the findings of this study and the observations of Whyte, Reisman, Remmers (1957), and others.   The unthinking conformer, who often does not *want* to think for himself, probably makes up the largest single group of Americans, and perhaps of humanity everywhere.   A good many people not only question the good sense or the ethics of "most people" (a view that is hard to argue with, on some factual grounds); they unwittingly propose to make the situation worse by having all decisions made by an elite of presumably wiser people. This would, of course, progressively worsen the ignorance, compliant passivity, and blind helplessness of the mass, until the day arrived when their outraged human potentialities exploded into violent—and probably blindly useless—revolution.

The crux of the problem is this: each generation tends to perpetuate its strengths and weaknesses of character, largely unchanged. A sizable minority of adults are heavily Amoral or Expedient in character. They treat their children this way and their children strongly tend to turn out just about like their parents. This fraction of the population provides our criminals, probably most of our psychotics, and a great many more who are never institutionalized but who lead drifting, fear-ridden, or hate-ridden lives. From among this group come the actively evil members of society: the viciously hate-filled sadists, the conscienceless exploiters, the men and women whose terrible greed corrupts our law-guarding forces in community after community. Such people are sick, with crippled, distorted perceptions of life. But they are also dangerous and must be firmly controlled lest they destroy the rest of us, or corrupt our morals into "getting ours, too," or turn us so revengefully against them that we descend to their level of immorality in fighting them.

A much larger segment of the adult population, perhaps over 50%, are largely Conforming or Irrational-Conscientious in their character dynamics. These people, often with a sense of high moral righteousness, treat their children in such a way that their children turn out to be either passively compliant sheep in search of a shepherd, or self-entrapped slaves to unalterable dogma. Most such people lead blameless lives, by and large. At least, their sins are apt to be ones of omission, rather than commission. Always a few of the slaves to "conscience" must be guarded against, however, for some of the greatest martyr-makers of history have been of this breed, not to mention a number of the martyrs. There are few things more terrible in their irresistible force than a self-righteous monomaniac who puts an abstract "principle" above real human considerations. A killing joylessness is the least penalty of such rule; and savage cruelty in the name of "righteousness" has all too often been known.

In the Prairie City sample, only about a quarter of the subjects showed any significant degree of rationality and genuinely ethical intent in their behavior. Detailed proof is lacking, certainly, but this seems like a rather generous estimate to make even for the American population as a whole. Probably, about this proportion has existed for many generations back; and this much, at least, can reasonably be expected to occur among the future children of these Rational-Altruistic people. It is heartening to note that the total group of adolescents in the study largely chose these people to be their leaders. Allowing for human frailties, it does look as though a preponderance of our national leadership in the adult world, too, is probably recruited from this group. (The record of chronic corruption in almost every large city does not seem, on the face of it, to speak quite as well for local leadership in the political area.)

Nonetheless, some events in the past decade of our national affairs reinforce the warning that eternal vigilance is the price of liberty—and of an ethical society. There are dangerously immoral individuals and even small groups in our society, as in every society. They have threatened to erode our capacity for human loyalty by playing on our fears and by sowing distrust and hate. They have used sophistry and dishonesty in the name of "truth." There seems to be a basic health and intuitive good sense in the mass of Americans which eventually rejects such threats to our ethical integrity as a society.

Some signs of erosion may be discerned, however; and another kind of danger has overtaken our national behavior. This is the rapid spread of a curtailment of our freedom to know and to decide on issues vital to our survival, our freedom, and our American Constitution.

This appears to be done in all sincerity, many times, in an excessive fear for "security." In other places it is done in an honest but essentially antirational, antidemocratic insistence that "father knows best." This wall of secrecy is all too easily misused by the vain to hide their mistakes, and by the unscrupulous to hide their dishonesty. The greatest danger, however, is the corrosion this implants and fosters in the very heart of our American way of life. It substitutes question denying, arbitrary decision by the few for open, public debate by the many. It may be true that most people, as yet, are neither very wise nor very rational; but it is no way to make us more rational—one of the keystone tenets of our republic—to deny us facts and thus to deny us the "freedom to choose" (Murphy, 1958).

The life of the United States, to date, is a brief second in the sweep of human history. We founded it in a passionate belief in the need and the right of all men to become able to reason for themselves, to speak for themselves, and to choose for themselves. We founded America, too, in the profound conviction that *every* man has an inalienable right to "life, liberty, and the pursuit of happiness." A respect for individual integrity, a belief in the necessity of ethical justice for all, these are what we first said we meant by "Americanism."

As the final pages of this chapter will remark, there does seem to be some partial but growing evidence that these ethical imperatives are not just one among many, equally plausible ways of life. Instead, they seem more and more to represent some basic, crucial facts about human nature, if it is to be maximally developed and gratified. Whiting and Child make a similar observation, from the most relevant kind of cross-cultural data, "The confirmation (of our predictions) has been sufficient, we feel, to suggest strongly that there are some principles of personality development which hold true for mankind in general and not just for Western culture" (1953, p. 305).

The brief time we have tried to give life to these principles, here in America, is no assurance, however, that we or our children will surely sustain them. Slow moral erosion can insensibly corrupt any society. Indeed, that may be the lesson of most human history, by a statistical count of vanished societies. Nonetheless, we were the first society in history to center our very form of government consciously and explicitly around these ethical principles. If most of us, still, are not often able to act by these principles in our daily lives, it is not in the spirit of our society to give up because we cannot yet wholly succeed.

We are often accused by members of other societies of being incurably naive in our conviction of the perfectability of man. We are viewed, and often rightly so, as uncritical devotees to the myth of inevitable "progress." Progress certainly does not look inevitable from any long-range view of human history. One major nuclear war, for example, could easily put a permanent end to the complex technology we have built so rapidly. Even more gravely, we can see that only yesterday a centuries-old fabric of decent humaneness which had been painfully evolved in Europe, disintegrated into the most terrible orgy of sadism and mass murder the world has ever seen. A wholly new word had to be invented to describe it: genocide. The fabric there has been rewoven; but who can guarantee it will withstand future eruptions of the evil urges within some men?

Yet, a persistent hopefulness is better than a hopeless resignation. We Americans may be brash and naive; but progress can only come by continuous trying. In the present international world of science, with its central faith in that same rational ethic that inspired our American constitution, it is just beginning to be conceivable that we may be able to collect some unarguable facts about human nature which will once and for all demonstrate that the ethical principles held by the Rational Altruist are not just a nice sentiment, but a set of directions for living based on the deepest, most inexorable demands of human nature. If it could be shown that consequences *everybody* desires can *only* be achieved by following these principles, then there would be at least a chance of removing many ethical issues from the realm of argument based on subjective opinion. There is, to be sure, a powerful resistance to this solution built into the very nature of us human beings; but if there is a *chance* that we could become more rational, it might be well to try it.

TOWARD A SCIENTIFIC BASIS FOR ETHICS

The results of the Prairie City Study, together with a great many other observations by many students of human behavior, suggest the following line of logic:

1. The ethical principles described for the Rational-Altruist seem to be universally desired by sane people everywhere; *in other people*, at the very least. Who would say that he prefers to live with people who cannot be reasoned with? Who would really want to live with people who are hostile or coldly indifferent, rather than friendly? Who would choose to live with people who are undependably erratic and unpredictably unstable? Who would choose to live with unscrupulous, untrustworthy people on whom one dare not turn his back? No one in his right mind, anywhere, seriously wants this kind of life. (True, the question of "sanity" needs defining, but substantial agreement on that seems reachable in most instances.)

If man is by nature a social being, as seems an inescapable fact, then he cannot stand to be rejected or continually frustrated by other people. No matter what disappointed cynics may protest, or psychopaths try to overlook, it is an observable fact that friendly, considerate treatment by others is essential to the genuine happiness of every human being.

2. There is only one sure way to obtain genuinely friendly treatment from others, for any length of time. That is to treat them in the most friendly, considerate way possible. (Note Tables 7 and 9.)

3. There is only one sure way to breed a reasonable attitude and effective reasoning powers in other people. That is to be consistently and patiently reasonable with them, giving them progressively greater opportunities to try out their own decisions. (Table 7.)

4. The only way to beget dependably stable, sincerely motivated, ethical behavior from others is to treat them in exactly this way. (See Tables 7 and 9.)

It must be recognized that the one-to-one relationship that so largely holds true for the parent behavior–child reaction equation does not necessarily obtain, in the short haul, in contacts between adults.

Deeply fixed preconceptions and reactions can keep some adults from responding ethically to ethical treatment. Even among adults, however, only a very small minority is this recalcitrant in attitude. The process of generating rational, independent reasoning may be much slower, in an adult who never yet developed it. Even with very recalcitrant youths or adults, though, these principles apply in the long run. That is not to say that they always will succeed; but *only* these methods ever *do* succeed.

5. Intelligent self-interest thus dictates, if nothing else does, that the basic human needs outlined in 1 can only be fulfilled successfully by the methods described in 2, 3, and 4. In other words, the most practical rule for real personal happiness is the golden rule.

6. A proviso must be added: what one *thinks* he wants is not always what he really wants most of all. Deep, accurate self-knowledge seems to be essential for the most effective ethical behavior, and for one's own happiness.

7. The great majority of people, youths as well as adults, recognize, admire, and seek to emulate these principles. (Note Tables 5, 13–15.)

In the Prairie City group, for example, the Rational-Altruistic children, who showed the highest degree of genuinely spontaneous, rational morality, were without exception admired and sought as friends and leaders.

8. If this set of observations can be verified systematically, with much larger samples, especially in different societies, we would be approaching the place where we could say as a matter of inarguable fact, not just opinion, that certain universal needs of human beings make the qualities of the Rational-Altruistic pattern the ones which create the deepest satisfaction for everyone. These ethical needs of humans would then be seen to be as innate and matter-of-fact as the need for food and water.

To be realistic, however, requires facing a grave obstacle on the road to mature character for everyone. At present, we act toward others largely as we were acted toward by our parents, not necessarily as we *ought* to act. To alter this age-old pattern of character transmission requires a great deal more self-restraint and a great deal more effortful, thoughtful foresight than most of us have learned or find really welcome. What most of us have to cope with in ourselves is a welter of childishly intense desires, often curbed only by sheer force, mixed with some milder, more satiable urges. We are a turmoil of unorganized, undirected, highly irrational thoughts, out of which we wrest an acceptably logical idea only now and then. We are a mass of preconceptions, only reluctantly willing or able to entertain a really new, different outlook. We have loving impulses but we also have a great many aggressively selfish desires; and we experience more intense resentments and hatreds than polite society is ever supposed to admit. This is not a pretty picture, and the terms are somewhat vague, but it seems to be generally accepted as true by most students of human nature. (Indeed, it is no little achievement to be able to view this picture without turning away either in disgust or in despair.)

This present state in which most of us find ourselves is itself the chief obstacle to be overcome. The problem of achieving ethical rationality is this: the aligning and harmonizing of violently powerful emotional forces is a necessary *precondition* for rational thought.

This harmonizing can *only* be accomplished through the intrinsically non-rational (not *anti*rational) means of harmonious experiences with other people who have great emotional importance for oneself. (Cf. Sullivan, 1953.) The intellect can be used to select and arrange such an experience, but the crux of the interaction is an emotional experience which has little to do with rational thought.

Thus we come to the paradox that points to a solution: not *either* intellect *or* emotion, but intellect *and* emotion are essential components of rationality.

As a corollary, non-rational symbols and action systems, such as are a nexial part of most religions, may be essential to all of us, if we are to experience the *sensations* and *emotions* that represent and embody the ethical interaction. A rational theory of ethics would therefore have to provide for these kinds of non-rational experiences, while at the same time providing for regular, rational examination of the course and the moral consequences of one's actions. Perhaps this is one of the reasons why ethics and religion have always been intertwined.

This is decidedly not a recommendation for a surrender to irrational experience. It may point, however, to the serious dangers inherent in an arid intellectualism which is sterilized of affective experience: if we do not provide, indeed urge, participation in interactional experiences which provide expression and fulfillment for these non-rational aspects of our natures, they can build up growing tension and frustration until they explosively erupt and overwhelm our reason. The recurrent group insanity of our cyclical wars may be an illustration of this phenomenon, on a massive scale.

Whatever the pertinent facts that can be discovered through much more extensive study, both hope and conservative expectation are in order. There seems to be a chance, at least, to establish ethical principles on a basis of objective observation of behavioral causes and effects, not just on exhortation or an appeal to our "better nature." Since some kind of moral order is a universal characteristic of human societies (Warner, 1959, pp. 486–487), the more objectively tested and clarified the principles, the better, it would seem.

Appendix

OVERVIEW OF THE RESEARCH

The design of the Prairie City character research was not fully and neatly crystallized before it was begun. When the overall project was inaugurated in Prairie City in 1942, to study all the 120 children of the 1933 group, there were no well-developed methods for studying moral character in terms of everyday behavior; nor was it foreseen how methods of "depth" psychology could be used to get at the inner sources of moral behavior. During the middle 1940's, Havighurst, Taba, and others developed or applied many tests of attitude and ability, as well as measures for determining moral reputation among adults and peers. It was on such methods that the study was based which was reported in *Adolescent Character and Personality*.

In 1945, the special group of thirty-four children was picked for intensive developmental study, adding interviewing and projective testing to the battery of measurements already in annual use. Actually, while the thirty-four children thus selected were evenly distributed along the full range of moral reputation in the 1933 group, the 1946 study which occasioned the gathering of the new kinds of data was not primarily focused on character development. Rather, it was focused on the relationship between the children's personalities and the social roles they performed in their peer group. Thus, the question of character was held in abeyance until data were gathered through the children's sixteenth year.

It was in 1948 that Havighurst proposed a new study of moral character, to be conducted by a research team along the lines of the earlier studies. Peck proposed the psychological hypotheses and the character typology which were thereafter used; but it required the work of the entire staff for six months before the conceptual framework, the conference procedure, and the rating definitions were judged ready to be applied to the case data. It was halfway through this preparatory period that Havighurst proposed the use of ratings, in order to provide quantitative measures of whatever variables were to be studied. This six months, incidentally, seems to have been a reasonably successful compromise between freezing an inadequate design too early and dragging out the formulation of the research plan beyond the point of diminishing returns. The steps, briefly outlined, were as follows:

1. *Collection of Data.* A wide variety of observational, interview, rating, and test data had been gathered, over a period of eight years. There was no particular theoretical emphasis which dictated the selection of data, beyond the general proposition that evidence on personality and attitudes would probably be useful, as well as evidence about overt behavior and reputation.

2. *Development of a Conceptual Scheme for Describing Character.* When the time came to make a systematic study of the dynamics and development of character, it was evident that an organized set of hypotheses was needed. Only in this way could one choose and define the variables to be measured. Therefore, a theory was postulated which consisted of five "developmental" levels of character (character types), and those specific capacities, attitudes, and personality characteristics which seemed most relevant to moral behavior.

3. *Qualitative and Quantitative Assessment of Each Individual Subject.* A research team was formed, of ten people trained in the fields of psychology and sociology. For the first six months of its work, the team refined the conceptual framework for analyzing the cases. Variables were defined in detail, and clarified. (This process continued through the next several months, as well, until all variables were judged acceptably clear and distinct.) In the year that followed, the research group made an intensive study of one case a week. This required, for each case, independent analyses of the various kinds of data, collation of these results into an organized case study, and ratings on some seventy-odd variables by the research-team members.

The results of the clinical-conference procedure were a comprehensive case study on each subject and a set of ratings for each subject on variables which represented the hypotheses about the components of character.

4. *Analysis of the Quantitative Measurements.* The ratings on the personality traits were intercorrelated and factor-analyzed, and individual personality patterns were derived. The relationships between personality and moral character were then analyzed.

In terms of methodology, this was not a purely inductive process, the discovering of regularities in the data with no use of prior hypotheses. Rather, it was a deductive-inductive approach. It postulated certain hypotheses about the psychological components of moral character, then tested these against the case data to see if the theory fitted the observed facts. Where significant patterns were found, taking all cases together, this was interpreted as general substantiation of the theory. Beyond this, where unforeseen relationships emerged, it might be said that the new patterns represented inductive discoveries.

This mixed kind of approach does not possess the purity or the rigorous precision of the classic experimental method. However, it may be inescapable in an exploratory approach to the extremely complex phenomena of human conduct. Perhaps, by their nature, the important aspects of moral conduct can never be validly measured in a laboratory setting, or with the simplified logic of the controlled experiment. In this research, at any rate, it seemed appropriate to study the subjects' behavior in everyday life, whatever limits this might impose on precision of measurement.

5. *Comparison of the Character Data with Independent Measures of Family and Peer-Group Experience.* When psychological patterns associated with moral character had been found, these patterns were compared statistically with measures of family characteristics and peer interaction. From such comparisons it was possible to determine some significant facts about the kind and degree of influence of family experience and age-mate relations on the formation of character in this research population.

This, in brief, was the plan of the research. It is also the plan of this Appendix, which presents the details of the research procedure.

THE DATA

Interviews

Date	Interviewer	Assignment
1943–44	A	Interviewed children of T group
1945–46	B	Interviewed mothers of children of lower socioeconomic status
1946–47	C	Interviewed mothers of T group
1947–48	D	Interviewed special cases of T group
1949	E	Interviewed special cases of T group
1950	F	Interviewed special cases of T group

Projective techniques

Date	Instrument
December, 1943	Emotional Response Test
March, 1944	Moral Ideology Test
April, 1944	Essay, "The Person I Would Like to Be Like"
April, 1944	Essay, "If I Were Sixteen"
April, 1945	Essay, "The Person I Would Like to Be Like"
January–February, 1946	Essay, "The Person I Would Like to Be Like"
May, 1946	Rorschach Test
December, 1946–January, 1947	Thematic Apperception Test
February, 1947	Essay, "The Person I Would Like to Be Like"
February, 1947	Essay, "If I Were Sixteen"
November, 1947–May, 1948	Rorschach Test
May, 1948	Sentence Completion Test
May, 1949	Rorschach Test
May, 1949	Essay, "The Person I Would Like to Be Like"
May, 1949	Thematic Apperception Test
April, 1950	Essay, "A Good Kind of Person in Our Community Is"
May, 1950	Essay, "The Person I Would Like to Be Like"
May, 1950	Essay, "When I'm Twenty-Two"
May–June, 1950	Thematic Apperception Test

Sociometrics

The sociometric instruments can be divided into two classifications: (1) sociometrics the children completed themselves, and (2) another kind of sociometric in which various adults in the community gave their ratings and opinions of adolescents. The general term used for this latter is the Adult Ratings, covered below.

The sociometric instruments completed by the children were as follows:

Date	Instrument
December, 1943	Guess Who—Peers (5 character traits)
April, 1944	Portrait Guess Who—Who's Who in Our Group (5 character traits)
March, 1944	Volberding Guess Who Test (adjustment traits)
February, 1946	Guess Who We Are (7 character traits)
February, 1946	Portrait Guess Who (7 character traits)
December, 1946	Tryon and Henry Guess Who (personality traits)
April, 1947	Tryon Sociometric Guess Who (social traits)
April, 1949	Tryon Sociometric Guess Who (social traits)
May, 1949	Portrait Guess Who (7 character traits)
April, 1950	Guess Who We Are (7 character traits)

Mental tests and achievement records

The results of the following tests were available for the study:[*]

Date	Instrument
1943–44	Stanford-Binet, Form L
1943–44	Iowa Silent Reading Test, Elementary Form Am
1943–44	Progressive Achievement Test (Primary Battery; only the Reading Test was used, for retarded children who were not ready for the Iowa Test)
1943–44	Minnesota Paper Form Board, Form AA
1943–44	Minnesota Mechanical Assembly Test
1943–44	Chicago Girls Assembly Test

[*] Reports of the testing of this age group have been published in: Robert J. Havighurst, and Leota Long Janke, "Relations between Ability and Social Status in a Midwestern Community. I. Ten-Year-Old Children," *The Journal of Educational Psychology*, 35, No. 6 (Sept. 1944), 357–368; Robert J. Havighurst and Fay H. Breese, "Relation between Ability and Social Status in a Midwestern Community. III. Primary Mental Abilities," *ibid.*, 38 (Apr. 1947), 241–247.

1943–44	Cornell-Coxe Performance Test
1943–44	Porteus Maze, Vineland Revision
1943–44	Chicago Interest Inventory, Junior Form (modeled after the PEA, 8,2b and 8,2c tests, designed by Mrs. Janke and Mr. Havighurst)
1943–44	Goodenough Draw-a-Man Test (Administered by Eleanor Volberding to fifth graders in March, 1944)
1943–44	Otis Self-Administering Intelligence Test
May, 1946	Metropolitan Achievement Tests
December, 1946	Thurstone Primary Mental Ability Tests
April, 1947	Stanford-Binet, Form M
April, 1947	Wechsler-Bellevue Performance Section (Replacing the Cornell-Coxe, which was given in 1943–44)
April, 1947	Iowa Silent Reading, Advanced Test, Form Am
April, 1947	Minnesota Mechanical Assembly (Modified) boys only

All of these instruments were administered by field workers from the University of Chicago, with two exceptions—the Otis Self-Administering Intelligence Test, given in the ninth grade, and the Metropolitan Achievement Tests, given annually in the elementary schools in town. For these two tests, the results were recorded from the local school records.

Questionnaires

Date	Instrument
1943–44	Chicago Interest Inventory
May, 1944	California Personality Test (Elementary Form)
May, 1943	Adult Guess Who Test
May, 1944	Pintner Aspects of Personality
June, 1944	Family Relations Questionnaire
1946–47	Chicago Interest Inventory (Revised)
January, 1947	Student Beliefs Test
May, 1947	Family Relations Questionnaire (Revised)
May, 1947	How Bad Is It?
May, 1947	How Would You Feel?
January, 1948	Student Beliefs Test (Revised)
March, 1948	How Would You Feel?
February, 1946	California Personality Test (Secondary Form)
May, 1948	PEA Interest Inventory 8,2b
May, 1949	Adult Guess Who Test

Reputation ratings by adults

Date	Instrument
November, 1943	Confidential Check List of Personal Characteristics
March, 1944	Portrait Matching (Character Sketches)
March, 1946	Confidential Check List of Personal Characteristics
1946–47	Portrait Matching (Character Sketches)
1947	Teachers' Behavior Rating Scale
1949	Portrait Matching (Character Sketches)
1950	Confidential Check List of Personal Characteristics

Physical data

A series of some seventeen measurements over the ten years were taken on each subject by a trained anthropometrist. Height and weight data were given systematic treatment. Rates of growth converted into inches per year and pounds per year were calculated from every measurement of the special group. Average and standard deviations of actual height and weight were computed from data on the entire age sample in Prairie City. From these, as well as descriptive reports, an estimate was made of where each subject was with respect to accomplishment of the adolescent growth cycle.

A summary report on the physical status and previous growth and health history was made to the clinical conference on each subject. This report ordinarily contained a description of the person as obtained from observers, interviewers, and/or test personnel. Pertinent data on health were obtained from interviews with subjects and their parents and from the school records.

The subjects' sizes (height and weight) with respect to the means and SD's of the group were then given. An estimate of date of menarche for the girls was obtained jointly from analyses of the anthropometric materials and from a special set of interviews on this point. The boys' voice changes, stature, beard growth, etc., were noted by the same interviewer. These, in conjunction with anthropometric data, allowed an estimate of how far each boy had progressed into physical maturity.

These data, of course, have little direct bearing on moral character. But often they were of use in clarifying ideas about how much energy a person could expend, why one was listless and another not, and so on. Occasionally it was difficult to understand why a particular person was rejected by peers until data on maturity, probable nutritional status, appearance, cleanliness, strength and skills, irritability due to fatigue, and other factors in the physical picture, were taken into account. This proved not to have an immediate bearing on estimates of moral character; but it was vital to a complete understanding of the personalities and reputations of the subjects.

Relative value of the instruments

In view of the large amount of time and effort spent in administering, scoring, and analyzing the above instruments it seems pertinent to inquire into their value. For the purposes of our study, structured self-report questionnaires were not so useful as the interviews and projective tests. And those which proved most useful, the Student Beliefs and the Interest Inventory, were interpreted not merely in terms of specific scores, but in terms of their contributions to a pattern of inferences that resulted from the use of these tests along with interviews and sociometric and projective techniques. While the range of scores on an adjustment questionnaire such as the California Personality Test showed a very rough relationship to the distribution of adjustment in the group, as judged by all other data, in any single case the scores by themselves turned out to be nearly as often misleading or inaccurate as they were accurate evidence.

We did think that it might be interesting to know what picture a child wanted to present, as in the case of a poorly adjusted child who gave a high score on an adjustment questionnaire. However, it proved much more efficient to look into the interview and projective material to find the child's concept of himself and also the picture he wanted to present to the world. The questionnaires themselves turned out to be rather unreliable as indicators of the child's attitudes and adjustment; thus not much could be done with them.

A procedure which appeared fruitful and gave some reliable results in relation to the known facts of the child's life was a study of individual items. This was used on the California Personality Test in its three forms, and the two forms of the Family Relations Questionnaire. This, too, was a laborious procedure, with results that might have been obtained much more efficiently from other sources. For example, it seemed possible to get a much better picture of the actual family relations through a brief inspection of the interview material than could be done reliably from the California Personality Test and the Family Relations Questionnaire. Similarly, we found it more rewarding to look to the projectives for the child's attitudes toward his home than to take the rather meager—and often questionable—

inferences that were possible from the yes-no responses in the questionnaires.

While a question may be raised concerning the validity of our inferences from such sources as the projectives and the interviews, and we do not have a completely independent criterion against which to test these inferences, yet the judgment of the clinical conference, after attempting to use all the various instruments and procedures described above, was that the projectives and interviews contributed more, and in a more unequivocal fashion, than did the sociometrics; and far more than the questionnaires.

It would be unfair to conclude this section without pointing out that questionnaire forms have some value and some real advantages for studying large groups. Our experience merely suggests that when one wants to understand and assess a particular individual, instruments of the questionnaire type are not worth a great investment of time and energy, especially when the results they give are compared with those of the free-response techniques, exemplified by the projective tests and interviews.

THE CASE-STUDY OUTLINE
AND THE CONFERENCE PROCEDURE

The case-study method was selected as the best way of assembling and integrating all the information we had gathered about each child. Furthermore, our previous experience with the method had led us to believe that it permitted far deeper insights into the complex picture of inner feelings and motives which a human being shows than did the alternative method of devising so-called "objective" tests of moral and personal characteristics and intercorrelating the results of such tests for the group as a whole. We felt it would be possible to untangle the cause-result web in each individual case much better by the case-study method, and in the end arrive at more insightful explanations of moral behavior for the whole group.

Perhaps the simplest way to convey the framework we developed for analyzing the cases, and the procedure we followed, is to present the "Conference Outline" in the form in which we used it.

Committee on Human Development
Prairie City Moral-Character Study

Part One
Conference Procedure

There are three stages in the conference: analysis of instruments, presentation and interpretation of data, and summary evaluation of the case.

I. *Analysis of Instruments*
The analysis of instruments precedes the meeting of the conference. It is the responsibility of different staff members, each working alone on one or more instruments. Each individual works "blind," using only the information from the instrument or instruments for which he is responsible. He writes a report according to the outline given in Part Two (see below), making whatever contributions his data permit. This report is circulated to all other members of the staff before the conference.
The following instruments are used as the bases of these reports:
A. *Interviews*
   1. Interviews by Field Workers with the Subject, with the Parents, and with Other People in the Community.
B. *Subject's Reports: Check Lists*
   2. California Personality Test
   3. Conscience Questionnaire
   4. Family Relations Questionnaire
   5. Interest Inventory
   6. Student Beliefs Test
C. *Subject's Reports: Free Response*
   7. Emotional Response Test
   8. Moral Ideology Test
D. *Projective Techniques*
   9. Thematic Apperception Test
   10. Rorschach Test
   11. Essays
   12. Sentence Completion Test
E. *Ratings*
   13. Reputation Ratings by adults and age mates
   14. Behavior Ratings by teachers
F. *Sociometric Techniques*

      15. Character Guess Who, Who's Who in Our Group, Social Personality Guess Who, etc.

      16. Friendship Sociograms

  G. *Observation Reports*

  Recent data contributed by field worker at the time of the conference

  H. *Other Instruments*

  After the moral-character study has been completed for the group of special cases, it may be desirable to investigate relationships with such other measures as intelligence and achievement tests, physical-status indices, etc.

II. *Organization and Presentation of Data*

      (First Conference)

  A. *Preparation*

  Preceding the conference, reports are prepared summarizing, in the areas stated below, all of the information from instruments analyzed in Stage I. A staff member is assigned the responsibility of preparing a report on a given area for each case. The areas for which these reports are prepared are:

  1. Moral Behavior

    a. Reputation

    b. Behavioral anecdotes

  2. Motivation Patterns

    a. Perceptual pattern and goal system

    b. Attitudes in major relationships

    c. Behavioral self and self concept

  3. Developmental Pattern

    a. Family history

    b. Sources of moral-value code

  A description of these areas is given in Part Two (see below).

  B. *Presentation*

  These reports, summarizing the data by areas, are presented in the conference. Following each individual presentation, the conference staff critically evaluates the report for accuracy and coverage of facts as well as appropriateness of interrelationships deduced from the data. The gist of the conference discussion on each point is recorded by the secretary of the conference, and forms an important part of the final report.

  C. *Case Report No. 1*

  Following this conference, a document is prepared summarizing the presentations made above, together with the critical discussion that took place in the First Conference meeting.

This is distributed to each staff member to be used as a basis for the next step.

The report may also be used as a basis for comparisons between cases.

III. *The Rating Procedure*

Following the First Case Conference, each staff member rates the subject on the characteristics listed in the Trait-Rating List. The completed set of ratings is turned in to the secretary of the conference no later than three days before the Second Case Conference. The secretary compiles all the ratings and presents them for discussion and/or revision at the Second Case Conference.

IV. *Summary Evaluation*

(Second Conference)

A. *Preparation*

Preceding the Second Conference, staff members prepare reports summarizing and evaluating the data presented in the First Conference. These reports are prepared according to the framework stated in Part Three (see below). The main areas of the framework are:

1. Adequacy of Moral Behavior
   a. Effect on others
      (1) Honesty
      (2) Loyalty
      (3) Responsibility
      (4) Respect for Integrity of Others
      (5) Kindness
      (6) Moral Courage
      (7) Self-Control
   b. Effect on self

B. *Presentation*

As the report prepared by the assigned staff member is presented for each area, it is followed by critical discussion. The emphasis in this conference is on the combined effect of motivation pattern and conformity to social expectations, and on evaluation of the resultant pattern of moral behavior.

C. *Discussion of Ratings*

Following the reports, the ratings on the case are presented to the conference in tabular form, by the secretary. All trait ratings which show a range of more than four points on the decile scale (e.g., 2–6), as the various members have rated the case, are discussed. An effort is made to arrive at a consensus within a four-point range (e.g., 2–5), by referring to case data, interpreting them, and discussing the reasons for the difference of opinion among the staff members. If no consensus can be reached, the ratings are considered final. Other trait ratings on which there is agreement within a four-point spread may also be discussed at the desire of conference members. Unless changed, they stand as final ratings.

D. *Case Report No. 2*

Following the Second Conference, a report is prepared which summarizes both the presentations made above and the critical discussion. All final averaged ratings on the Trait List variables are included in the report.

The report is organized to permit comparisons between cases.

Part Two
Outline for Case Analysis

This framework is used in two of the steps set forth in the Procedure (Part I, above):

I. Analysis of Instruments

II. Organization and Presentation of Data (during the First Conference)

The various areas of the framework are described below:

I. *Moral Behavior*
   A. *Moral Reputation*
      1. With *Adults* in Community
         a. Honesty
         b. Responsibility
         c. Loyalty
         d. Respect for Integrity of Others
         e. Kindness
         f. Moral Courage
         g. Self-Control
      2. With *Peers*
         a. through g., as above
      3. With *Family*
         a. through g.
   B. *Behavioral Anecdotes*
      This section provides for anecdotal data, from current or past

observations. Its purpose is to provide evidence on overt behavior for each of the seven traits: e.g., Honesty, Responsibility, etc.

1. Family Traits
   a. through g.
2. Peer Traits
   a. through g.
3. Community
   a. through g.

II. *Motivation Patterns*

A. *Perceptual Pattern and Goal System*

1. Perception of External Reality (Intellective Functioning)
   a. Mental ability
   b. Creativity and imagination
2. Perception of Other People
   a. Observation: accuracy of perception of how people behave
   b. Insight: accuracy of recognition of what other people want, and how they feel
   c. Empathy: degree of ability to "feel with" others' emotions, aims, and behavior from their point of view
3. Locus of Concern: on a continuum from complete self-centeredness or selfishness to altruism, i.e., concern for others that equals or exceeds concern for self
4. Nature of Major Goals
   This section has no predetermined, fixed set of categories. Each case will show its own specific pattern. The main object here is to locate the "drives" or "needs" which are most strongly emphasized. Some possibilities are: affection, dominance, succorance, achievement, self-expression, superiority, orderliness, sensual pleasure, etc. (See Murray's list, and Henry's "self" statements on T cases.)
5. Attitudes in Major Relationships: does subject feel friendly or hostile; seek emotional closeness or distance; is he personally interested or impersonally detached; does he feel he should act morally, and in what respects?
   a. Subject toward parents; by extension, toward any authority figure, or authority in general
   b. Subject toward peers
      (1) Same-sex
      (2) Cross-sex
   c. Subject toward community (people and institutions)

d. Subject toward persons subordinate to him in age, social status, authority status, etc.

B. *Behavioral Self and Self Concept*

1. Nature of Impulse Control
   a. Emotional maturity: a continuum from undifferentiated emotionally responsiveness (cf. Pure C on Rorschach) to situationally appropriate, differentiated responsiveness (cf. FC on Rorschach)
   b. Awareness of impulse life (i.e., emotional reactions, and action tendencies)
   c. Control system
      (1) Degree of identity or dissociation of inner impulses and outer behavior
      (2) Nature of control: repressive (unconscious) conscious-suppressive, conscious-adaptive, etc.
      (3) Strength and stability of control—consistency
      (4) Rigidity or flexibility of control
2. Resultant Behavior (Covert and Overt)
   a. Methods of maintaining balanced control: conformity through identity of personal motives with aims externally defined as "moral," deferred actions, displacement into substitute outlet, rationalization of behavior, projection, etc.
   b. Constricted or spontaneous behavior?
   c. Anxiety or feeling of comfort?
   d. Rationality of behavior: is it based on accurate judgment; does subject realistically assign responsibility for acts; does he attribute his own motives and acts to others, via projective defense mechanisms?
   e. Direction of punishment in moral sphere: toward self, toward other people, against concrete acts, against special groups of people, etc.
3. Consistency of Value System Shown in Subject's Behavior: are subject's moral principles stably generalized or situationally determined; are they integrated or compartmentalized?
4. Subject's Rationale
   a. Public values
   b. Private values
      These include "What I Am" and "What I'd Like to Be." The ego-ideal concept may enter here, though it also

includes *unconscious* values as well as those the subject can state.

    c. Concept of self as a moral being

        (1) Concept of self as a good or bad person: described specifically for each of the seven traits

        (2) Feelings of righteousness or guilt, assurance or anxiety, or tension

        (3) Sense of identity or dissociation of outer behavior and inner impulse

        (4) Rationale for own behavior; ways of justifying it to self

    5. Congruence of Behavioral Self with Self Concept

III. *Developmental Pattern*

    A. *Family History*

        1. Nature of Family Members

        These descriptions are made in the same terms as used for the subject, in sections I and II above.

        a. Mother

        b. Father

        c. Other significant figures

        2. Formative Experiences (Descriptive and Inferential)

        3. Extrafamilial Figures and Experiences

    B. *Sources of Moral-Value Code*

        1. Degree and Nature of Identifications

        a. With mother

        b. With father

        c. With other people

        2. Source of Final Ideal System and Pattern of Moral Behavior

Part Three
Summary Evaluation of Moral Character

This framework is used for the Second Conference. It follows the two stages above:

    I. Analysis of Instruments

    II. Organization and Presentation of Data (during the First Conference)

The purpose of this framework is to permit combined analysis of personal motives and response to social expectations, in order to state both *how* and *why* the subject behaves morally or otherwise.

I. *Adequacy of Moral Behavior*
   A. *Effect on Others*
      Assess functioning in each of the following moral-trait areas, discuss subject's behavior at home, with peers, in school, and in the community.
      1. Honesty
      2. Loyalty
      3. Responsibility
      4. Respect for Integrity of Others
      5. Kindness
      6. Moral Courage
      7. Self-Control
   B. *Effect on self*
      Assess degree of calmness or anxiety concerning moral behavior; degree of spontaneity or "forced" control; degree of satisfaction or dissatisfaction with own behavior, and its results; etc. (cf. Part Two, IIB, above).

THE TRAIT DEFINITIONS USED IN THE STUDY

In order to permit measurement, definitions of certain personality "traits" were constructed. The definitions were intended to help us rate each adolescent on each trait, along a ten-point scale. We therefore tried to define at least the high, middle, and low points on the scales, to indicate the kind of attitudes or behavior the scales were intended to represent. These details may be found in an earlier report (Peck, 1951). Here are the general trait definitions:

   1. *Potential Intelligence:* highest level of intellectual functioning shown, whether in the highest of a series of standard test scores or in performance on projective tests. It may be only a "flash" of better ability to assess and integrate data, if potential is higher than usual functioning. Expressed in IQ points.
   2. *Functioning Intelligence:* usual level of intelligence the subject shows in his daily behavior. This may be represented by standard test scores, as on the Binet, or it may be better represented by the estimate of functioning intelligence from the projectives. This criterion emphasizes behavior in typical, practical problem situations, not just performance in school subjects. Expressed in IQ points.

3. *Observation of Human Behavior:* degree to which subject accurately recognizes the usual behavior patterns of the people around him, can predict what they are likely to do, and how they are likely to react to a given action. In essence, this involves the perception of the social patterns around him.

4. *Insight:* capacity to understand other people's reasons for acting as they do. This is primarily a matter of intellectual apprehension and comprehension of people's motives: it may or may not involve sympathy for others' aims and intentions. That is not relevant here. Further, this should not be confused with "insight" into one's own nature, feelings, and motives. It refers only to the understanding of other people.

5. *Empathy:* capacity for "feeling with" other people; for experiencing, at least to some extent, the same emotions they are experiencing at the moment.

6. *Locus of Concern:* a continuum from egocentric to sociocentric concern; the degree to which the subject cares what happens to other people in the same way that he cares what happens to himself.

7. *Attitude toward Father:*
   a. Outer acceptance of father's authority, rules, and directives
   b. Positive Feeling
   c. Negative Feeling

8. *Attitude toward Mother:*
   a. Outer acceptance of her rules and directives
   b. Positive Feeling
   c. Negative Feeling

9. *Attitude toward Peers*
   a. *Same-sex*
      (1) Feeling tone in overt behavior with peers
      (2) Inner feeling (evidence from projective materials and, by inference, from quality of peer interaction)
   b. *Opposite-sex*
      (1) Feeling tone in overt behavior with peers
      (2) Inner feeling

10. *Attitude toward Younger Persons:* (this variable was omitted from final analyses).

11. *Range of Moral Horizon:* the social distance from himself to which the person extends his sense of obligation to be-

have morally, and does behave so. The range extends from self, through kin and neighbors, to townspeople or age group, to ethnic or racial group, to the larger society of America, and potentially to all people everywhere.

12. *Maturity of Emotional Reactivity:* this concerns not overt behavior, necessarily, but the nature of the subject's immediate, internal emotional reaction to reality stimuli, ranging from reactions which are appropriate in kind and degree to the nature of the precipitating situation, to reactions which are either excessively violent or inappropriately emotionless.

13. *Impulse-Behavior Identity:* degree to which outer behavior is a direct expression of spontaneous inner impulse.

14. *Heteronomy-Autonomy:* degree to which behavior is self-initiated and guided by internal, personal standards of judgment, a measure of independent ego control of behavior. A continuum from "morality by constraint" (where the constraint may be external pressures or uncriticized, irrationally introjected sanctions) to "morality of consent," where the social purpose of moral rules is understood, where they are freely chosen by the subject as a system for participation in society, and where he feels free to modify or alter the letter of the rules in order to carry out their underlying purpose.

For rating, emphasize the "constraint-consent" factors. The resultant morality of the subject's behavior is irrelevant, since a person may ignore many of the usual moral rules and still be thoroughly ego directed in all he does. We are concerned here with the degree of autonomy, not with positive morality, as such.

It seems that a psychopath, ruled by "id" forces we might say, would not rate high here, since "autonomy" is defined as the operation of an independent, rational ego, which organizes and channels both id and superego directives without being dominated by them.

15. (a) *Assignment of Responsibility:* degree to which subject realistically assigns responsibility for behavior of self and others.

(b) *Rationality of Behavior:* the realism of judgment the person shows, and the effectiveness with which he chooses his actions to achieve his ends. This does not necessarily imply that a person who is highly rational in moral situations has highly moral goals. This variable includes, but is not limited to, the area of moral behavior.

16. (*a*) *Consistency of Personal Values:* this describes the degree of internal consistency of subject's major life aims and values, and the consistency with which they are expressed in action. Morality is irrelevant here. The question is the degree of congruity or contradiction within the system. It is basically a measure of "personality integration," as that term is usually used. It reveals the presence or degree of inner conflict (among drives).

(*b*) *Consistency of Positive Morality:* this describes the degree to which the subject's overt behavior is consistent with the code of positive morality defined in this research. (Cf. the moral "traits.") For example, to what degree is the subject consistent through time on any given trait, and consistent from one trait to another? The motivation for such behavior is irrelevant here.

17. *Guilt about Outer Behavior:* amount of guilt felt, on the average, about subject's overt behavior. "Guilt" is here defined as a private feeling that what one does is bad, whether or not it is socially observed or disapproved. It is a self-evaluation, divorced from any reaction of other people. It is distinct from "shame," which is here defined as that embarrassment or discomfort felt when some other person becomes aware of an act that is *socially* defined as "bad.

"Guilt" is further distinguished from "anxiety" by its primarily self-referent quality. "Anxiety" about deprivation or punishment by others as a consequence of one's actions, need contain no self-criticism or self-censure. Therefore, a person may be highly anxious about how others will weigh the morality of his actions without feeling any "guilt," i.e., without censuring himself because his act is "bad" by his own, personal standards. Guilt is presumed to be the result of conflict between ego acts and superego directives.

18. *Guilt about Inner Impulse:* amount of guilt felt, on the average, about inner impulses to act, regardless of whether or not they are expressed in action. Either impulse or guilt reaction may be included or excluded from the subject's conscious awareness, without affecting this rating.

19. *Accuracy of Self-Perception:* degree to which conscious or preconscious self-perception is congruent with the be-

havioral self. (This is not restricted to "behavior" in the overt sense. See the conference outline, IIB, 1, 2, 3.) This includes, but is not limited to, the moral-character area. It involves any discrepancy between how one acts and how he thinks he acts, between actual abilities and projected goals, etc.

20A.–20H. *Sources of the Subject's Morality System:* a moral-value system is the total set of rules for behaving; beliefs about prohibited or approved actions. The life goals of the person, insofar as they have moral connotations, are a relevant part of this system. Empirically, the family seems the most likely source of such a system; other sources—people, groups, institutions, vicariously experienced figures—are given weight as the subject shows divergences from or distinct differences within the parentally installed system, for which divergences or differences a definite source can be ascertained. When we observe that the child is different in moral code from the parent in certain respects, we then ask why and from where this feature is derived.

A total of ten points is distributed among the possible sources. For example, mother and father may receive all ten, and all the others zero; or points may be assigned to several sources, according to their inferred significance.

For 20A–D the same process of reasoning obtains as for the ratings on 20W–Z. That is, the moral code of the subject is compared with that of each of the parents, or parent surrogates, and older siblings. If there is marked correspondence between the beliefs of the child and those of the mother, for example, a large share of the total of ten points may be assigned to 20A. The rest are assigned to the one, two, or more other sources according to the proportional weight they seem to have contributed to the formation of the child's moral code. In another case, it may be the father, a parent surrogate, or an older sibling whose morality system the child's most resembles. The chief criterion is the degree of similarity between the child's code and the source figure's code. It is pure inference to assume a causal relationship here, but there may be direct evidence in the projectives to support such an inference. When the child reveals feelings of admiring and wanting to emulate an older family figure, and where he shows many of the same values as this figure, in his actual behavior, the validity of the inference would seem to be considerably strengthened.

For sources 20E–H, the above-mentioned process of reasoning-by-exclusion obtains. That is, when the child's moral code differs from the family code in some respect, weight is given to an extrafamily source. Conversely, when the child accepts and acts by a code that is encouraged by the church or school, for example, but where this code has also been presented and encouraged by the parents, from the child's earliest years, it is assumed that the chief source is the parents. The institution, in this example, may act to reinforce home training, but the fact of a code having been established prior to the child's contact with groups outside the family suggests that the family, and not the external institutions, is the primary source of his code.

A. *Mother*

B. *Father*

C. *Parent Surrogates*

D. *Siblings*

E. *Peers:* weight is given here when the subject has internalized elements of the peer code which are not mere extensions of the parental code. Peers are those people in the milieu at or near his age and with whom he characteristically interacts.

For example, a child from a strict, conservative, ethnic-church-centered family, who rejects precepts of loyalty restricted to same-sect group, in favor of loyalty to the entire peer group, or who accepts a peer belief in the value of standing up for a moral principle, whether or not his parents approve it, would receive some weight on peers as a source of his moral code.

F. *Institutions:* weight is given here when it appears that the child has adopted some values from school, church, community organizations, etc., which were not presented or instilled by the family. For example, a child from a disorganized, chaotic lower class home which offers no incentive for responsible, hard work or concern about consistent honesty who nevertheless works hard in school, and adopts its code of honesty, loyalty, etc., would probably receive several points on 20F. In the usual case, where it appears that the institutions serve to uphold and continue a code that the family has already fostered in the child, fewer points will probably be assigned.

G. *Figures Vicariously Experienced:* this pertains to the heroes and heroines ("good" or "bad") whom the child encounters via movies, radio (TV in urban areas but not in Prairie City), newspapers, books, and comic books. The same criterion applies here, of giving one or more points when the child's code contains values derived from this source that were not previously presented by the family.

H. *Other Adult Figures:* this category includes adults in the community, or older relatives who have not acted in a parental role. There must be positive evidence that one or more of such persons has contributed to the child's code, in contrast to the parentally taught values, or in areas where the family did not present any moral guides and values.

20W.–20Z. *Primary Identification:* this assumes that every child acquires important ways of behaving and feeling by taking them over directly from some emotionally significant person in his life experience. Who is the subject most like in his feelings, attitudes, and action tendencies? It is further assumed that the most basic identifications occur in the first years of life and are formed through experiences with parents or parent surrogates (which may include much older siblings). The range of possible models is restricted to the family complex. The best evidence is a comparison of the subject's behavioral and emotional patterns with the patterns shown by each of the possible models. A second source of evidence is feelings and attitudes which the subject reveals on projectives, where he is responding to stimuli that call up deep, spontaneous associations he makes to each of the parentlike figures.

W. *The Mother:* the actual mother is the only one considered here as an identification figure.

X. *The Father:* same is true.

Y. *Other Parent Surrogates:* the continued presence of another adult over a period of time is necessary—it takes care of cases where stepmother or stepfather, grandparent, aunt, uncle, etc., has acted *in loco parentis* during formative years and has had noticeable influence.

Z. *Siblings:* These are important as parent surrogates for

possible identification when there is a considerable gap in age (more than five years), and/or the parental figures are absent through death, occupational separation, etc., or where continuous care of the child is delegated to such an older sib.

In rating identification a total of ten points is to be distributed among the four possible categories. It is possible to assign 10, 0, 0, 0; 9, 1, 0, 0, etc., 8, 2, 0, 0; 8, 1, 1, 0, etc. When 10 is given to one person, complete, unequivocal identification is with that one person. Since our culture acts to press persons toward identification with the same-sex parent, it should be a rare occurrence to find a case in which 10 is given the opposite-sex parent. It might occur in cases where complete separation of parents and child had taken place. In the more general case, with both parents present, it will be infrequent that the residues of very early identifications with both of the parents will not remain in some force. *In the absence of data to the contrary,* it can be assumed that expressions of feelings of sensuous pleasure, emotional passivity, and submissiveness are attributable to identification with the female figure. Conversely, *other data absent,* feelings of being active, aggressive, dominative, and "masculine" are derived from identification with the male figure. *However,* care must be taken to observe the characteristics of the parent in question; e.g., a passive, weak father might be, through identification, the source of such feelings in a boy, and masculine traits in a girl might stem from identification with an active, dominative mother.

The distribution of the ten points is a rough estimate of the proportions of the life patterns of the subject following from his respective identifications. This is an extremely complex judgment which can never be more than a crude estimate, lacking, as we do, a continuous depth analysis of the child and parents. It is not assumed that these ratings can account for the whole of the life pattern but rather that they assess that part generated by direct identification.

Character-type rating definitions

For each of the motivation types constituting this profile a rating is made which represents a comparison by the rater of the amount and quality of that motivation in the individual being rated, against the conference estimate of the norm for the American adolescent population as given in the following definitions. The definitions below have been set up so as to place this norm at 5.5; in other words, the average in amount and quality of a given motivation is expressed by a rating of 5.5, and we should expect to find 10 per cent of the American adolescent population at each of the extremes defined below.

For the purpose of this study a motivation is defined as a tendency (behaviorally effective desire) involving significant relations with other people. By "behaviorally effective" is meant a desire for which there is either overt evidence that the desire has been expressed in behavior, or conviction on the part of the rater that it might be so expressed at some time, in view of the life circumstances the individual can be expected to meet. The latter part of the definition is an endeavor to include in the rating, motivations which are not quite strong enough to have resulted in actual overt expression to date, but which are strong enough to manifest themselves in behavior under stress or as a result of the various changes in the particular individual which time may bring. The above definition meets the two criteria of significance for this study: (1) that a factor must relate to actual or potential behavior, (2) that a factor must relate to *moral* behavior.

For the following definitions of *high* rating for each motivation type, eight variables have been used as common to all motivations, together with any other factors which seem significant for a given motivation. These variables are mostly represented in the trait list. However, they are presented here as guides to qualitative assessment of the subject. In making the type rating do not refer mechanically to your trait ratings even if some of the traits are applicable here. These variables are *hypothesized* as relevant. They may or may not be, in the final analysis. They have been used for the *high* rating only, since (*a*) this is the pattern which defines the type most clearly, and (*b*) these variables are not necessarily significant when discussing *middle* or *low* ratings. These variables follow, in the order in which they are used in each definition: Impulse Control, Conformity to Group Patterns, Overt Conformity to Moral Code (this is the conference-defined moral code, not necessarily that of the community), Range of Moral Horizon, Locus of Concern, Internalization of Principle, Capacity for Guilt and/or Shame (note that this does not refer to amount of guilt or shame actually experienced, but to ability or capacity to feel them), Rationality.

21. *Amoral:* having the tendency to secure immediate gratification of impulse without regard for the welfare of others.
    High
    1. *Impulse Control.* Tendency to express impulse, of whatever kind, immediately.
    2, 3. *Conformity to Group Patterns, Overt Conformity to Moral Code.* Between socially disapproved outbreaks of impulse, there may be conformity to the moral code and to group patterns, but there is a tendency to select groups whose patterns allow the most impulse expression.
    4. *Range of Moral Horizon.* There is a tendency to treat everyone with the same lack of consideration when it comes to impulse expression; but apart from this there may be friendliness and warmth—may be known as "charming but irresponsible," if this is true.
    5. *Locus of Concern.* Fairly continuous acting out of impulse to gratify self without taking account of others or their welfare. This is not necessarily impulse to *im*moral behavior, which would mean *anti*social, destructive, malicious impulse, but impulse which simply disregards morals, and which may or may not result in serious destruction of others and their welfare, depending upon circumstances and not upon motive. This kind of behavior has usually resulted more than once in severe punishment or severe social disapproval.
    6. *Internalization of Principle.* Little or no internalization of moral principle.
    7. *Capacity for Guilt and/or Shame.* Capacity for some guilt and/or shame may be present, but it is ineffective in guiding behavior.
    8. *Rationality.* Little or no reasoned consideration of action or its consequences.
    Middle
    Subject normally controls impulse well enough to avoid serious injury to others' rights or interests. But he occasionally resorts to immediate impulse gratification which represents a minor infraction of the moral code (such as playing hooky from school two or three times a year, stealing a watermelon in the summer, leaving a chore undone once in a while). He may gossip occasionally about others but seldom to a destructive degree. He does consider others' reactions and the effects of his behavior on them, although absence of external control or unusual pressure

from inner impulse now and then leads him to ignore these considerations. Tendency to occasional rudeness, or self-indulgence; may show some amount of quarreling, biting criticism, or scolding.

Low

1. *Impulse Control.* Tendency to control impulse, of whatever kind, immediately. This control may be a rational selection of morally acceptable means for impulse satisfaction. It may involve repression or suppression to the extent of constriction.
2. *Conformity to Group Patterns, Overt Conformity to the Moral Code.* This is average or above.
5. *Locus of Concern.* In guiding his behavior, subject takes into account the reactions of other people; whether this is for selfish or unselfish reasons is irrelevant here.

22. *Expedient:* having the tendency to secure maximal self-gratification, with regard for the welfare of others only as a means to an end. Tendency to get what subject wants with a minimum of giving in return. Consistent behavior in disregard of others' welfare whenever it conflicts with subject's welfare as he defines it. When, however, others' reactions are important to the subject's security and/or gratification, he may behave in a conventionally moral way, but will do so only so long as the advantages of so behaving outweigh the advantages of immediate selfish gratification. That is, subject may interest himself in others' satisfactions, but only if this brings him maximum gratification for his own wishes in the long run.

High

1. *Impulse Control.* High degree of impulse control, to avoid punishment and to secure the rewards of social approval.
2. *Conformity to Group Patterns.* Apparent conformity to social patterns, actually powered by purely selfish considerations for the most part, not by a respect for the social rules and patterns themselves.
3. *Overt Conformity to Moral Code.* Ultimate inconsistency in moral behavior, but not necessarily in reputation.
4. *Range of Moral Horizon.* It is possible for the individual to show a high degree of overt moral behavior toward a wide range of people, but, as suggested above, this will vary with situations.
5. *Locus of Concern.* High on narcissism, i.e., almost completely self-centered.

6. *Internalization of Principle.* Little or no internalization of moral principle.

7. *Capacity for Guilt and/or Shame.* Low or absent capacity for guilt or for shame.

8. *Rationality.* May have well-organized set of personal values and rational system of means for achieving ends; moral considerations do not enter this system.

   Outright manipulation of others for own purposes is evidence here. On the other hand, subject may adapt himself to expectations without any such manipulation; his expediency may take the form of ignoring or failing to observe such expectations when they do not suit him.

Middle

Clearly tends to be selfish, e.g., may cheat on an exam. Tends to ask, "What do I get out of this?" in a new situation, but will not operate this way when it seriously endangers other people's satisfactions. Will subordinate personal to social considerations when the latter are clearly heavily involved.

Low

Tendency either to gratify impulse immediately without considering ultimate effect on self or others, or to behave in conformity with the moral code (conference) because of internalized principles or concern with the welfare of others as well as self. In the latter case, gratification of purely selfish wishes is subordinated to considerations of a more socialized nature.

23. *Conforming:* having the tendency to conform to the patterns of behavior of the groups of which self is a member. It is important to note that a person may be highly conforming in behavior without rating even average on this motivation. The important consideration is *why* he conforms, not whether he conforms. It is only if he conforms because he wants to conform, because he values conformity for its own sake, that he can be rated high. In general, there are two types of conformers. One is chameleonlike in his ability to adapt his behavior to new patterns when he encounters them. The other is more rigid; he learns a fixed set of ritualized behaviors, probably during childhood, and tends to follow these the rest of his life. His pattern of behavior in a particular life area may or may not be consonant with a general moral principle; however, his reason for behaving this way is that it is the prescribed ritual, not that he recognizes or is concerned about the moral issues involved. This pattern of habitual behavior is followed whether

or not it is the normalized pattern in groups the subject encounters later on in life. It is not possible for this second type to rate 10. The chameleon type of conformer seems to depend for guidance upon the outside social structure in which he finds himself, whatever it may be. The ritual conformer seems to have internalized particular patterns more strictly, so that the immediate external structure may not be so much a source of rules as is his inner pattern if he finds himself in a new group different from the one in which he learned "the rules."

High

1. *Impulse Control.* Impulses are either held in check or expressed only in group-approved ways.
2. *Conformity to Group Patterns.* Tendency to do what others do in any given situation, regardless of moral considerations. Identification of self-interest with conforming behavior.
3. *Overt Conformity to Moral Code.* This will be incidental to the moral code of the group, and the group's conformity to it.
4. *Range of Moral Horizon.* Morality of behavior toward a wide range of people will depend on that of the group.
5. *Locus of Concern.* Locus of Concern may range from low to above average.
6. *Internalization of Principle.* The few moral principles which may be internalized are always subordinate to the desire to conform to the mores of the group. Has a strong need to be given a clear, firm external structure of rules and procedures. Tendency to be primarily an imitator, reflector—never an originator.
7. *Capacity for Guilt and/or Shame.* The worst punishment for the high conformer is the feeling of shame at non-conformity, or inability to meet group expectations.
8. *Rationality.* There is little rational thinking-out of moral principles or the ultimate purposes of social action.

Middle

Most of the time he goes along with his group, rarely objecting in any overtly serious way to moral decisions the group has made. It is possible, however, for him effectively to object to the majority decisions. Tends to be a moderately solid member of the peer group, and has a fair amount of peer-group morality.

Low

1. *Impulse Control.* May be very low, or very high control, because of rational, irrational-internalized, or egocentric-expedient motives.

2. *Conformity to Group Patterns.* Tendency to act independently, on a personal basis of judgment, whether or not this corresponds to the customary practices of the group. May be an outstanding non-conformist.

7. *Capacity for Guilt and/or Shame.* Capacity for shame is low. If behavior is guided by internalized principle, capacity for guilt may be high.

24. *Irrational-Conscientious:* having the tendency to behave in accordance with externally originated principles of conduct which have been introjected, operate autonomously to guide and criticize behavior, and are not subject to rational criticism by the self. This body of principles may be thought of as the superego or conscience. Tendency to do what the individual believes to be morally "right" in all situations. Tendency to judge others and often self in harsh, black-and-white terms (no middle ground, an act is either "right" or "wrong"), and to perceive others more as actors in expression of principles than as persons in their own right. Subject tends to get caught occasionally in moral paradoxes, e.g., conflicts between implications of two principles. Honesty and kindness can conflict if pushed too far, for instance. Subject cannot compromise such principles easily because of their absolute quality.
High

1. *Impulse Control.* Impulse control is exceptionally high, amounting at the least to thorough channeling of impulse expression, and at the most to constriction.

2. *Conformity to Group Patterns.* Conformity to group may range from low to high, but in case of conflict between group decisions and a moral principle of the subject's, the subject acts by his own dictates rather than by those of the group.

3. *Overt Conformity to Moral Code.* The important factor in guiding behavior is the individual's internalized code. Any conformity to the conference moral code is coincidental with this.

4. *Range of Moral Horizon.* Depending entirely on the content of the body of principles, range of morality may be very broad, or quite narrow.

5. *Locus of Concern.* Locus of Concern may range from low to high average.

6. *Internalization of Principle.* The internalized body of principles is well organized, and covers almost all moral relationships and situations of which the subject has cognizance.

7. *Capacity for Guilt and/or Shame.* Capacity for guilt is high

(regarding both inner impulse and outer behavior). Actual guilt may be fairly low, if desires do not conflict with super-ego principles, and if behavior is in similar accord.

8. *Rationality.* Rationality is low.

Middle

Subject has a set of irrational moral principles which keep him conforming to the moral code in some major areas of behavior. He almost never would commit a major violation of the moral code such as deliberate grand larceny. These principles may be roughly organized but are not firmly integrated into a consistent, thoroughly directive system.

Low

Tendency to vary behavior with situations, individuals, group patterns. Behavior is seldom governed blindly by superego directives. This may be a result either of lack of superego directives, or of internal directives which are readily accessible to realistic assessment.

25. *Rational-Altruistic:* having the tendency to act with consideration of others and their ultimate welfare. This is carried out both in terms of the possible effects of action over a time-span and on any other people who might be concerned, and in terms of a rationally held body of principles as to what constitutes the greatest good for the greatest number. These principles may and perhaps must be originally derived from introjection. They have been modified and differentiated by conscious, rational assessment of their human significance. Perception of others primarily as persons rather than actors only. Willingness to "let circumstances alter cases." Does not blindly impose his principles on persons and situations.

High

1. *Impulse Control.* Control system well organized and highly effective; not rigid, but flexible.
2. *Conformity to Group Patterns.* Conformity to group is not low; may be very high, depending on the morality of the group.
3. *Overt Conformity to Moral Code.* The morality of behavior tends to be high.
4. *Range of Moral Horizon.* High morality of behavior shown toward a wide range of people.
5. *Locus of Concern.* Tendency to consider other people part of the time, and to avoid behavior which is destructive of their welfare, regardless of self-centered considerations. High on "respect for integrity of others."

6. *Internalization of Principle.* The body of internalized principles is fairly well organized, but may have a number of inconsistencies, some irrationality, some difficulty in application in various milieu, some difficulty in accepting others' ideas as to what is best for them.

7. *Capacity for Guilt and/or Shame.* High capacity for guilt over violation of principle, but actual guilt is probably low, since behavior will normally be in accord with principle.

8. *Rationality.* Usually assesses situations accurately and acts in a way well calculated to produce the desired moral effect. Shows reasonable foresight, whether or not this is the result of deliberate, conscious planning. Seldom makes a morally wrong decision of any serious consequence, even if acting on irrational premises.

Middle

Subject has some firm, moral principles which he has begun to inspect and analyze. He has been able to assess some of his principles in terms of their social effects and to modify his behavior to carry out the spirit rather than the letter of the original rules. Most of the time his behavior is governed by habitual conformity, uncriticized superego directives, etc. Rational investigation of moral issues is only an occasional occurrence.

Low

2, 3. *Conformity to Group Patterns, Overt Conformity to Moral Code.* Subject may be highly conforming to group patterns and/or the moral code (conference), but he is conforming by reason of uncritical acceptance of social stereotypes rather than by any rational process.

5. *Locus of Concern.* More concerned about self than about others.

6. *Internalization of Principle.* If internalized principles are important in guiding subject's behavior, they do so quite irrationally, and may constitute a very highly controlling system.

8. *Rationality.* If subject is rational, it is only to further personal ends without regard to moral considerations.

26. *Ambitiousness:* refers to the goals a person sets for himself and to the eagerness and persistence with which he pursues them.

27. *Emotional Stability:* the degree to which a person appears outwardly calm, cool, and collected, and the consistency with which he presents this appearance.

28. *(a) Absence of Overt Hostility:* the degree and frequency with which a person refrains from inflicting injury on others.

(*b*) *Absence of Covert Hostility:* this measures the presence and intensity of emotions such as anger, rage, hate, dislike, and violent distaste—which do not reach expression in direct verbal or motor behavior. This tends to be visible to other people only in subtle or disguised forms—often no more than vague uneasiness in an observer is its perceived manifestation. This sort of hostility may be a chronic, diffuse feeling of the subject, not dependent on immediate stimuli, or it may be specifically directed toward persons or situations. One may have high overt expressions of hostility and low covert—i.e., the feelings are discharged. Data are mainly derived from projective materials, and projective interpretations of other instruments.

29. *Trustfulness:* the degree to which a person exhibits faith in the moral integrity of others.

30. *Superego Strength:* this contains the idea of "behaviorally effective motivation." It is the degree to which behavior is directed by, or in accord with, a present and functioning superego. To amplify, this depends on the presence of superego principles; for a person with little or no conscience, no feelings of guilt about immoral acts performed or anticipated, cannot be considered to have much superego strength. A second factor is the degree to which superego directives are integrated into behavior; i.e., a person with only self-punitive superego "voices" which do not forestall immoral be-behavior does not have an integrated system of principles to which behavior itself is synchronized. Thus, guilt per se is not a direct measure of superego strength, unless the present or potential anxiety it arouses leads the person to control his behavior accordingly.

31. *Severity of Parental Control:* both the amount of control the parents exert over their child and the extent to which they employ physical and/or mental punishment as a means of control. Whenever possible, data on parental control during infancy and early childhood should be given weight.

32. *Introspectiveness:* the extent to which a person examines his behavior and experiences in order to gain a better understanding of himself—what his goals are and what they should be.

33. *Optimism:* the extent to which a person is cheerful, looks on the bright side of life, and has faith in the future.

34. *Creativity:* the extent to which a person invents and then uses new ways of doing things.

35. *Consistency of Parental Control:* refers to the degree to which parental methods of control are predictable both through time and on logical grounds. Whenever possible, data on parental control during infancy and early childhood should be given additional weight.

THE RATIONALE, RELIABILITY, AND VALIDITY
OF THE RATINGS

The main objective in using a rating system in this study was to achieve a single set of quantified measurements on each subject which would describe that subject with as perfect accuracy as possible. When each case study was completed, we wanted to be able to say, "This is the way he thinks, feels, and acts, and these are his reasons for doing so"; and we wanted to represent this picture as fully and objectively as possible by a set of scores on psychodynamic and behavioral traits. The advantages of quantified scores are that they permit point-to-point comparison of one case with another; and they also permit analysis of all the cases, as a group. This, in turn, permits the discovery of any systematic relationships which exist among psychological and social dimensions. This could not be found by taking one case at a time.

There are several alternative ways in which such ratings can be obtained. One way is to have each judge make "blind," totally independent ratings based on his analysis of a particular set of instruments. This has two obvious disadvantages. First, he must base his ratings on incomplete evidence. He would have no opportunity to check inferences drawn from projective tests—about social attitudes, let us say—against sociometric and observational reports on the subject's social behavior. Any erroneous conclusions he reached would then affect the accuracy of any pooled rating (with other judges' scores). His inadequately based judgment would distort the final pooled rating, and there would be no way to take out that error.

Secondly, any subjective errors he might make in assessing the data could not be corrected, and they would likewise introduce an irremovable inaccuracy into the pooled-rating picture of the case.

A second method is to give each judge all the raw data and all the test analyses on the case and have him rate the case from this evidence. This permits independent rating (or semi-independent, since his judgment would doubtless be influenced to some degree by the interpretations of the experts who must necessarily analyze the various instruments). This gives him all the data, but it still leaves room for subjective, idiosyncratic errors in assessing and rating the case. This would introduce an indeterminate and uncorrectable error into the pooled rating of all the judges.

There is still another practical difficulty which can only be resolved by the conference discussion method. It is this: in making judgments about complex attitudinal and behavioral phenomena, it is crucially important to have clear and stable agreement on the *definition* of each variable which is to be rated. It is necessary to correct any judge who purposely or unwittingly redefines a variable when he rates a given case. This is a problem which seems to arise chronically in assessment studies of human beings.

Having faced these problems in previous researches, we decided on the case-conference method as the best attainable procedure for achieving the closest possible approximation to a valid, accurate picture of each subject, represented by ratings. It still presents some questionable features, in theory; but in practice, as will be shown further on in this discussion, there is evidence that it did achieve dependably valid results in this research.

To recapitulate the procedure briefly: all the raw data and all the expert instrument analyses were compiled, and they were then studied by each judge. Following this, a case conference was held, at which the evidence in each area of the case outline was reviewed and discussed, until all the judges could substantially agree in saying "This is the person, as he really is." Thereafter, each judge separately reviewed the case documents (including the conference discussion) and rated the subject on the various specific traits.

At the second conference on each case, all the judges' ratings were reviewed. Where there was substantial disagreement on some trait, it was discussed until reasonably close agreement was reached; or until it was clear that the disagreement could not be resolved. The average of the eight judges' ratings on each trait was then taken to be the score for that subject on that trait.

In short, a deliberate effort was made to reconcile any greatly differing interpretations, and to arrive at a description on which all the judges could largely agree. A judge could, however, maintain a different opinion from the majority, and have his own view recorded. Thus, the ratings by the eight judges were not intended to be totally independent. Nonetheless, there was still a good deal of room for genuinely independent rating, in the sense that each judge, even after the case conference, evaluated the case on the basis of his own thinking. The many cases where one or another pair of judges correlated as low as .40 to .50 with each other, testifies to the fact that they found room for some wide differences of opinion. In almost every one of the thirty-four cases, there were one or more variables on which the judges differed by a seven-point spread, or more, on a ten-point scale. (The average reliability of the prediscussion ratings, for ten judges, was .96, nonetheless.)

From one point of view, this represents less than the ideal of total agreement on "the true picture" of the case; but it also indicates that there was no arbitrary pressure on the judges to arrive at identical ratings. Even after the case-conference discussion, the judges found considerable freedom for independent thinking about the proper ratings to assign to the subject. Consequently, the high reliability (.97) of the final pooled ratings does not appear to be importantly an artifact of arbitrary pressure on the judges—either from the case-conference document or from the group discussion.

There were, moreover, two sets of ratings which showed very high reliability, although they were made in a completely independent manner. The first was a rating on overall Moral Effectiveness, or "goodness of character." This was made six months after the case conferences ended. The judges reported that they rated chiefly on their overall impression of each child, referring back to the case documents in only a few cases, to check on an occasional question. The average degree of correlation (Kendall's W coefficient) for the five judges was .94, without any discussion between judges prior to their ratings. (Ultimately, this rating was not used, since after the factor analysis it turned out to correlate highly with Moral Stability, and to be related to other variables in almost exactly the same degree, so that the Moral Stability measure seemed sufficient.)

TABLE 19.* THE RELIABILITY OF THE RATINGS ON DEVELOPMENTAL-TASK ACHIEVEMENT

	Age-Mate Adjustment	Sex-Role Acceptance	Emotional Independence	Development of Moral Values
Average of six interjudge correlations	.82	.67	.67	.78
Highest interjudge, r	.92	.75	.86	.86
Lowest interjudge, r	.74	.61	.59	.71
Reliability of the average of 8 judges' ratings Spearman-Brown for- (mula)	.98	.94	.94	.97

* Adapted from Table 1, page 318, in R. J. Havighurst, *Human Development and Education*.

The second set of independent ratings is represented in Table 19. At the same time that the research staff were studying the thirty-four adolescents with regard to moral character, they were also rating these same subjects on Developmental Task Achievement. These ratings were based on the same collection of data as were the moral character and personality ratings. However, there is an important difference: during the case conference, there was never any discussion of the subjects in terms of their developmental task achievement. The judges did not discuss either the case or the ratings with each other. Consequently, the ratings on the "tasks" were independent ratings. The reliability of these ratings was very high: .94 to .98.

In one sense, of course, this evidence is tangential to the question of the validity of the personality and character ratings. However, it demonstrates that the same judges, when rating the same subjects on a different set of dimensions, in an independent way, achieved a high order of reliability. This would seem to indicate that their ratings on the character traits accurately represent the data, and are not merely an artifact of group discussion.

Such evidence is usually taken to indicate good validity. The fact that the judges were all trained and experienced experts in human assessment might also carry some weight. The very fact that their individual backgrounds and primary fields of professional interest ranged from the disciplines of psychology to sociology to education suggests—qualitatively, at least—that when they agreed in rating a case, it was agreement dictated by the data, not by commonly shared preconceptions or irrational biases which unknowingly moved them to make similar ratings. (Anyone who knows scientific research workers, as people, will also appreciate that their individualism is not apt to yield meekly to group pressure, just for the sake of agreement.)

There are two major kinds of validity problems, however, which exist in the kind of research design used here. The first kind of validity problem in this particular study arises from the fact that the personality and character ratings were all made by the one team of judges. In practice, the cases were studied one at a time, over a period of a year. No systematic comparison of different cases was made while these case studies were in progress. (Anyone who has made clinical case studies can testify that sight of "the forest" usually gets lost in the "trees" after several cases have been analyzed.) Subjectively, the research staff reported at the close of the case study stage that they could foresee few clear, specific patterns of relationship that might be revealed by a statistical analysis of the entire group of cases. However, the possibility of unconscious assumptions producing some built-in or halo-effect relationships among the variables cannot be ignored.

In the personality trait–Moral Effectiveness correlations in this study, there is some internal evidence that an artificial halo effect was not systematically operating. If preconceived biases had been dictating spurious correlations, there are many places in the correlation table where high coefficients should appear which did not, in fact, emerge. For example, it was hypothesized that inner attitudes toward father, mother, and peers would be significantly related to morality. There was an unexpected lack of significant correlations for these variables, when the data on all thirty-four cases were analyzed. Similarly, such traits as Empathy and Absence of Covert Hostility did not show the expected level of correlation with morality. Of course, such evidence is not conclusive proof that where high correlations did appear, they were not somehow artifacts of circularity in the rater's reasoning.

Finally, there were three separate sets of ratings by judges outside of the character study staff, which cast some light on the validity of the staff's ratings on the personality and character type variables. One set was explicitly included in the data for the case studies. A second set was imbedded in the data but not isolated nor specifically studied during the case conferences. The third set of ratings was independently made and was not examined until the case studies were concluded.

The first set comprised the adults' and peers' ratings of the subjects on six moral traits (averaged, to give an overall rating). Because these ratings were judged significant data in themselves concerning the child's perceived moral status in his social world, they were listed in the case documents. However, they were not considered by the staff to be necessarily prima facie evidence of actual morality. This is reflected in the .73 correlations of the staff's Moral Effectiveness rating with overall adult and peer ratings on character. The staff found fairly frequent occasion to differ with the peers and/or adults in assessing a given child's character. The fact that the correlation is still high, in the staff's opinion, reflects an agreement with adults and peers on the facts of the subjects' morality. Still, it cannot be proved that such agreement is not an artifact of including the adult and peer character ratings in the case data.

The second set of measures consists of peer ratings on social-behavior traits. These were derived by extracting certain items from the 1946 and 1947 social-personality sociometrics and computing social-trait scores.

Some extracts from 1946–47 sociometric interpretations were included in the individual case documents, as were the *moral* ratings by peers. At the time of the case conferences, however, no specific dimensions of social behavior had been identified or scored on the basis of peer ratings. The 1946–47 peer ratings on social traits were not analyzed or correlated with the character ratings until two years later. In short, the peer "social" ratings seemed to be independent of the conference ratings on character and personality. They were based, of course, on the *peers'* observations of much the same individual behavior on which the character study ratings were based. They would not be a usable criterion, if that were not the case.

For the purpose of testing the validity of the conference ratings, a comparison can be made between the conference ratings and the peer ratings. Here were two sets of people, each viewing the same behavior, and each assessing it in ways which ultimately permitted quantitative comparison. As Chapter VI has shown, several different kinds of statistical comparisons all revealed a significant, high degree of agreement between these two separate assessments of the same individuals. This is the more impressive when it is noted that the peer social traits were not identical in definition with the character traits the conference was rating. Insofar as these peer "social" ratings can be considered an independent criterion of the validity of the conference ratings, they show just about the order of relationship one would expect if the staff's ratings were valid, making allowance for differences in variate definitions and for the somewhat different standards one would expect adolescents and the character-study staff to use in assessing character.

The third set of ratings consists of the 1947 research group's assessments of the children's families. Of course, these have no direct relationship, as a validating criterion, to the personality and character ratings on the children. What can be said is that the relationships between these family ratings and the character ratings, which are statistically very significant, are of the nature one would expect, reasoning from what is currently known of family influences on child personality formation. This logical congruence scarcely represents anything like direct evidence that either the character ratings or the family ratings are valid; it merely suggests that both these sets of ratings *may* be valid, insofar as their mutual relationships agree with, rather than contradict, current psychological knowledge.

To summarize, the ratings on moral character by the conference, by adults in the community, and by peers all tend to agree significantly. The peer "social" ratings constitute the most nearly independent criterion for validating the conference ratings, and tend to indicate quite good validity.

There was no independent criterion against which the personality ratings could be tested; by the nature of the phenomena, such a criterion would be difficult to find, except by having another group of experts independently assess the children. Here, particularly, the high reliability of the interjudge ratings in the character study is the evidence most suggestive of validity. Finally, the logical congruence of all these various sets of ratings with the independent measures of family characteristics suggests that the various ratings probably are valid, although this is indirect evidence at best.

THE STATISTICAL ANALYSIS OF THE PERSONALITY DATA

The direct factor analysis

In order to study the relationships among the personality and character ratings, all their intercorrelations were computed. It was evident from the clusters in the resulting matrix that what had originally been defined as some thirty personality traits actually represented a much smaller number of separate characteristics. Therefore, a factor analysis of the personality traits was performed in order to identify these characteristics (see Table 20). The results classified the measures into six factorially distinct clusters. It should be noted that these are not six "factors" in the technical sense. Actually, a three-factor system was found; but within it were six clusters of variables which were statistically distinct from one another, and which represented psychologically separate and meaningful dimensions that it was desirable to retain. Hence the term personality "vectors" has been used, rather than "factors." We are indebted to William Stephenson for supplying the model and the rationale for this treatment of variables which represent "mixed factor types" (Stephenson, 1953). The composition of the six personality vectors is as follows:

P1: Moral Stability

Vector P1 is most heavily loaded on the following traits:

16b. Overt Conformity to the (conference-defined) Moral Code (.93)
27. Emotional Stability (largely a measure of overt conformity to expected, "controlled" behavior) (.91)
11. Range of Moral Horizon (a measure of the range of people toward whom the subject is overtly moral) (.87)
8a. Overt Acceptance of Mother's Expectations (.81)
28a. Absence of Overt Hostility (.70)
9b1. (Positive) Overt Relations with Opposite-Sex Peers (.55)

TABLE 20.   FACTORIAL PATTERN OF THE PERSONALITY CHARACTERISTICS

Trait	Before Rotation				After Second Rotation			Personality* Vector					
	I	II	III	IV	I″	II′	III′	1	2	3	4	5	6
2, Functional IQ	.77†	.38	.25	−.18	.51	.17	.72		2				
3, Observation	.81	.26	.14	.10	.58	.05	.63		2				
4, Insight	.83	.33	.34	.03	.48	.11	.81		2				
5, Empathy	.42	.10	.28	.19	.16	−.01	.49				4		
6, Locus of Concern	.86	.13	−.08	.32	.73	−.09	.48		2				
7a, Outward Acceptance of Father's Code	.28	−.41	−.10	−.37	.19	−.47	.02						−6
7b, Positive Feeling toward Father	.51	−.09	.33	−.21	.17	−.22	.55				4		
7c, Negative Feeling toward Father	.06	.35	.22	−.18	.00	.32	.28						
8a, Outward Acceptance of Mother's Code	.47	−.27	−.66	−.23	.81	.14	−.20	1					
8b, Positive Feeling toward Mother	.71	−.11	.16	.06	.42	−.29	.53		2				
8c, Negative Feeling toward Mother	−.51	.63	.08	.05	−.31	.73	−.15						6
9a1, Outward Feeling toward Same-Sex Peers	.73	.17	.16	−.18	.49	−.02	.59		2				
9a2, Inner Feeling toward Same-Sex Peers	.36	−.19	.33	−.12	.03	−.28	.44				4		
9b1, Outward Feeling toward Opposite-Sex Peers	.57	−.06	−.22	.36	.55	−.20	.16	1					
9b2, Inner Feeling toward Opposite-Sex Peers	.38	−.35	−.21	.54	.34	−.44	.01						−6
11, Range of Moral Horizon	.84	.19	−.31	.04	.87	−.03	.30	1					
12, Emotional Maturity	.90	.14	−.06	.11	.74	−.09	.51		2				
13, Identity of Impulse and Behavior	.26	−.17	.68	.34	−.26	−.23	.65				4		
14, Heteronomy-Autonomy	.86	.28	.35	.07	.49	.05	.84		2				
15a, Assignment of Responsibility	.90	.14	.13	.21	.63	−.10	.66		2				
15b, Rationality	.92	.25	.11	.08	.69	.01	.67		2				
16a, Inner Consistency	.92	.05	−.06	.04	.73	−.18	.51		2				
16b, Conformity	.65	.15	−.66	−.35	.93	−.02	−.11	1					
17, Guilt about Outer Behavior	−.32	.19	−.33	.30	.00	.26	−.43				−4		
18, Guilt about Inner Behavior	−.52	.62	.04	.16	−.30	.73	−.19						6
19, Self-Perception	.89	.21	.10	.08	.66	−.02	.65		2				
27, Emotional Stability	.80	.19	−.43	−.23	.91	−.02	.18	1					
28a, Absence of Overt Hostility	.57	−.17	−.49	−.17	.70	−.31	−.07	1					
28b, Absence of Covert Hostility	.64	−.57	−.18	.24	.49	−.71	.16					5	
30, Superego Strength	.40	.62	−.46	−.12	.71	.50	−.02			3			

* P1: Moral Stability, P2: Ego Strength, P3: Superego Strength, P4: Spontaneity, P5: Friendliness, P6: Hostility-Guilt Complex.

† With an N of 34 children, loadings of .20 or less are considered to be not significantly different from zero. Loadings above .40 are the only ones of significance in the table.

It seems to be more a descriptive than a psychodynamic factor. It represents behavior which conforms positively to the established moral code, particularly as that code is defined and encouraged by the mother. Not much of the underlying motivation can be directly seen by looking at the traits pure for P1. At most, we could say that a person who exemplified this vector is one who is conventionally moral, socially conforming to both the maternal and peer codes of approved behavior, and shows no hostility or emotional discomfort in doing so.

However, if we take into account certain other traits which are highly loaded on P1 though they belong mainly to the cluster which defines vector P3 (see below), we begin to see the underlying dynamics of the P1 vector. These traits, while they do not represent P1 purely, are:

12. Emotional Maturity (.74)
16a. Internal Consistency of Values (broadly, a measure of "personality integration") (.73)
6. (Socialized) Locus of Concern (.73)
30. Superego Strength (.71)

We might infer that the person high on this characteristic conforms, not so much from pressure to do so, but because he enjoys it and finds it the most comfortable and satisfying way to live. He does tend to be genuinely concerned for others' welfare, and to have firm beliefs about the way he should act. While P1 is also loaded .69 on Rationality, and lower but positively on the perceptual traits, the emphasis seems to lie on willing acceptance of social and moral norms without too much inquiry into their actual value for moral purposes. The P1 vector may therefore be best defined as a willing, rather uncritical, acceptance of conventional morality and a strong tendency to observe its dictates in overt behavior.

P2: Ego Strength

It is difficult to find a simple phrase that encompasses this closely woven complex of traits. The traits and their loadings are as follows (I and III refer to factors I and III):

12. Emotional Maturity (I—.74, III—.51)
6. (Socialized) Locus of Concern (I—.73, III—.48)
16a. Internal Consistency (integration) (I—.73, III—.61)
15b. Rationality of Behavior (I—.69, III—.67)
19. Accurate Self-Perception (I—.66, III—.67)
15a. Accurate Assignment of Moral Responsibility (I—.63, III—.66)
3. (Accurate social) Observation (I—.68, III—.63)
2. Functioning Intelligence (I—.51, III—.72)
4. Insight into Others' Motives (I—.48, III—.81)
14. Autonomy (I—.49, III—.84)

9a1. (Positive) Relations with Same-Sex Peers (I—.49, III—.59)
8b. Positive Feeling toward Mother (I—.42, III—.53)

Graphically, this is a cluster of traits which lie quite closely together, roughly midway between I and III factor axes. They constitute a global cluster which might be called a distinct entity. This is the assumption, of course, in saying that they define a distinct vector, correlated on the one side with factor I (P1) and on the other with factor III (P4), which are themselves orthogonal vectors.

P3: Superego Strength

This vector is represented by just one trait, the original rating on superego strength. In the factor system it is loaded .71 on factor I (P1), .50 on factor II (P6). While it would not be orthodox practice to base a factorial *axis* on one variable, what we have done in retaining superego strength as a separate variable is simply to acknowledge the fact that it emerged as a separate, distinct characteristic from the factor analysis. Of course, it has direct psychological pertinence to the study.

P4: Spontaneity

This might as easily be termed "Friendly Spontaneity," for it is striking that this is closely bound up with positive feelings toward other people. The "pure," loaded traits are as follows:

13. Identity of Impulse and Behavior (.65)
7b. Positive Feeling toward Father (.55)
5. Empathy (.49)
9a2. Positive Feeling toward Same-Sex Peers (.44)
17. Guilt about Overt Behavior (−.43)

The hypothetical representative of P4 (factor III) is a good-natured, impulsive individual who likes people and can establish emotional rapport with them. He may or may not conform to moral expectations, but if he acts contrary to others' best interests he does so because he is bent on following his own desires, not because he is aggressively aware of the moral implications of what he is doing, or because he wants to take advantage of people.

Here, too, is a dynamic pattern reported by psychoanalytic and client-centered therapists. The person who is self-acceptant, who likes himself as he is, tends strongly to like and be acceptant toward others. This is almost the reverse case of P6, where guilt about one's inner self is highly associated with hostility toward other people.

P5: Friendliness

This, like vector P3, is defined by one variable: 28b, Absence of Covert Hostility. It is loaded .49 on factor I (P1) and −.71 on factor III (P6). To use a less complicated, inverted concept than the original trait name, after checking case data to insure that it would be appropriate, this characteristic was renamed "Friendliness." From the case data, that appears to be an apt description of the attitude of the children who received a high score on this variable.

P6: Hostility-Guilt Complex

This name was chosen after inspecting the traits which are pure for vector P6:

18. Guilt about Inner Impulse (.73)
8c. Inner Feelings of Hostility to Mother (.73)
7a. Acceptance of Father's Code (−.47)
9b2. Inner Liking for Opposite-Sex Peers (−.44)

In addition, there are two traits loaded on P6 which are also loaded on P1:

28b. Absence of Covert Hostility (−.71)
30. Superego Strength (.50)

This constellation is composed of dynamic characteristics which strikingly resemble a classic syndrome in psychoanalytic theory. To begin with, it demonstrates a close association between intense hostile feelings and strong feelings of guilt about one's inner impulses. This corresponds well with the psychoanalytic assumption that guilt is the product of inturned hostility. More than this, however, the rating on Covert Hostility indicates that there remains a great deal of negative feeling toward other people and the outer world.

Futhermore, the hostility is most intense toward the mother. Yet there is active rejection of father's expectations, but not consistent departure from mother's code in overt behavior (loading on 8a is .14). Finally, there is a tendency to be inwardly hostile to opposite-sex peers. If boys alone were the subjects, this would seem a quite clearly defined case of the unresolved Oedipal conflict. Since the data come equally from boys and girls, a more general formulation appears possible: that of an unresolved mother tie, with bitter underlying hostility, but with so much guilt attached to it that as often as not the person is unable to act as he would like.

The loading on Superego Strength, which is not too high, thus bears out a theory we developed some time ago. That is, that the hostile, punitive "superego" which is internalized early from punishing parents, and is not subsequently accessible to reality testing (modification to suit new circumstances), is different not in degree but in *kind* from the principles of conscience which are incorporated as a guiding influence in the character structure of the person who conforms willingly, or who even more actively tests, applies, and adapts his behavior rationally, from a desire to be considerate of others as well as realize his own wishes.

P6 thus appears to represent a way of adapting to society which is grudging at best. A person of this type, if he conforms (which he may or may not do: loadings on 16b, −.02; 28a, −.31; 15b, .01; 17, .26; etc.) does so because he anticipates and fears punishment. He has little positive regard for other people, and little understanding of their feelings and aims.

It is noteworthy that although we did not rate sexual attitudes as such, there is a definite implication of failure to break the dependent attachment to mother, however hostile; and failure to make a positive, satisfying relationship to people of the opposite sex. This is inferential, of course, but on checking back to the case studies of the children highest on P6 one can see that they do have conflictful, frustrated sexual attitudes. For our purpose, however, we are chiefly concerned with the fact that Hostility-and-Guilt emerges as a clear entity. As will be seen in more detail below, this kind of punitive conscience is no necessary guarantee of even superficially socialized behavior. It is strongest, in fact, in the Amoral type group, though negatively correlated with Amoral motivation when the ratings of all the thirty-four children on the Amoral dimension are considered.

Computing individual scores on the personality vectors

Since the personality measures had been condensed from thirty to six, it was desirable to compute for each child a standard score on each of the six personality vectors. The traits were selected which contributed most of the variance on a given vector. These were for P1 traits 11 (loading of .87); 16b (.93); and 27 (.91). These were taken to be approximately equal, hence were given equal weights of 1. The variables highly loaded on P2 were 2 (I: 51, III: .72); 3 (.58,

.63); 4 (.48, .81); 12 (.74, .51); 14 (.49, .84); 15a (.63, .66); 15b (.69, .67); 16a (.75, .51); 19 (.66, .65). Although the composite loadings on these traits (sum of the squares of the two correlation figures) ranged from .86 to .96, it was decided to take them as roughly equivalent, and give a weight of one to each variable.

The scores on P3 were those originally obtained on trait 30, superego strength. The P5 scores were those obtained on trait 28b. P4 was defined by traits 5 (.49); 7b (.55); 13 (.65); and 17 (−.43). (The scores on 17 were reversed, in order to permit simple addition with the scores on the other P4 variables). In computing the loading of P4, scores on traits 13, 7b, 5, and 17 were given weights of 4, 3, 2, and 2, respectively. P6 was largely defined by traits 8c (.74) and 18 (.73), which were therefore chosen and each given a weight of 1.

The scores a child got on the traits defining vector P1, for example, were summed. When the sums for all the subjects were obtained, the resulting array was converted into a standard score array. In the end, this gave for each subject a standard score on each of the personality vectors.

Studying the children via obverse factor-analysis: A cross check

A different way to arrive at subgroups within a population is to correlate the subjects with each other, rather than intercorrelate the traits. Ruth Cooper undertook an "obverse" factor analysis of such a subject-by-subject correlation matrix, in order to discover if this inductive treatment of the data would verify the character-type hypotheses, and also a different set of empirical "type" descriptions presented by Havighurst and Taba in *Adolescent Character and Personality*.

In order to use as many measures as possible, relevant to both the Peck and Havighurst-Taba typologies, Miss Cooper not only included the thirty personality traits used in the direct factor analysis, but an additional thirty-five variables drawn from peer and teacher ratings, self-report inventory scores on attitudes and interests, mental tests, family relations ratings, and the conference ratings on Developmental-Task Achievement. Upon analysis, ten bipolar factors were found. These were defined by individual subjects who presented a distinctive pattern on the variables studied. They could properly be said to constitute a set of twenty types, or patterns, of moral motivation and behavior; although, since most of the children were represented on two or more of the factors, few subjects could accurately be described as of one "pure" factor type, nor can one fully describe each child, since only some aspects of his make-up are represented by those obverse factors in which he has a significant loading. A comparison of the results with the character-type scale nonetheless shows substantial congruence with that typology, insofar as direct comparison is possible.

The ten bipolar factors were identified as follows:

A. Passive, Friendly Submissiveness vs. Active, Hostile Self-Assertiveness
B. Social, Emotional, and Intellectual Maturity vs. Social, Emotional, and Intellectual Immaturity
C. Self-Denying Adherence to Principle vs. Self-Indulgent Expediency
D. Self-Advancing Conformity vs. Self-Defeating Non-Conformity
E. Affectionate, Trustful Outgoingness vs. Hostile, Suspicious Withdrawal
F. Hostile Moral Compulsiveness vs. Friendly Amoral Impulsiveness
G. Emotionally Stable, Realistic Conformity vs. Emotionally Unstable, Irrational Non-Conformity
H. Outgoing, Kindly Realism vs. Withdrawn, Hostile Fantasy
J. Willing Acceptance of Parental Code vs. Hostile Rebellion Against Parental Code
K. Carefree, Good-Natured Spontaneity vs. Anxious, Hostile Constriction

The adolescents who fall at each type level of the character scale can by described in terms of their obverse factor patterns, in a way analogous to the analysis of their personality patterns using the vectors derived from the direct factor analysis. In the following discussion, the designating letter of the obverse factor is given in parentheses (−A) where the child's factor loading was .25 to .40; where the loading was above .40 there are no parentheses around the letter identifying the factor: A. The factors not shown for a child (which comprise most factors) were the ones on which he had no significant or near-significant factor loading (less than .25). By citing the meaning of the factors on which a child had such loadings, at least some highlights of his moral behavior pattern can be seen. It may be of interest to the reader to compare those characterizations with the ones above, based on the personality vectors.

The Amoral-Impulsive Group

T-78 [−E, (−F), (−J)]: Hostile, suspicious withdrawal, with lesser elements of hostile rebellion against parental code and of friendly, amoral impulsiveness. (The inconsistencies, as earlier analyses have shown, accurately reflect real "inconsistencies" in T-78's behavior at different times. Where internal inconsistencies occur in cases below, they similarly reflect actual inconsistencies in the child's feelings and behavior.)

T-25 [−A, −H]: Active, hostile self-assertiveness combined with withdrawn, hostile fantasy "escape."

T-89 [−G]: Emotionally unstable, irrational non-conformity.

T-42 [−D]: Self-defeating non-conformity.

T-99 [(−F)]: Insofar as T-99 is described by any factor—which is not very significantly—it is by friendly, amoral impulsiveness.

The CEA Type Complex

T-95 [(−A), (−F)]: Such definition of T-95's character as is given by these factors consists of active, hostile self-assertiveness mixed with friendly, amoral impulsiveness.

T-55 [(B), (−D), −H, (−K)]: This adolescent's major feature is withdrawn, hostile fantasy, with self-defeating non-conformity and anxious, hostile constriction added. There is also, however, a trace of social, emotional, and intellectual maturity mixed in.

T-64 [(A) (−F)]: Passive, friendly submissiveness, combined with friendly, amoral impulsiveness.

The Expedient Group

T-08 [−B]: Social, emotional, and intellectual immaturity.

T-52 [(−A), D]: Self-advancing conformity combined with some active, hostile self-assertiveness.

T-22 [−C]: Self-indulgent expediency.

T-76 [(−C), (−F)]: Self-indulgent expediency plus friendly, amoral impulsiveness.

The IAE Type Complex

T-16 [−B, (−E)]: Social, emotional, and intellectual immaturity, plus hostile, suspicious withdrawal.

T-37 [A, −G, H, (−J)]: Here is the very mixed, conflicted make-up seen above for T-37: Passive, friendly submissiveness; outgoing, kindly realism; yet with emotionally unstable, irrational non-conformity and some hostile rebellion against the parental code.

The Conforming Group

T-11 [(A), −D, (−H)]: Passive, friendly submissiveness, mixed with self-defeating non-conformity and withdrawn, hostile fantasy.

T-17 [(−D), E, −H]: Affectionate, trustful outgoingness; but withdrawn, hostile fantasy is also present, and some self-defeating non-conformity.

T-04 [(A)]: Passive, friendly submissiveness.

T-57 [A, (−D), (E)]: Passive, friendly submissiveness plus affectionate, trustful outgoingness, though with a trace of self-defeating non-conformity.

T-34 [E]: Affectionate, trustful outgoingness.

T-88 [−C, G]: Emotionally stable, realistic conformity, mixed with some self-indulgent expediency.

T-39 [−B, G]: Emotionally stable, realistic conformity, mixed with social, emotional, and intellectual immaturity.

T-49 [(F)]: What small part of T-49's character is described by the obverse factors is her hostile moral compulsiveness.

The Irrational-Conscience Group

T-79 [F]: Hostile moral compulsiveness.

T-83 [(−B), D, (−K)]: Anxious, hostile constriction, plus social, emotional and intellectual immaturity, modifying a trend toward self-advancing conformity.

T-28 [C, (F), (J)]: Self-denying adherence to principle, supported by hostile moral compulsiveness and willing acceptance of the parental code.

The Group with a High Secondary Component of Rational-Altruism

T-40 [(B), (C), (−D)]: Social, emotional, and intellectual maturity, with conflicting elements of self-denying adherence to principle and self-defeating non-conformity. (T-40 had an A-R character-type profile)

T-60 [(−A) E, (J), (K)]: Affectionate trustfulness is the dominant note, with carefree, good-natured spontaneity and willing acceptance of the parental code supporting it; yet there is also a trace of active, hostile self-assertiveness (*at times,* as the case material reveals).

T-86 [H]: Outgoing, kindly realism.

T-50 [(B), −E, (−J)]: Here is a mixture of social, emotional, and intellectual maturity with hostile, suspicious withdrawal and some hostile rebellion against the parental code.

T-53 [(E), F, H, K]: Outgoing, kindly realism, carefree, good-natured spontaneity, and some affectionate, trustful outgoingness, yet with an element of hostile moral compulsiveness.

The Rational-Altruistic Group

T-47 [A, H]: Outgoing, kindly realism plus passive, friendly submissiveness.

T-51 [B]: Social, emotional, and intellectual maturity.

T-03 [(−F), G, (H)]: Emotionally stable, realistic conformity plus outgoing, kindly realism, with a trace of friendly, amoral impulsiveness.

T-06 [B]: Social, emotional and intellectual maturity.

The obverse factors incompletely represent the individual subjects' character and personality. Of the 340 factor-loading figures, only three are above .60—the highest is .67—and only ten are .50 or higher. It seems all the more striking, therefore, that the characterizations which they do permit agree quite closely with what would be expected from the character-type hypotheses. Since about half the variables included in the obverse analysis came from independent ratings and inventory scores, the degree of congruence thus demonstrated tends to reaffirm the accuracy of the character-type scale and its associated personality patterns (Cooper, 1952).

However, the finely discriminating analysis which this obverse procedure yields, also casts new and additional light on the relationship between personality and character structure. If the obverse factor descriptions within each character type group are examined, a common note generally distinguishes each group. Thus, in the Expedient group, T-52's self-advancing, self-assertive expediency compares with T-22's and T-76's self-indulgent expediency (T-08's "immaturity" is obviously low on moral quality, but in a way not specifically defined by the obverse factors). Similarly, the Amoral group all show one or another kind of impulsive amorality or immorality, as described by the obverse factors. This is a quality shared only by the CEA subjects, who were placed next to the Amoral group on the Maturity of Character scale, on theoretical grounds.

What the obverse analysis adds is a differentiation *within* the character-type groups. It shows that there can be several kinds of personality and behavior patterns which would be evaluated morally as Expedient, or as Amoral. Thus, this method reproduces the fine differences between individuals which may not separate them in terms of the quality or maturity of their moral character, but which further helps to describe and explain the exact nature and reasons for their unique behavior patterns.

Correlation of the Character and Personality Variables

The separate type ratings were singly correlated with each other and with the personality variables (Peck, 1951). As might be expected, though, few simple relationships were found this way, except that the Amoral rating correlated negatively and the Rational-Altruistic rating correlated positively with most of the presumably positive personality characteristics. Only by considering each character-type rating in the context of the other four type ratings a person received could a meaningful analysis be made. Thus, an average rating on Conforming motivation contributed to a quite different overall picture of morality when it occurred in a person who was highest on Expediency, than in the case of a person highest on Rational-Altruism. Then, too, a score of 7 on Conforming motivation might be the highest score in one person's character profile, yet be outweighed by a higher score on another type, in another person's profile. In short, this was one of the frequent instances when the atomizing of human behavior into singly treated variables seemed to be an inappropriate representation of what, in fact, was a complex *Gestalt* that could only be understood when treated as such.

Since there is presently no known way, however, to handle a five-variable pattern quantitatively, it was necessary to resort to an even cruder abstraction. Ultimately, it was decided to group the cases according to the dominant type rating in each profile. There were five subjects whose highest type score was for Amoral. These five were put together and termed the "Amoral group." Four other subjects who had their highest score on Expediency were classed together as the "Expedient group." In this way, each person was placed in a character-type group, as was explained in Chapter IV. Thereafter, the analyses were based on this classification.

THE STATISTICAL ANALYSIS OF THE FAMILY DATA

Since it seemed clear from the outset of the study that moral attitudes and behavior are probably affected strongly by experiences in the family, an analysis of the family was indicated. The characteristic behavior of the parents, and the interaction pattern of the families, had already been rated by the Tryon-Henry conference, three years earlier. Since those ratings were made without any thought of their relevance to moral character, and since they were made by a different staff, they provided a completely independent picture of the thirty-four families. The family ratings were not inspected by anyone in the character study until several months after the close of the character conference.

Naturally, there was the limitation that they might not include all of the family characteristics crucial to character development; but they were carefully chosen aspects of family life, important to any aspect of child development. Adding the two variables which were rated in the character study, Severity of Parental Control, and Consistency of Parental Control, there were quantified measures for all the cases on the following ten aspects of family life.

A. Frequency and Variety of *Common Participation* among Members of the Family.
   How many activities do the members of the family indulge in as a group? For example, do they go on excursions together, to the movies together, etc., and how often?
B. *Regularity* in the Home.
   How much system is there to the home routine? For example, are there regular hours for meals, bedtime, when to be in at night, etc.?
C. Degree of *Approval-Disapproval of the Child* by the Parents.
   What is the general emotional tone of the parent-child relationship? For example, how much affection do the parents give the child? Do they accept him as a person? How much praise do they give him? How much do they criticize him?
D. Degree of *Confidence Sharing* between the Child and His Parents.
   To what extent does the child talk over his problems with his

parents? To what extent does he feel free to discuss with his parents anything that is on his mind?

E. Degree to which the *Child Shares in Family Decisions.*
Where does the home fall on an authoritarian-democratic continuum? To what extent does the child have a chance to express his views and to what extent do the parents consider his views before issues are settled?

F. Degree of *Trust and Faith in the Child* by the Parents.
To what extent is the child allowed freedom from close parental supervision? How much confidence do the parents have in the child's judgment?

G. Degree of *Parental Approval-Disapproval of Peer Activities.*
What is the parents' attitude toward the child's participation with age mates? For example, how much do they encourage or discourage him to have friends of his own? Are his friends welcome or unwelcome in the home?

H. *Interparental Relations* (the compatibility of the parents).
What is the general emotional tone of the relationship between the parents? For example, are they congenial or is there constant quarreling?

31. *Severity* of Parental Control.
This refers to both the amount of control the parents exert over their child and the extent to which they employ physical and/or mental punishment as a means of control.

35. *Consistency* of Parental Control.
The degree to which parental methods of control are predictable, both through time and in their nature.

Ultimately, of course, we were interested in the relationship of these family dynamics to the moral character variables. First, though, it seemed worth investigating the relationships among these family characteristics themselves. Therefore, these ten variables were intercorrelated, using Spearman's rank method (rho). The results are shown in Table 21. A factor analysis was then performed. The results are presented in Table 22. Four family "vectors" were identified within a two-factor space, in a manner analogous to the analysis of the personality data. The vectors are:

F1, Consistency in Family Life
    B. Regularity in the Home
    35. Consistency of Parental Control
    A. Common Participation in Activities

TABLE 21. INTERCORRELATIONS OF THE FAMILY CHARACTERISTICS

Characteristic	A	B	C	D	E	F	G	H	31	35
A, Participation		.38	.43	.53	.15	.43	.34	.68	.16	.37
B, Regularity	.38		.37	.55	−.11	.41	.41	.49	.59	.73
C, Approval of Child	.43	.37		.79	.63	.90	.80	.70	−.31	.43
D, Confidences Shared	.53	.55	.79		.49	.74	.75	.66	−.01	.55
E, Decisions Shared	.15	−.11	.63	.49		.57	.56	.34	−.66	−.09
F, Trust in Child	.43	.41	.90	.74	.57		.77	.70	−.31	.50
G, Approval of Peers	.34	.41	.80	.75	.56	.77		.61	−.26	.40
H, Interparental Relations	.68	.49	.70	.66	.34	.70	.61		.09	.55
31, Severity of Control	.16	.59	−.31	−.01	−.66	−.31	−.26	.09		.40
35, Consistency of Control	.37	.73	.43	.55	−.09	.50	.40	.55	.40	

TABLE 22. FACTORIAL PATTERN OF THE FAMILY CHARACTERISTICS

	Before Rotation		After Rotation		Vectors*			
	I	II	I′	II′	F1	F2	F3	F4
A, Participation in Same Activities	.56	−.24	.59	.10	F1			
B, Regularity in the Home	.55	−.53	.74	−.14	F1			
C, Parental Approval of Child	.90	.30	.58	.76			F3	
D, Confidences Shared	.90	.00	.75	.50			F3	
E, Sharing in Family Decisions	.42	.67	−.02	.78		F2		
F, Trust and Faith in the Child	.90	.25	.60	.70			F3	
G, Parents' Approval of Peers	.82	.25	.53	.66			F3	
H, Interparental Relations	.84	−.16	.78	.33			F3	
31, Severity of Parental Control	.00	−.93	.50	−.77				F4
35, Consistency of Parental Control	.59	−.44	.72	−.03	F1			

* F1: Consistency, F2: Democracy, F3: Mutual Trust, F4: Severity.

F2, Democracy-Autocracy
    E. Sharing in Family Decisions
F3, Mutual Trust and Approval among Family Members
    H. Good Interparental Relations
    D. Confidences Shared with Parents by Child
    F. Parental Trust and Faith in the Child
    C. Parental Approval of Child
    G. Parental Approval of Child's Activities
F4, Parental Severity
    31. Severity of Parental Control

It is of interest to compare these factors with the aspects of family life selected for study by the Fels Parent Behavior Scales (Lorr and Jenkins, 1953). A second-order factor analysis of seven first-order factors derived by Roff from thirty Fels PB Scales indicated that these scales center around three issues: (1) how far the home sustains and encourages dependence or how far it denies dependency satisfactions;

(2) how far its child training reflects democratic practices and values or authoritarian and undemocratic methods; (3) how far the house is characterized by strict orderliness or by a lax and unorganized pattern.

The last two factors in the Fels scales reproduce the two "pure" factors measured in this study: Democracy and Consistency. Their first factor, support of dependency needs, might be considered partially analogous to the Mutual Trust and Approval vector used in this study. Such a comparison suggests that the particular family characteristics chosen for this research are considered salient aspects of family life by other investigations of child development, whether the issue is one of personality formation, social development, or character development.

Each family was assigned a standard score on each of the four family vectors, using a system of weighted sums from the appropriate variables, as was done to obtain the children's scores on the personality vectors. These family scores were the ones used in the computations of Chapter V.

Bibliography

Adorno, T. W., E. Frenkel-Brunswick, D. Levinson, and R. N. Sanford. *The Authoritarian Personality*, New York, Harper and Brothers, 1950.

Axline, Virginia. *Play Therapy*, Boston, Houghton Mifflin, 1947.

Bettelheim, Bruno. *Love Is Not Enough*, Glencoe, Illinois, The Free Press, 1950.

Brinton, Crane. *A History of Western Morals*, New York, Harcourt, Brace, 1959.

Cooper, Ruth. An Obverse Factor Analytic Study of Adolescent Personality and Character Traits, Unpublished Ph.D. Dissertation (microfilm), University of Chicago, 1952.

Cronbach, Lee. *Educational Psychology*. New York, Harcourt, Brace, 1954.

Dewey, John. *Reconstruction in Philosophy*, Boston, Beacon Press, 1948.

Erikson, Erik. *Childhood and Society*, New York, W. W. Norton and Company, 1950.

Fenichel, Otto. *The Psychoanalytic Theory of Neurosis*, New York, W. W. Norton and Company, 1945.

Freud, Sigmund. *Civilization and Its Discontents*, London, Hogarth Press, 1953.

Fromm, Erich. *Man For Himself*, New York, Rinehart and Company, 1947.

Fromm, Erich. *The Sane Society*, New York, Rinehart and Company, 1955.

Glueck, Sheldon, and Eleanor Glueck. *Unraveling Juvenile Deliquency*, New York, The Commonwealth Fund, 1950.

Harlow, Harry F. "The Nature of Love," *American Psychologist*, 12:13, 673–685, 1958.

Hartman, Walter. The Moral Values Held in an Adolescent Peer Culture, Unpublished M.A. Thesis, Committee on Human Development, University of Chicago, 1949.

Hartshorne, H., M. A. May, and F. K. Shuttleworth. *Studies in the Organization of Character*, New York, The Macmillan Company, 1930.

Havighurst, Robert J. *Human Development and Education*, New York, Longmans, Green and Company, 1953.

Havighurst, Robert J., and Hilda Taba. *Adolescent Character and Personality,* New York, John Wiley and Sons, 1949.

Hollingshead, A. B. *Elmtown's Youth,* New York, John Wiley and Sons, 1949.

Jones, Vernon E. "Character Development in Children," in Leonard Carmichael (Ed.) *Manual of Child Psychology,* Second Edition, New York, John Wiley and Sons, 1954.

Jung, Carl. *Modern Man in Search of a Soul,* New York, Harcourt, Brace, 1933.

Kardiner, Abram, and associates. *The Psychological Frontiers of Society,* New York, Columbia University Press, 1945.

Ligon, Ernest. *Dimensions of Character,* New York, The Macmillan Company, 1956.

Lorr, Maurice, and Richard Jenkins. "Three Factors in Parent Behavior," *Journal of Consulting Psychology,* 17, 306–308, 1953.

Lynd, Robert S. *Middletown in Transition,* New York, Harcourt, Brace, 1937.

McGuire, Carson, and Rodney Clark. "Age Mate Acceptance and Indices of Peer Status," *Child Development,* 25, 141–154, 1952.

Murphy, Gardner. *Human Potentialities,* New York, Basic Books, 1958.

Murray, Henry. *Explorations in Personality,* New York, Oxford University Press, 1938.

Nicolson, Sir Harold. *Good Behavior,* Garden City, N. Y., Doubleday and Company, 1956.

Ojemann, Ralph H. "School-Community Programs," *Mental and Physical Health, Review of Educational Research,* 26, 479–502, 1956.

Peck, Robert F. "Measuring the Mental Health of Normal Adults," *Genetic Psychology Monographs,* No. 60, 197–255, 1959.

Peck, Robert F. The Psychology of Moral Character, Unpublished Ph.D. Dissertation (microfilm), University of Chicago, 1951.

Peck, Robert F., and John Parsons. "Personality Factors in Work Output," *Personnel Psychology,* 9:1, 49–74, 1956.

Peck, Robert F., and John Thompson. "The Use of Individual Assessments in a Management Development Program," *Journal of Personnel Administration and Industrial Relations,* 1:2, 79–98, 1954.

Phillips, Beeman, and M. Vere DeVault. *Psychology,* The Steck Company, Austin, 1959.

Piaget, Jean. *The Moral Judgment of the Child,* Glencoe, Illinois, The Free Press, 1949.

Powers, Edwin, and Helen Witmer. *An Experiment in the Prevention of Delinquency,* New York, Columbia University Press, 1951.

Rapaport, Anatol. *Operational Philosophy,* New York, Harper and Brothers, 1954.

Redl, Fritz, and David Wineman. *Children Who Hate,* Glencoe, Illinois, The Free Press, 1951.

Redl, Fritz, and David Wineman. *Controls From Within,* Glencoe, Illinois, The Free Press, 1952.

Reisman, David. *Individualism Reconsidered,* Glencoe, Illinois, The Free Press, 1954.

Reisman, David, and associates. *The Lonely Crowd,* New Haven, Yale University Press, 1950.

Remmers, H. H., and D. H. Radler. *The American Teenager,* Indianapolis, Bobbs-Merrill, 1957.

Rickman, John. "The Development of the Moral Function," *The Yearbook of Education, 1951,* London, Evans Brothers, 1951.

Roback, A. A. *Psychology of Character,* London, Kegan, Paul, 1952.

Roback, A. A. "The Character Aspect in Recent Psychology and Psychiatry," *Present Day Psychology,* New York, The Philosophical Library, 1955.

Rogers, Carl R. *Client-Centered Therapy,* Boston, Houghton Mifflin, 1951.

Sears, Robert, Eleanor Maccoby, and Harry Levin. *Patterns of Child Rearing,* Evanston, Illinois, Row, Peterson, 1957.

Stephenson, William. *The Study of Behavior,* Chicago, University of Chicago Press, 1953.

Sullivan, Harry Stack. *The Interpersonal Theory of Psychiatry,* New York, W. W. Norton and Company, 1953.

Warner, W. Lloyd. *The Living and the Dead,* New Haven, Yale University Press, 1959.

Warner, W. Lloyd, and William E. Henry. "The Radio Daytime Serial" *Genetic Psychology Monographs,* 37. Provincetown, Mass., Journal Press, 1948.

Warner, W. Lloyd, and associates. *Democracy in Jonesville,* New York, Harper and Brothers, 1949 (*a*).

Warner, W. Lloyd, Marchia Meeker, and Kenneth Eells. *Social Class in America,* Chicago, Science Research Associates, 1949 (*b*).

Whiting, John W. M., and Irvin Child. *Child Training and Personality,* New Haven, Yale University Press, 1953.

Whyte, William H. *The Organization Man,* New York, Simon and Schuster, 1956.

Index